THE WRATH OF JONAH

THE WRATH OF JONAH

The Crisis of Religious Nationalism in the Israeli-Palestinian Conflict

ROSEMARY RADFORD RUETHER
HERMAN J. RUETHER

1817

Harper & Row, Publishers, San Francisco

New York, Cambridge, Philadelphia, St. Louis
London, Singapore, Sydney, Tokyo

Grateful acknowledgement is made for permission to use the following: Appearing on page xi, adaptation of a map from THE ARAB AWAKENING by George Antonius. Copyright © 1969 by Geroge Antonius. Published by Hamish Hamilton Ltd. Appearing on page xii, adaptation of a map from THE BIRTH OF ISRAEL by Simha Flapan. Copyright © 1987 by Simha Flapan. Reprinted by permission of Pantheon Books, a Division of Random House, Inc., and by permission of the Estate of Simha Flapan.

Unless otherwise noted, Scripture quotations contained herein are from the Revised Standard Version of the Bible, copyright © 1946, 1952, 1971 by the Division of Christian Education of the National Council of the Churches of Christ in the U.S.A., and are used by permission. All rights reserved.

Library of Congress Cataloging-in-Publication Data

Ruether, Rosemary Radford.
    The wrath of Jonah.

    1. Israel (Christian theology)   2. Zionism.   3. Nationalism—
Palestine   4. Nationalism—Religious aspects.   5. Jewish-Arab
relations.   6. Holocaust (Jewish theology)   7. Holocaust (Christian
theology)   8. Judaism—Doctrines.   9. Islam—Doctrines.
I. Ruether, Herman J.   II. Title.
BT93.R84   1989   291.1'77'095694   88-45672
ISBN 0-06-066837-7

89   90   91   92   93   RRD   10   9   8   7   6   5   4   3   2   1

This book is dedicated to Kathy Bergen,
a valiant woman working for justice and peace
between Israelis and Palestinians

Contents

Acknowledgments

Many people have contributed to this work through reading parts of the manuscript and offering criticism and corrections. We wish to thank Dr. Ibrahim Abu-Lughod of Northwestern University and Dr. Deborah Gerner of the University of Kansas, Dr. Ghada Talhami of Lake Forest College, Dr. Marc Ellis of Maryknoll School of Theology, Dr. Wolfgang Roth and Dr. Phyllis Bird of Garrett-Evangelical Theological Seminary, Dr. Bruce Rigdon of McCormick Theological Seminary, and Dr. Klaus Herrmann of Concordia University, Montreal. Dr. Salem Tamari of Birzeit University provided invaluable material in his lectures on the sociology of the West Bank. Beth Goldring and Louise Cainkar of the Database Project on Palestinian Human Rights, Chicago, Illinois, made their resources available. We also thank Barbara Harr, Helen Hauldren, and Linda Koops, who did the typing of this manuscript.

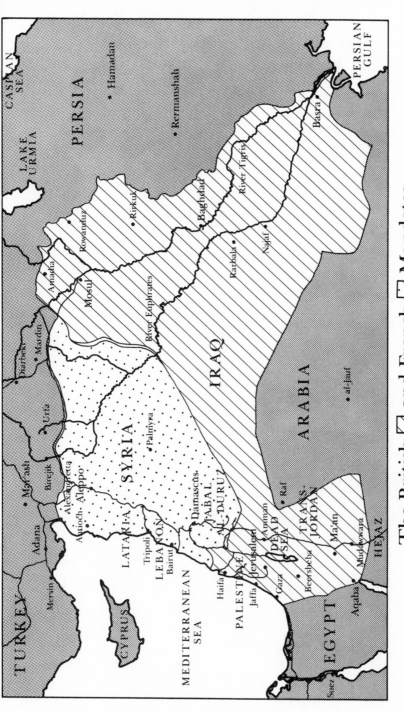

The British ⬚ and French ⊞ Mandates
In Syria-Palestine and Iraq

Territories Captured
in 1948 and 1949

Israel according to
UN partition plan

Arab territories
captured by Israel beyond
UN partition borders

Remaining Arab
territories in Palestine

River Litani

GALILEE

Haifa

SEA OF
GALILEE

Nazareth

River Jordan

Tulkarm

Nablus

Tel-Aviv
Jaffa

Amman

MEDITERRANEAN SEA

Jerusalem

DEAD SEA

GAZA

Beersheba

SINAI

NEGEV

Aqaba

Introduction

God repented of the evil which he had said he would do to them; and he did not
do it. But it displeased Jonah exceedingly, and he was angry. And he prayed to
the Lord and said, "... I knew thou art a gracious God and merciful, slow to
anger, and abounding in steadfast love, and repented of evil." ... But God said to
Jonah, ... "You pity the plant, for which you did not labor.... Should not I pity
Nineveh, that great city, in which there are more than a hundred and twenty
thousand persons?"

JON. 3:10; 4:1, 2, 9, 10, 11

In this book we examine the religious and ideological underpin-
nings of Zionism, and of the Christian support for Zionism, and
the tragic unfolding of the Zionist project in the Israeli-Palestinian
conflict. Several concerns have motivated the undertaking of this
study, and we wish to state these concerns clearly at the outset. Both
of us are very aware that the intense atmosphere of ideological
debate and mutual misinterpretation may mean that our intentions
in writing this book may be misunderstood. We wish to be correctly
understood, at least, by persons of good will who are genuine
friends of a just peace between the Palestinian and Israeli peoples.

We write as persons concerned about human rights and global
justice. The two of us also write as Western Christians with special
concerns about injustice, violations of human rights, and an unending spiral of violence in the Middle East, sparked particularly by the
unresolved conflict between Israel and Palestinian nationalism,
which both claim the one land of Israel/Palestine. We are concerned
about this particular conflict for several reasons, including our
deep feelings of identification with both the Jewish and the Palestinian peoples. These feelings are rooted, on one side, in the study
of the history of Christian anti-Semitism and a concern to right that
evil history. This particularly motivated Rosemary to write a book,
published in 1974, on the Christian roots of Western anti-Semitism
(*Faith and Fratricide*).

Herman, although sharing these concerns over injustice to Jews
in Western Christian society, has also had a long interest in Islam

and Muslim peoples, which has led him to study their history, first in Asia and then in the Middle East and in the United States. These interests led Rosemary and Herman to spend a teaching term at the Tantur Ecumenical Institute, between Jerusalem and Bethlehem, in the winter of 1987. During this teaching term Rosemary taught a course — attended by both American students and some Israelis concerned about peace — on Western anti-Semitism, the Holocaust, Zionism and its conflict with Palestinian nationalism. This was a course she had taught several times before, but its content took on a new reality in the context of a setting literally situated between the Israeli and the Palestinian "worlds." Herman taught a course, to students and faculty, on Islam, its foundations and development. The idea for this book crystallized during that teaching term.

In this book we wish to express our concerns for the injustice that has been done to the Palestinian people by both Israel and Western Christian peoples who sponsored and continued to sponsor the Zionist state and to justify its ideology. We are acutely aware of the intolerable suffering of Palestinians who have endured more than forty years as refugees or as politically repressed people under Israel and in various "host" Arab countries. The continued bombings of refugee camps and beatings of Palestinians in the occupied territories are the ongoing expression of this plight.

We are also concerned about the Jewish people, both in Israel and throughout the world. We are concerned that many have been drawn into an identification with an ethnocentric nationalism that was bound to result in the moral debacle that such nationalism presently faces. Jews in Western societies have long been teachers and prophetic leaders in the struggle for more just societies, societies that allow peoples of many races and religions to live together in justice and peace. It saddens us to see many Jews locked into a defensive stance toward Israel's obvious failure to express a like concern for democratic pluralism. In this book we seek to probe the reasons for this failure and the way in which Western Christian bigotries have contributed to it.

In writing this book we have been haunted by many poignant experiences and encounters with Jewish and Palestinian friends. We will recount some experiences to stand for the many. On the one side, we recall a kaleidoscope of meetings with doctors, lawyers, scholars, community organizers, and human rights activists in the

Palestinian community on the West Bank and the Gaza Strip. Our overwhelming experience of this Palestinian community was of a suffering people, assaulted in every part of their human and political rights by the Israeli occupation and yet morally resilient, unbeaten, and "steadfast" in their determination to remain rooted in their homeland. This, of course, does not mean that they are impeccable. We do not assume that any group of people need be impeccable in order to have human and political rights. Palestinians have sometimes been poorly served by their national representatives. They have been drawn into factional quarrels and military tactics that had no real chance of success. Yet, despite their factional divisions, there has emerged and been sustained over many decades of suffering an enormous sense of moral unity in the rightness of their cause.

On the other side, we recall many experiences with Jewish friends, some of whom seem forced into convoluted efforts to defend the rightness of Israel's policies, efforts that rang hollow to us. Other Jewish friends seem overwhelmed by a profound sadness that is denied public expression. This sadness was especially communicated to us by a Jewish woman who was staying with our family one summer. Coming down for breakfast one morning, we saw her standing at the table with the newspaper before her and her body wracked by sobs. On the front page of the paper was the story of the release of the Israeli settlers who had been convicted of assassination attempts against the Palestinian mayors. These settlers were given minimal fines and allowed to go free.

Our friend's tears were the expression of her deep disappointment at the failure of the Israeli court to do appropriate justice in this case. This for her was one more example in the worsening pattern of injustice in the relation of the State of Israel to the Palestinians. Her disappointment in Israel's failure to be a just state was like a deep wound in her Jewish psyche that bled but had to remain hidden. Most of the Jewish world did not want to hear her complaint, and she was afraid to reveal it to the gentile world.

This book is written out of concern for both of these wounded people: the one, wounded in body but not in spirit; the other, militarily strong but wounded in soul.

We have titled this book *The Wrath of Jonah* because the story of Jonah in Hebrew Scriptures is about two themes that are also central to this book: repentance and mutual acceptance between nations, as peoples equally created and loved by God. In the Book of Jonah, Jonah is depicted as a reluctant, angry, and resentful prophet. This reluctance, anger, and resentment are directed at God because God has called him to a task that expresses God's universal mercy upon all peoples. Jonah does not want God to be a universal God, slow to wrath and bountiful in mercy toward all nations. Rather, Jonah wants God to be a punitive and partisan God who punishes the enemies of Israel.

The Book of Jonah was written in the post-Nehemiah period (fourth century B.C.E.), after the return of Jewish leaders from the exile into which they had been cast by the Babylonian conquest of Palestine in the early sixth century. This book was meant to promote tolerance and coexistence of Jews with other communities within the Persian empire in this period after the return of Jewish religious leadership in Jerusalem. It was a gentle satire on a type of self-righteous Jewish religious exclusivism that had arisen after the return.

The story avoids the more immediate feelings against the Babylonians (who had caused the exile of the leaders of the Southern Kingdom of Judah in the early sixth century) by projecting its tale back to the time before the destruction of the city of Nineveh in 612 B.C.E. Nineveh was the capital of the Assyrian empire, which had caused the destruction of the Northern Kingdom of Israel in the latter part of the eighth century. Because of this conquest, which scattered the northern tribes of Israel and replaced them with Assyrian settlers, no city was more hated in Jewish tradition than was Nineveh.

In the story, God commands Jonah to go to Nineveh and preach repentance to its people. But Jonah, knowing that God is merciful and will relent in his threatened destruction of the Ninevites if they repent, runs the other way. Jonah goes to the coastal port town of Joppa and takes the first boat going west. But God forces Jonah to carry out his commanded prophetic mission. God raises a storm; he has Jonah thrown overboard, swallowed by a fish, and belched up on the shore. Jonah is forced to direct his steps to Nineveh and deliver God's call to repentance.

To Jonah's great disgust, the Ninevites repent of their evil ways. The Assyrian king proclaims a fast to express the repentance of all the Ninevites, from the greatest to the smallest, including even the cattle and sheep. All put on sackcloth, refrain from eating or drinking, and cry out for God's mercy. The Assyrian king hoped thereby to avert divine judgment against the city: "Let everyone turn from his evil way and from the violence which is in his hands. Who knows, God may yet repent and turn from his fierce anger, so that we perish not?" When God saw that the Ninevites had repented, God changed his mind and did not carry out the threatened destruction of Nineveh.

This, however, greatly displeased Jonah, and he was angry with God. Jonah wanted vengeance against the Assyrians and the destruction of their capital city. Instead, God forced him to be the emissary of their repentance and salvation. God then tried to instruct his angry, chauvinist prophet in the true nature and ways of God. God is not the God of one people only. God created and loves all nations; all are the work of God's hand. God does not wish for the destruction of any nation but rather that all repent and should be saved. By implication, God wants the Judaites and the people of other nations to live together in the peace that springs from repentance and obedience to the one God who created them all, rather than in violence and desire for the annihilation of the others.

What kind of repentance seems to be called for in order for Israelis and Palestinians to live together in justice and peace today? This is the question that underlies this book. We do not, in this book, attempt to advocate a particular political solution to this conflict. In our view, there might be several political solutions: two states, Jewish and Palestinian; or one binational or cantonal state. What must come first, underlying any authentic search for a political solution, is a deeper change of attitude toward each other, or "repentance." This change of attitude means that both recognize that two national communities have arisen in Palestine in the twentieth century. Although neither was there as a national community before the twentieth century, both are there now. And for either to try to deny that the other exists, as a national community, is an exercise in futility.

These two national communities are not "mirror images" of each other, as some Jews tend to think, regarding the Palestinians as having sprung up primarily as a negative response to Jewish nationalism. Both communities have their own different histories that have led them to their national identities. If there had been an Arab nationalism and a British Mandate for Palestine in the first half of the twentieth century, but no Zionism, there would have undoubtedly arisen a Palestinian nationalism to express the desire of the Palestinian Arab community for liberation from British colonialism and for national self-determination.

Unlike the Palestinians, the immediate forebears of almost all the Israelis were not present in Palestine before the twentieth century, and most of them not before 1948. The Israelis came from other lands, and their coming was facilitated by Western colonialism. But it is inadequate to call Israel a "colonial settler state," to be compared with white European settler states in Africa or other colonized areas. For two millennia, Jews in Muslim and Christian countries kept alive, through their religious traditions, a vivid image of this region as their ancestral homeland. But this longing had remained latent and without political expression. So, for Arab peoples, who had lived for thirteen centuries in the context of Muslim control of Palestine, the advent of Zionism in the modern period came as something unexpected and incomprehensible.

This belief—that this area is the Jewish peoples' homeland—must be understood as a powerful sense of Jewish identity, quite apart from whether it gives them a political "right" to found a state there, much less to displace anyone else in the process, and apart from whether many of the Jews who inherit this longing for Palestine are actually descended from later proselytes, rather than from ancient Hebrews. Jewish ethnicity is a religiously rooted communal cultural identity, not a racially transmitted characteristic. Through the centuries, many people who were Jews have ceased to be Jews, and others who were not Jews have become Jews.

Palestinian nationalist ideology has already made major shifts toward the accommodation of Israel as a state in part of their (Palestinian) ancestral homeland. This shift is primarily a practical, political one, not an ideological shift. Although Palestinians continue to believe that Zionist nationalism is illegitimate and that all Palestine should belong to the Palestinians, they are ready to have half a loaf rather than none. This shift needs to be accepted and tested in good faith rather than dismissed out of hand, as has been the response of Israel and the United States to Palestinian concessions for the past fifteen years.

Although Israel, world Jewry, and the United States continue to see the Arabs and Palestinians as the chief impediment to peace, it has become evident to us that, in fact, it is Israel and the United States that are the chief impediments. This impediment lies not only in the Zionist concept of Israel as a Jewish state (which resulted in the expulsion of most of the Palestinians within the 1949 borders of Israel) but also in Israel's present insistence on holding onto the West Bank and the Gaza Strip, which were conquered in 1967. Underlying both of these conquests is the refusal to recognize, alongside Jewish nationalism, a parallel Palestinian nationalism and right to self-determination.

What can help bring about a repentance that can allow Israeli Jews and the world community to recognize the rights of Palestinian national self-determination? We believe that one important step toward repentance lies in telling the truth about the history of both people. Israeli rejectionism has been clothed in many layers of falsification about the sociologies and historical relations between these two people. Many Jews have accepted these falsifications as the true story. Knowing the true story will be essential to putting the pieces of two fragmented worlds together in one coherent picture. It is for this reason that we have spent what might seem like an inordinate amount of space, for a book of theological and ethical critique, on telling history.

An Israeli political scientist, in a public lecture that we heard, declared that the Israelis and the Palestinians each have one half of a puzzle, but the problem is that they have two halves of different puzzles. This is an insightful, but finally destructive, analysis. It suggests that each national community has a vision of itself that excludes the other and that their stories can never fit together, that the disparities between the way each side tells its story is finally an intractible difference in point of view. We believe, in contrast, that there are not two different truths about what actually happened, for example, in the flight of the Palestinians from their homes in 1948. It must be pieced together and told as one coherent story, communicated across the two communities. Revisionist Israeli historians and critical Palestinian historians have already amply laid the basis for this unified history. Knowing a common story of the past is an essential first step in fitting the two halves of the puzzle into one picture of two peoples who must live together in one land.

But telling the true history can simply be received with cynical *Realpolitik* if the hearers are not truly concerned with ethical values. Such cynicism unfortunately has become too typical of the type of Israeli leaders who have come to power with the founding of the state in 1948. Most of them, such as David Ben-Gurion, Shimon Peres, and Moshe Dayan, as well as those who came to power in 1977, Menachem Begin and Yitzak Shamir, have known very well the truth behind these various official dissimulations. But they have believed that it was necessary to deceive the other Jews, the "beautiful souls" who might quail before the facts of rank injustice perpetrated by Jews. Thus, there needs to be that change of heart that is the essence of true repentance. There also needs to develop the collective organization and assertion of political influence on the State of Israel that can curb the expansionists in the military government.

The conditions for this change of heart lie in a diminishment of both fear and contempt for the Palestinians and the multiplication of Israelis who have come to know Palestinians, not in the sense of information about Palestinians, but in the sense of being able to enter into and experience the Palestinian reality. Contemporary Israeli and world Jewry's fears of annihilation, while exaggerated, are nevertheless real, rooted both in the trauma of the Holocaust and in the transference of the Nazi face of unrelenting hostility and genocide to the Arabs. Palestinians cannot be expected to address this pathological fear that Jews have of them, since it makes little sense to their own experience as refugees and as an oppressed community with no state, little land, no army worth mentioning, and so little political clout that only by suffering endless assaults does it keep itself before the attention of the world at all.

Various powers, particularly the United States, might help assure Israel that recognition of Palestinian political self-determination is, not only not a radical danger to its existence, but worth risking in order to end the violence of the occupation and the chief cause of the hostility of the Arab world. But the only real basis that can, finally, allow Israelis to take that risk is the sort of relationship with Palestinians that can build mutual trust. Without mutual trust, no armies are strong enough, no buffer zones wide enough to protect one from one's enemies. With mutual trust, armies and buffer zones become unnecessary. This book cannot create that trust, which can be built only through new relationships based on new political realities. But we hope that it may make some contribution to the critique of the ideologies that prevent Israelies and Americans from asking the right questions.

A brief remark on the use of the word "anti-Semitism" is in order. In the context of the Arab-Israeli conflict, the term *anti-Semitism* is misleading because, originally, *Semitic* referred to numerous languages, especially Hebrew and Arabic, spoken by Jews *and* Arabs. *Anti-Semitism* was coined as a Western racist term in the late nineteenth century and has always and only meant anti-Jewish hostility. It has never included anti-Arab hostility. Today anti-Semitism is often criticized by Western Christians or by Jews who are not at all critical of their own or other people's anti-Arab stereotypes. However, because *anti-Semitism* has become an established term, we use it in this book, recognizing that it means only hostility to Jews. But sometimes other terms, such as *anti-Jewish,* will be used for clarity. We use the term *anti-Arab* to refer to unjust stereotypes of Arab people and Arab culture.

THE WRATH OF JONAH

PART 1.

CLASSICAL FOUNDATIONS: THE THREE MONOTHEISTIC FAITHS

1. Peoplehood, Covenant, and Land in Judaism, Christianity, and Islam

Those who believe in the Qur'an and those who follow the Jewish Scriptures and the Christians and the Sabians, any who believe in God and the Last Day and work righteousness, shall have their reward. . . . The Jews say: "The Christians have naught to stand upon;" and the Christians say: "The Jews have naught to stand upon," Yet they profess to study the same Book. . . . But God will judge between them in their quarrel on the Day of Judgment.

QUR'AN, SŪRA II: 62,113
ALI TRANSLATION (see n. 53)

THE LAND OF CANAAN: CROSSROADS OF EMPIRES

Palestine or Canaan, including the east bank of the Jordan River, was occupied by hunting-gathering peoples who lived in caves and open-air camps as early as 100,000 B.C.E. New migrations of peoples have continually entered the area from the north, the Aegean and Anatolia; from the east, along the Fertile Crescent route from Mesopotamia; from the south, along the seacoast from Egypt; and from the southeast, from the Transjordan. More developed settlements began in the ninth millennium B.C.E. in areas such as Jericho. The first city wall of Jericho dates from 8000–7000 B.C.E. The early Bronze Age (3000–2400 B.C.E.) saw an urbanization of Palestine, with walled cities such as Megiddo, Ai, Arad, Hazor, and Urusalim (Jebus or Jerusalem). In the third and second millennia B.C.E., Palestine was an area of mixed population organized into small city-states, particularly on or near the valleys and plains.

Beginning in 2800 B.C.E. the region became dominated by Egypt, the first great empire of the eastern Mediterranean. Egypt controlled the region until 1700 B.C.E., when a people from Syria, the Hyksos, controlled Canaan and ruled in Egypt until 1430 B.C.E. The Egyptians reasserted control until 1350 B.C.E. and then lost it until 1154 B.C.E.

to the Hittites, who originated in Asia Minor. Thus, beginning in the early third millennium, Canaan was controlled by adjacent empires, located either in Egypt or in imperial powers to the northeast (Assyria, Babylonia, Persia) and, then, in the northern Mediterranean (Rome-Byzantium). Only during brief periods, usually interludes between imperial powers, did the local people control the region.

In the late second millennium B.C.E., new settlers broke down the old system of small city-states under a distant overlord and, instead, began to create tribal national monarchies. These tribal monarchies — the Philistines along the southern coastal plain; the Judeans and the Israelites in the central hills, Jordan valley, and Galilee; the Moabites east of the Dead Sea; and the Edomites in the Negev — competed with each other for power and territory.[1] For seventy-three years, between 1000 and 927 B.C.E., the Hebrews, under David and then Solomon, were able to assert hegemony over the whole region, reigning from the Jebusite capital, Jerusalem, which had been captured by David.

After 927 B.C.E. the Hebrew united kingdom of Judah and Israel broke into two warring kingdoms. The rising power of Assryia began to assert hegemony over the two kingdoms in the ninth century. In 722 B.C.E. the Northern Kingdom of Israel was swept away by the invading Assryians. The Assyrians asserted control by taking tens of thousands captive and scattering them throughout their empire and, in turn, importing colonists loyal to them to settle the region. The southern Hebrew kingdom of Judah, reduced to a small region around Jerusalem, suffered a similar fate in 586 B.C.E., when it was captured by the Babylonians. Then the upper stratum of its population was deported to Babylonia.

In 538 B.C.E., the Persian empire swept the region. Under King Cyrus, a part of the deported Jewish population was allowed to return. Many chose to stay in Babylonia, however, and became the source of the historic Jewish community in Babylonia (later, Iraq). The Jewish community in Judea between 538 and 330 B.C.E. was an integral part of the Persian empire, not an independent state. In 330 B.C.E. the region was conquered by Alexander the Great and, for the next 175 years, was ruled by successor Hellenistic states from Egypt and then from Syria. A brief interlude between imperial powers allowed a quasi-independent Jewish kingdom to arise under the Hasmoneans from 142–70 B.C.E.

Beginning in 63 B.C.E., Canaan, now called by the Romans *Palaestina*, was ruled by Rome and then by its Christian Greco-Roman successor state, Byzantium, until C.E. 614. After a brief interlude of Persian control, Palestine was conquered by the Arab Muslims in C.E. 638. The Muslim control over the region also fell into the pattern of domination from the three imperial centers of Egypt, Syria, and Byzantium. Between C.E. 638 and 1085 an Arab Muslim state controlled the region from Damascus. After a period of conflict, in which Crusader states from the West asserted control for two hundred years, the Mamelukes ruled the area from Egypt from C.E. 1291 to 1517. Then, from C.E. 1517 until 1918, the region was ruled by a third Muslim empire, the Ottoman Turks, ruling from Constantinople (renamed Istanbul).

The basic pattern of political organization in antiquity was built up from tribal confederations and city-states, which asserted control over the surrounding land and its peasantry. The city became the political, economic, and religious center and knit the community together in a common *gens* or people. Beginning with Egypt, imperial power arose, subjecting these city-states and tribal confederations to tributary status. The local people retained their own religious cults and cultural identity, often with local self-government, but their elites took on the culture of the conquerors. In the Hellenistic and Roman periods, the cult of the emperor knit the empire together in a quasi-religious unity. The Jews and, later, the Christians came into conflict with the Hellenistic and Roman empires by resisting allegiance to this imperial cult.

The Christianization of the Roman empire was the first time an imperial power demanded religious uniformity of all its subjects, although the Christian empire allowed the Jews to retain their own religion. The Muslims followed a similar pattern of religious imperialism, demanding that all their pagan subjects become Muslims. But they allowed Jews and Christians to retain their own religions, in a subordinate relation to the ruling Muslims. After the Christianization of Palestine, a small remnant of Jews remained in rabbinic centers, such as Tiberias and Sepphoris. Jews were forbidden to enter Jerusalem after the Romans crushed the second Jewish revolt in C.E. 136; they were not allowed to enter the city again until the Muslim conquest in C.E. 638. With the Muslim conquest, most of the people of Palestine became Muslims, although a strong Christian community and a tiny Jewish one remained. All three religious groups became Arabized in language and culture.

This brief survey should make it clear that, from the point of view of historic residence, the Jews have no exclusive claim on the land. The Arabized Jewish, Christian, and Muslim people have the longest continuous residency and are themselves an amalgam of all the peoples who have entered and colonized the region. Beginning with the ancient Canaanites, the region has synthesized successive peoples and cultures. Its history should point us, not to the exclusive right of one religious-ethnic group to rule, but rather to the reality of many peoples and cultures who have cross-fertilized each other. All three monotheistic faiths—which have seen this area as the cradle of their religious beginnings and as their "Holy Land"—need to seek to live together in justice and peace in this land.

In the following sections of this chapter we will discuss the claims of the peoples of each of the three monotheistic faiths to this region as their Holy Land. The story will begin with the Hebrews, or Jews, and their reinterpretations of their relationship to the land in the period of the Hebrew Scripture. It will then continue by discussing how the peoples of each of the three faiths who laid claim to this biblical legacy interpreted their identity as a people, their relationship to the land and to each other. Rabbinic Judaism, Christianity, and Islam each saw itself as an elect people in relation to a monotheistic God, a God who had elevated each of them to unique chosen status as a historical community. How did each faith community understand this unique chosen status in relationship to others making rival claims? How did each faith community define the relationship of its peoplehood to the Holy Land, vis-à-vis its complementary claims to be a universal people living in all lands?

COVENANT PEOPLE AND PROMISED LAND IN HEBREW SCRIPTURE

The ancestors of the Hebrews entered Canaan around the nineteenth century B.C.E. as one of many seminomadic tribes from the desert and eastern areas who sought pasturage. The basis of a Hebrew claim to the land from the collective ancestor Abram (Abraham) may well go back to this period.[2] Since the land claim was reformulated in the Davidic period, it is not possible to reconstruct its original form. But it seems to have envisioned the right to graze animals and pitch the tribal tents in a hill region from Shechem (Nablus) to Beersheba. Abraham is said to have owned only one piece of land, a field with a cave on it near Hebron, which he bought for four hundred shekels from Ephron the Hittite as a family burial place (Gen. 23:3–20).

Abraham's claim to the land did not displace other people, particularly the people of the cities. When Abraham is told by God in Gen. 13:14–17, "Lift up your eyes and look from the place where you are [from a hill near Bethel], northward and southward and eastward and westward; for all the land which you see I will give to you and to your descendants for ever.... Arise and walk through the length and breadth of the land for I will give it to you," what seems to be envisioned is a region where he and his clan and animals can claim rights of pasturage.

About 1200 B.C.E. some descendants of the Hebrews, who had become enslaved in Egypt, escaped and wandered for a period of time in the Sinai and then moved north to the Transjordan, where they eyed the land of Canaan. In the Book of Joshua, a confederacy of Yahwist tribes is described as laying claim to a territory from the Transjordan through the central hill regions to the mountains north of the Galilee. These people are not nomads looking for a migratory region in which to pitch their tents and graze their animals but conquerors who seek to wrest the walled cities from the Canaanite agricultural settlers and city builders. Significantly, throughout the first six books of the Bible (the Hexateuch) the term *land of Israel* never appears. The land is referred to throughout as the *land of Canaan*, thus making clear that the Hebrews saw themselves as taking away or wresting rights to settle in a land previously settled by another people, the Canaanites.

Joshua is described as sweeping through the land, taking city after city by the sword, putting the people and even animals to death. He ranges from Jericho in the Jordan valley to the walled cities of the central hill country and north to the hill regions above Galilee, where a confederacy of cities is gathered around the central city of Hazor. In Joshua 24 the mighty deeds of God on behalf of the tribes of Israel are described as the basis of a formal covenant between God and Israel. The Hebrew confederacy under Joshua is pictured as being given overlordship over the area of the conquest, with land allotments for each of the twelve tribes. In response to this gift of the land, the tribes of Israel put away their former gods and serve Yahweh alone as God. The covenant of God with the twelve tribes at Shechem makes explicit that this land was not originally theirs, but was taken from its original settlers and city builders: "I gave you a land on which you had not labored, and cities which you had not built, and you dwelt therein; you eat the fruit of vineyards and olive yards which you did not plant" (Josh. 24:13).

However, the Joshua account cannot be read literally as history. It is a schematic theological construct from the perspective of later land claims. Archaeological work has shown that no such sweeping Israelite conquest of walled cities took place in the late thirteenth century B.C.E., the probable time of the settlement. For example, the city of Ai, which Joshua 8 describes as being conquered by the Israelites, was actually destroyed in 2400 B.C.E., and the Joshua account may have been created to explain this settlement of a long-ruined Canaanite walled city. It is more likely that the Hebrew tribes infiltrated gradually into the unsettled hill areas and then consolidated a tribal confederation and began the takeover of the cities. Some theories see this as a peasant revolt that included Canaanite peoples.[3] Tribal unity was created by allegiance to the sole cult god Yahweh. This period of tribal unification led to a power struggle against rival tribe monarchies, especially the Philistines. This period is represented by the first Israelite tribal monarchy under Saul (1 Sam. 13–16).

About 1000 B.C.E. the Hebrews under David were able to push back the Philistines and create a small empire that asserted hegemonic control over not only the territory from Beersheba to Shechem but also over an arc of cities and tribes in the Transjordan, the northern hills to the Lebanon border and some of the coastal plain. David brought the kingdoms of Israel and Judah together in a united monarchy and asserted control over the regions of Moab, Ammon, Edom, the desert tribes, and the Aramaean states west of the Galilee. The Philistines remained in control of the southern coastal region. This empire was further expanded and consolidated into administrative units under David's son Solomon. The wealth of Solomon's empire was created by extensive international trade by sea and land routes to Africa, Asia, Arabia, and Anatolia.

However, this does not mean that non-Hebrew peoples were displaced from the land. Ancient empires were hegemonic, not ethnically exclusive. The ancient kingdom of David and Solomon was, not a "Jewish state" in the modern sense of an exclusive ethnic-religious nationalism in which only Jews were members, but rather a Jewish overlordship amid diverse people, most of whom retained their own cults and acknowledged the Davidic king as overlord. The ethnic pluralism of the Davidic kingdom is clearly shown in the descriptions of David's generals as including Philistines, Hittites, Ammonites, and Moabites.[4]

During the Davidic period, the idea of a covenant between God and the Hebrew people, giving them the land, was developed and shaped into the pattern that survived in Scripture. By recalling God's covenant with Abraham, promising the land to his descendants, the kingdom of David and Solomon sought to give their own imperial hegemony a more ancient ancestry. They also expanded the purview of these claims, including not only the enlarged area over which they asserted some power but also an even wider area over which they did not have any real hegemonic power. Thus, the passage in Genesis describing God's covenant with Abraham was shaped in the Davidic period to read as follows:

On that day the Lord made a covenant with Abram, saying, "To your descendants I give this land, from the river of Egypt to the great river, the river Euphrates, the land of the Kenites, the Kenizzites, the Kadmonites, the Hittites, the Perizzites, the Rephaim, the Amorites, and Canaanites, and Girgashites and the Jebusites." (Gen. 15:18–21)

But this overlordship of the kings of Judah over both the northern Hebrew tribes and an expanded group of non-Hebrew peoples lasted less than a century. In 930 B.C.E. the northern tribes revolted against the Davidic monarchy. Warfare broke out between the divided kingdoms of Judah and Israel. As we have seen, the area soon afterwards fell under the hegemony of Assyria. From then on, Palestine would be a subject province of successive empires, with the exception of about one hundred years under the Maccabees. Jews would begin their Diaspora by being deported or migrating throughout the regions of these empires from Persia to Spain.

In the first millennia B.C.E., Jews only briefly held a united monarchy and asserted hegemony over the other people in the land. They never displaced the other people; most of the time, they were themselves a subject people under the hegemony of other imperial centers. Thus, despite assertions in Scripture that Israel should drive the other peoples out of the land little by little (i.e., Exod. 23 and 33), there is ample evidence to show that this did not happen.[5] Such assertions probably reflect a desperate hope over against a very different reality.

There remains in the biblical narrative an ambivalence about residency in the land, its seizure from other people, and the adoption of Canaanite city-state patterns of life and political power.[6] Tribal traditions viewed kingship and city life with suspicion. Yahweh was originally a God of a tribal confederacy whose ark migrated with the migration of the people. Urban life belonged to the "Baals" of the agricultural plains and walled cities. To build a temple and accept a king was temptation to "harlotry" with those alien gods.

The reference to the land as belonging to other people prevails in the Hexateuch. The phrase *land of Israel* begins to appear in 2 Kings and Chronicles but not in connection with the promise of the land by God. Rather, it is a factual term for tribal territories, as contrasted with other powerful neighboring peoples. Only the prophet Ezekiel makes extensive use of the term *land of Israel*, but that is in order to stress the absolute sovereignty of God over this land. If Israel is unrighteous, then God will lay waste this land and expel its people. When they repent, God will restore them to the land. Throughout Hebrew Scripture, *Israel* refers to a people who may or may not be in this particular land, a people who were brought out of Egypt by God, covenanted with God in the desert (Exod. 24, where there is no explicit reference to a promise of land), and called to be faithful to God's commandments.[7]

Sovereignty over the land remains in the hand of God. God may grant Israel the blessing of living in the land. But God can withdraw this blessing, just as God has withdrawn the blessing of living in the land to other, earlier peoples. Israel is said to "sojourn" in the land. Leviticus, speaking of the commandment to let the land lie fallow in the seventh year, says, "The land shall not be sold in perpetuity, for the land is mine; for you are strangers and sojourners with me" (Lev. 25:23).

Leviticus, Numbers, and Deuteronomy tie secure use of the land to faithfulness to God's commandments. Violations of the Law, particularly idolatry, are seen to "pollute" the land. God punishes such pollution of the land by laying it waste, withdrawing rain, and making it unproductive. The extreme punishment for unfaithfulness to God is expulsion from the land at the hands of enemies who take over the land and exile Israel's leaders. The land itself becomes an actor in hurling out those who pollute it. Leviticus says that the land had "vomited out" the previous inhabitants, who polluted it through forbidden sexual practices. Israel is warned that the same fate may befall it: "But you shall keep my statutes and my ordinances and do none of these abominations . . . lest the land vomit you out, when you defile it, as it vomited out the nation that was before you" (Lev. 18:26,28). Deuteronomy extends this warning to a general admonition against injustice. Those who show partiality and take bribes threaten the secure use of the land: "Justice, and only justice, you shall follow, that you may live and inherit the land which the Lord your God gives you" (Deut. 16:20).

In the biblical tradition, the land is not given over into Israel's hands as "private property" to which it has absolute "rights." Rather, Israel has usufruct of the land under God. But even this usufruct remains conditional upon obedience to God's commandments. This conditionality of Israel's gift of the land is restated judgmentally in the prophets of the eighth to sixth centuries B.C.E. For them, Israel had already sinned and polluted the land by its many abominations. And so God is laying waste the land and hurling Israel into exile. Thus Amos declares, "Your sons and your daughters shall fall by the sword, and your land shall be parceled out by line; you yourself shall die in an unclean land, and Israel shall surely go into exile away from its land." (Amos 7:17).

This exile is not seen as permanent. Postexilic revisions of the earlier prophets make explicit what was probably implicit in the eight-century prophets. If Israel repents, God's wrath will be softened. Israel will be restored to its land and live securely in it. Thus the last stanzas of Amos promise the following:

"Behold, the days are coming," says the Lord "when . . . , I will restore the fortunes of my people Israel, and they shall rebuild the ruined cities and inhabit them; they shall plant vineyards and drink their wine. . . . I will plant them upon their land, and they shall never again be plucked up out of the land which I have given them," says the Lord your God. (Amos 9:13,14,15)

In those prophets, permanent and secure possession of the land becomes part of a future vision of redemption. But any actual restoration to the land within unredeemed history would suggest that new sin and new divine judgment might again occur.

Some prophets (e.g., Hos. 1:9) even suggest that God might revoke the covenant with Israel. But, in the final biblical perspective, the covenant of God with the people of Israel is seen as permanent and irrevocable. God has chosen Israel as his people. Even when they sin and suffer in exile, they are not out of God's hand, for the exile itself reflects God's covenantal relation to Israel. The promise of the land, however, remains conditional. Its promise remains as an integral part of the fulfillment of the covenantal relationship in which Israel becomes obedient to God. But, at any particular time, Israel may find itself in exile in other lands. This exile is interpreted by the prophets as the judgmental side of God's covenant relationship with his people.

The Psalms and Later Prophets begin to individualize and universalize this concept of God's relationship to the land and its people. It can be said simply that "the righteous" shall dwell securely in the land, while "the wicked" shall not dwell in the land (Ps. 37). God's sovereignty can be extended over the whole earth. God can lay waste the lands of other nations because of their iniquity (Jer. 25:12–14). Although the unique relation between God, Israel, and the land of Israel remains the center of this vision of judgment and restoration, Isaiah can dramatically generalize it, as in this passage:

Behold, the Lord will lay waste the earth and make it desolate. . . . The earth shall be utterly laid waste and utterly despoiled; for the Lord has spoken this word. The earth mourns and withers, the world languishes and withers; the heavens languish together with the earth. The earth lies polluted under its inhabitants; for they have transgressed the laws, violated the statutes, broken the everlasting covenant. Therefore a curse devours the earth, and its inhabitants suffers for their guilt . . . The earth is utterly broken, the earth is rent asunder, the earth is violently shaken . . . its transgression lies heavily upon it, and it falls, and will not rise again. (Isa. 24:1, 4–6, 19, 20)

In Isaiah, the vision of Israel's redemption and restoration to the land is also extended to the nations, with Israel (Zion) as the center and the place of judgment and reconciliation:

It shall come to pass in the latter days that the mountain of the house of the Lord shall be established as the highest of the mountains, and shall be raised up above the hills; and all the nations shall flow to it, and many peoples shall come and say: "Come, let us go up to the mountain of the Lord, to the house of the God of Jacob; that he may teach us his ways and that we may walk in his paths." For out of Zion shall go forth the Law, and the word of the Lord from Jerusalem. He shall judge between the nations, and shall decide for many peoples; and they shall beat their swords into plowshares, and their spears into pruning hooks; nation shall not lift up sword against nation, and neither shall they learn war any more. (Isa. 2:2–4)

The perspective of Hebrew Scripture varies from a tribal, militaristic view of conquest of the land to a critical, ethical view of Israel's relation to the land. It also ranges from an ethnocentric to an increasingly universalistic view of the chosenness of Israel in relation to other people. The book of Jonah represents a high point of this universalist development. God creates, loves, and seeks to save the other peoples equally with Israel.

PEOPLEHOOD, COVENANT, AND LAND IN RABBINIC JUDAISM

The roots of rabbinic Judaism can be traced back to the exile of Jewish leadership to Babylonia in 586 B.C.E. The city of Jerusalem had been sacked and its Temple destroyed. In 536 B.C.E., the Persian king, Cyrus, allowed some of the exiles to return and to start to rebuild the Temple. But many declined to come. An autonomous Jewish community had long been established in the lands given to them to colonize by the Babylonian king.[8] Jews also dispersed in that period to Egypt. When Alexander of Macedon conquered the Persian empire and planted Hellenistic cities through Syria and Egypt, Jewish communities would grow up in these cities. The new religious institution that developed in the dispersion in Babylon and the Hellenistic cities was the synagogue, a house of study centered in teachers of the Law. These teachers identified covenantal life with God with study of the ancient writings and strict observance of the Law in daily life.

This shift from Temple to synagogue, from cult to study, was the basis of a religious revolution. Henceforth knowledge of the Law, including the laws of cultic sacrifice, would no longer be an esoteric lore known only to the priestly classes. A new learned elite would arise who would democratize knowledge of the Law, making it available to any male Jew. Judaism also became open to the proselyte. The God of the covenant was no longer a tribal God but a universal God. Potentially, all people could come to know him. This shift was already reflected in the passage from Isaiah cited above. Under Hellenistic influence, Judaism would be seen as a philosophical school. Becoming an authentic "son of the covenant," like becoming a "Hellene," would come to be seen as the product of an education.[9] Through study and observance of the Law, one entered into a way of life. The Gentile can enter into this way of life through becoming a proselyte. The born Jew also must become an observant Jew through study and practice of this way. The Pharisees were the masters and teachers of this way through which Israel was to walk with God.

Such a scribal class emerged, with the development of the synagogue, by 400 B.C.E. and was responsible for the shaping of the canonical Torah or Pentateuch. The Pharisees seem to have arisen in the Hasmonean period as one group of the *Hasidim*, or pious ones, who sought to shape the newly independent state along the lines of strict observance, so that it might become a "holy people, a priestly nation."[10] Another group of these *Hasidim* became repelled by the violations of the new Hasmonean line of priest-kings and withdrew to await the restoration of an authentic priest and king in messianic times. These became the Essenes. The Pharisees, however, remained in Jerusalem and undertook a struggle with the Hasmonean kings. They sought to subject their policies to strict religious observance of the Law. They were victorious in dominating the court during the brief reign of the widow of Alexander Jannaeus, Salome Alexander (76–67 B.C.E.). But the conflicts between her two sons for the throne brought the intervention and Roman takeover in 63 B.C.E.[11]

Josephus tells us that the Pharisees even petitioned for the Romans to take over, believing that they could better shape the internal religious life of Israel under foreign political rule. The foreign king would respect their exclusive sway over the religious life of the people, whereas the Hasmonean priest-king sought to dominate that religious life himself.[12] Whether such a petition happened in 63 B.C.E. or not, Josephus certainly means this scene to echo that of the academy at Yavneh where the rabbinic leadership sought to make such a settlement with the Romans. By ceding political domination to Rome, the Pharisees hoped to win acceptance of their control over the internal religious life of the people without political interference.

The Maccabean revolt (166–143 B.C.E.) against Hellenistic over-lordship created a new ideal of the religious revolutionary warrior and a new literature of apocalyptic to express this rebellion. After a century of independence, Palestine fell under Roman sway. Bands of guerrilla fighters, or Zealots, inspired by apocalyptic national-ism, were renewed in the first century C.E. Pietist groups that had been shaped in the Hasmonean period, such as the Essenes, with-drew into separatist communities where they lived a life of study and strict observance of the commandments. They sought to make atonement for the defilement of the land by an apostate temple priesthood and to prepare the way for a messianic redemption of the land.[13]

These movements of resistance and hope led, in C.E. 66–73, to the outbreak of a messianically inspired revolt against Roman rule. The Romans besieged Jerusalem, destroyed the Temple, and went on to destroy the strongholds of the Zealots at Masada and the Essenes's desert center at Qumran. The Pharisaic school of Hillel, led by their teacher, Johanan ben Zakkai, left Jerusalem before its fall and peti-tioned General (and soon-to-be Emperor) Vespasian to allow them to reestablish a center of study in the coastal city of Yavneh.[14]

In C.E. 132–136 messianically inspired warfare between Palestinian Jews and Rome broke out again. The revolt was led by Simon bar Kokhba, whose claims to be the messianic deliverer of Israel were supported by the leader of the Yavneh Academy, Rabbi Aquiba. This time the entire city of Jerusalem was razed by the Romans. A Hellenistic city was built next to it, and access to Jerusalem was for-bidden the Jews.

In C.E. 140 the rabbinic academy was reestablished, with Roman approval, at Usha in the Galilee under Simeon ben Gamaliel II. Under his son, Judah the Patriarch, the Mishnah, the Pharisaic tra-ditions of oral commentary on the law, would be published in C.E. 200. The century from C.E. 70 to the end of the second century C.E. thus saw a crucial transitional period in Jewish life and thought. Jewish religious and communal life lost its old focus in the Temple, the priesthood, and the sacrificial cult. It was adapted by the Pharisees, or rabbinic teachers, to a new focus whose center was the synagogue or house of study.

Under Pharisaic adaptation of Jewish law, the festivals and the laws of purity would now be observed in everyday life in the home. Pharisaic Judaism gave Jews a "portable priesthood" capable of being established wherever ten adult male Jews could be assembled. Covenantal life acceptable to God did not require possession of Jerusalem, or the Temple and its sacrifical cult. It is this Pharisaic revolution that made it possible for Jews to survive as a people without land or political autonomy.[15]

The revolution created by the rabbinic schools between C.E. 70 and 200 was simultaneously radical and conservative. The balance that had sustained Jews in the Diaspora for six hundred years was destroyed. No longer could Jews, gathered in their homes and synagogues, look to the national center in Jerusalem, with its temple cult, as a way of maintaining cohesion as a people. The Temple was in ruins. Jews could no longer enter the capital city. Much of Judaea was depopulated of Jews, replaced by Gentiles settled by the Romans. Jews who remained in Palestine were mainly in the Galilee. Study, instead of being an auxiliary to the national cult, now must replace it altogether.

Earlier Pharisaism had taught that temple purity is not limited to the temple cult and its priesthood but can be extended everywhere through observance in the home. Now they would teach that such hallowing of everyday life can *replace* the temple cult. The contrite heart and deeds of loving kindness are as effective in winning expiation of sin as temple sacrifice.[16] The rabbinic teachers created a bridge to a new religious system of internalized law that could replace the cult and laws of life in the land with its agricultural festivals. Yet, at the same time, they preserved the memory of this earlier life in the land and the temple cult by careful codification of its laws—laws that could no longer be observed in practice. Radical discontinuity between priestly temple cult and rabbinic school was denied by tracing the oral law back to Moses. The oral law was said to have been given at the same time as the written Law.[17] So all the rabbinic teachings were implicitly present from the beginning.

At the very moment when the temple cult had vanished as a reality, its ideal observance, according to Pharisaic law, was codified for unending study and commentary. One-sixth of the Mishnah, completed in C.E. 200, when the Temple was destroyed and the holy city inaccessible, has to do with minute regulations of the cult and priesthood. Many of the regulations in the other five sections of Mishnah have to do with life in the land of Israel and were not observable outside that land. Why, at the moment when most of these laws could not be observed, did a school of teachers set about fixing them forever in written form? What is reflected here, in its radical form, is the rabbinic conviction that study of the Law replaces the cult. If one carefully studies the laws of the cult, it is as if one had actually carried out these observances. Indeed, the cult is better observed through study than when it actually existed, for now it can be observed through ideal reflection that transcends its inadequate actuality. Morever, one no longer has to be in Jerusalem to fulfill the laws of the cult, for this ideal study and contemplation can be carried out anywhere. Wherever one studies the laws of cult and land, one creates them in ideal form. They become present in the minds of the studying community.[18]

The Judaism that emerged from the rabbinic schools simultaneously freed the Jews from the requirements of the national cult and residence in the land and fixed its laws in idealized memory. The rabbinic teachers made it possible to be a fully observant Jew anywhere in the world and to win a share in the world to come without residence in the land or pilgrimage to the Temple in Jerusalem. But, at the same time, they made sure that every Jew, in prayer and study, would turn to Jerusalem and to the Temple and remember them. They forbade the building of a new temple any place else in the Diaspora. In this way they made sure that it could exist only in this reflected form of study, as long as Jerusalem itself remained inaccessible and the Temple lay in ruins.

By fixing the land and the Temple in memory, the rabbis fixed them in hope as well. Three weeks of fasting and intense mourning lead to the Ninth of Ab, the day when Jews recall the destruction of the Temple in C.E. 70. Longing for restoration to the land and for the rebuilding of the Temple is kindled through study of the Law. Daily prayer also keeps alive this longing. Three times a day the (male) Jew recites the three benedictions that call upon God to show mercy to his people Israel and his city Jerusalem. The Fourteenth Benediction reads:

Be merciful, O Lord our God, in thy great mercy, toward Israel Thy people, and towards Jerusalem, Thy city, and towards Zion the abiding place of Thy glory, and towards Thy temple and Thy habitation, and towards the king-dom of the house of David, Thy righteous anointed one. Blessed art Thou, O Lord God of David, the builder of Jerusalem.[19]

Such daily reiterated remembrance of the land, the holy city, and the Temple continually generated a longing for their restoration. The rabbis combined faith that this restoration would be a part of future redemption with a rejection of political activism to bring about this restoration of land, city, and Temple. The Temple can be rebuilt and political autonomy in the land restored only through the return of an ideal Davidic king, the future Messiah. Meanwhile the pious Jew must remember and hope but refuse to act on this hope. He must be comforted in the knowledge that, if one studies the laws of the cult and the land, it is as if one had actually carried them out.

In this repression of messianic political action, the rabbis ac-knowledged the realities of a weak people who lacked the power to take over the government of Palestine from the political powers who ruled it. But the rejection of political activism perhaps also reflected the bitter memories of actual Jewish political power dur-ing Hasmonean times and the bloody conflicts that sought to restore political power in the first and second centuries C.E. Rab-binic law implicitly recalled the actual compromises with unrigh-teousness and impurity that inevitably followed upon real political power.

Forbidding the rebuilding of the Temple until the coming of the Messiah assured that there would be no more priestly class and tem-ple sacrifice under ambiguous historical circumstances. Waiting for the Messiah to restore the kingship also made sure there would be no more Jewish king or Jewish state in the land under ambiguous historical circumstances. These realities of Temple and kingship had to be preserved in ideal memory through study until they could be reestablished by God under redemptive conditions that would assure that such violations of the law could not accompany them.

Such rabbinic rejection of rebuilding the Temple and of restor-ing the cult, the priesthood, or the kingship before messianic times did not prevent communities of Jews from moving back to the land. Indeed, the rabbis were intensely concerned about the devastation of Judea after the 66–73 war and encouraged Jews to remain or return there.[20] Many Jews evidently were emigrating to other areas, especially to Syria, during this period. It came to be believed that resurrection would be assured for those who were buried in the land. So many pious Jews wished to have their bones returned to the land for burial to assure their share in the resurrection. Small groups of Jews through the centuries continued to be inspired to return and settle in the land, believing that fuller holiness could be obtained by observing those laws that could be observed in the land and that could not be observed elsewhere. But Jewish political power over the land was not to be taken from the hands of the Gentiles until the coming of the Messiah. Israel was to remain without political autonomy in the land until this could be restored under ideal circumstances. This belief most decisively separates rabbinic Judaism, with its adaptation to life outside the land, or even within the land under conditions of gentile overlordship, from modern Zionism.[21]

In the rabbinic writings, the religious meaning of the Diaspora, or life outside the land, contains two contrasted ideas. On the one hand, life outside the land is *galuth*, exile. Israel is seen as having been conquered and swept away from its own land to the lands of conquerors where the people suffer and are under the domination of alien powers. In common with the prophetic tradition, the rabbis interpreted this exile as punishment for sin. Israel had failed to observe the commandments and so had polluted the land and brought down divine wrath. Therefore the people of Israel were cast out and must suffer the punishment of exile and domination by others. They will atone for this sin and win God's favor by careful observance of the Law in the lands of their exile. This interpretation understands the Diaspora as alienation from full life in the covenant as God intends it. It also prescribes the way to win restoration to the land, through the Pharisaic way of study, not through the Zealot way of messianic politics.[22]

The concept of Diaspora as *galuth* would be developed into a powerful cosmic mysticism in medieval Kabbalism. The whole world would be seen as having fallen into sin and exile. Creation itself is in a state of fallenness and alienation from God. God in his transcendency has hidden his face. The *galuth* reflects a split in God's own essence, between divine transcendence and immanence, imaged as the male transcendent and the female immanent sides of God. God's female immanence has gone into exile with Israel, into the sorrow and darkness of the *galuth*. Only at redemption will these two sides of God be knit together and the unity and communion between God and Creation restored. On the Sabbath, the Sabbath Queen is welcomed, and the festival observances, including sexual intercourse between a husband and wife, symbolize and anticipate this reuniting of God with the Shekinah, God's female, immanent side.[23]

Restoration of Israel to the land thus becomes an integral part of a hope for the redemption of the whole cosmos. This includes the reconciliation of Creation with God and the transparent presence of God in and through Creation. This mystical view of the Diaspora as the *galuth* of the whole Creation, and even the alienation of God from Godself, was particularly developed under the pressure of Christian repression and persecution of Jews in medieval Europe. This heightening of tension and sorrow for the *galuth* and for the loss of life in the land burst its carefully set rabbinic bounds in the sixteenth to eighteenth centuries and led to new messianic activism, as we will see in the next chapter.

On the other hand, there was also, in rabbinic literature and in Judaism down to modern times, a different way of looking at the Diaspora as mission, rather than as *galuth*. This tradition would stress, not the defects of loss of the land, but the sufficiency of the prescribed rabbinic path of study, prayer, and deeds of loving kindness to replace the land and the temple cult. The *Shekinah*, the divine presence, is said to have left the Temple. Indeed, perhaps it never rested on the second Temple at all. But it is now present everywhere and rests on every house of study.[24] The scattering of the Jews among the nations does not reflect divine wrath and punishment but a divine summons to be the "light to the nations," a mission to make the true God and his commandments available to all peoples.[25] This can be done by witnessing to the oneness of God and the minimal laws of decency for all humans (the Noahite laws) amidst the nations. It also means calling the proselyte from among the nations into full standing in the covenant.

This view of the Diaspora as mission was particularly strong in the Hellenistic and Greco-Roman periods, when Judaism, in its rabbinic form, became a missionary faith. After Christianity came to power, it severely restricted Jewish proselytizing. Christianity sought to prevent Judaism from continuing to be a rival missionary religion. But proselytism never died out in Judaism.[26] Modern-day Jews exhibit the physical looks, as well as adaptations of culture, of all the peoples among whom they have resided these last two millennia. This fact witnesses, not only to the rape of Jewish women, but, even more, to the intermarriage of Jews, especially males, with the accompanying acceptance of Judaism by the non-Jewish spouse. It also indicates that individual, as well as mass, proselytism continued to occur.[27] Jews, although in a less overt way than Christians, have become a people drawn from many peoples.

THE TWO COVENANTS, THE HEAVENLY LAND AND THE EXILE OF THE JEWS IN EARLY CHRISTIANITY

The writing of the New Testament parallels the codification of Pharisaic tradition in the Mishnah by the rabbis. Shortly before the fall of Jerusalem in C.E. 70, the Christian "mother church" left Jerusalem for Pella in the Galilee. Unlike the Pharisees, who relocated at the same time in Yahneh, this Christian church disappeared from history. Christianity would henceforth be shaped by Christian churches gathered out of Jewish Diaspora communities and by their gentile converts. New Testament and patristic Christianity differentiated itself from its Jewish past by universalizing and spiritualizing the themes of city and Temple, peoplehood and land. This set its view of covenant and peoplehood in a disjunctive and supercessionary relationship to biblical Israel, over against its rabbinic rivals who claimed unbroken continuity with biblical Israel. Thus one should see the Christian Church and rabbinic Judaism as two peoples emerging at the same time from the *caesura* of the destruction of the Temple, each completing at the same time (C.E. 200) a new interpretive literature based upon Hebrew Scripture (Mishnah and New Testament), and each with rival claims to be the "true Israel."

The New Testament and patristic language that spiritualized and universalized the themes of land, people, and covenant have their roots in Hellenistic and apocalyptic types of Judaism of the previous three centuries. For example, Philo Judaeus (25 B.C.E.–C.E. 45), the leading exemplar of Alexandrine Hellenistic Judaism, regularly translated territorial realities into spiritual realities through Platonic allegorical hermeneutics. In his tract, *Migration of Abraham*, the patriarch's journey from Haran to Canaan is intrepreted as an allegory of the journey to the self from the outward world of the senses to the inward world of the soul.[28] For Philo, the Temple and the clothing of the high priest represented the cosmos, while the high priest himself stood for the divine Logos who mediates between the transcendent God and Creation.[29] This cosmological interpretation of the Temple and high priest could also be applied to the human body and soul as the microcosm. Thus Philo declares, "For there are, as is evident, two temples of God, one of them this universe in which there is also as High Priest His First-born, the divine Word, and the other the rational soul, whose Priest is the real Man."[30]

Transcendentalizing of territorial terms is also common in Jewish apocalyptic literature. In *2 Enoch* 55:2, the sage describes his ascent into heaven: "For tomorrow I shall go up on to heaven, to the uppermost Jerusalem to my eternal inheritance."[31] The prototype of the Temple and sanctuary is also thought of as existing in heaven, with God enthroned at its center (*T. Levy* 5:1). Apocalyptic writings regularly think of these territorial realities as being renewed in glorious, immortal form in the messianic age. Thus the Book of Enoch:[32]

And I stood up to see till they folded up that old house, and carried off all the pillars and all the beams and ornaments were at the same time folded up with it, and they carried it off and laid it in a place in the south of the land. And I saw till the Lord of the sheep brought a new house greater and loftier than the first, and set it up in the place of the first which had been folded up. (*1 Enoch* 90:28)

Some apocalyptic writers do not look forward to a glorifying of the present Temple, city, and land but to a total transcendentalizing of them, in which the present earth will be destroyed and replaced by a heavenly "land." So the Testimony of Job says:[33]

The whole cosmos will pass away and its glory will be destroyed.... My throne subsists in the holy land and its glory is in the world of the imperishable. The rivers will be dried up and the arrogance of their waves will descend to the depths of the abyss. But the rivers of my land where is my throne do not dry up, nor will they disappear, but they shall be forever. (*T. Job* 33)

Transcendentalizing of the land also occurs in rabbinic writings where "inheriting the land" is equated with "having a share in the world to come," in the sense of an eternal heavenly age. For example, in the *gemara* on *M. Sanhedrin* 10:3, the ten tribes who disappeared in the Assyrian exile are said to return in the time of redemption, not to the physical land, but to the world to come.[34]

The Christian understanding of the Church as the community of the new covenant has roots in messianic Judaism. The Essenes, whose literature was recovered in the library from Qumran, saw themselves as initiates into a renewed messianic covenant. This renewed messianic covenant had been foretold by Jeremiah, who looked forward to a messianic covenantal community. The people of this new covenant would never again violate the commandments, for the Law would be internalized in each person's heart. It would no longer need to be taught by one person to another (Jer. 31:31–34). The new covenanters at Qumran saw themselves as the people of the messianic covenant, over against a fallen and sinful Israel that gathered around the apostate priesthood and polluted Temple in Jerusalem. They were the true Israel. Those from apostate Israel who wanted to have a share in the messianic age must repent and become members of their community.

Early Christianity began as a Jewish messianic sect with a self-understanding similar to that of the New Covenanters at Qumran. The early Christians soon gathered into themselves more spiritualizing and universalizing interpretations of the type found in Hellenistic Judaism. But whereas those Jewish apocalyptic and philosophical traditions retained a continuity with the territorial realities thus transcendentalized, Christianity came to interpret the relationship more disjunctively. Philo, for example, explicitly says that the spiritualizing interpretation of Temple and Law does not allow one to neglect their outward manifestations. Rather one should observe these outward duties more faithfully.[35] The outward rite is the sacramental expression of the inward spiritual truth. Christianity, by contrast, came to understand the new spiritual Israel, Temple, priesthood, and land to annul and supersede the "material" expressions of these inward truths. Spiritualization and messianic fulfillment combined to allow the Christian both to negate the historical expressions of these things and, at the same time, to claim to have inherited their spiritual reality on a high plane of life.[36]

For Paul, Christ, present in Christians through baptism, is the spiritual power of right relation to God. Christ has superseded the

Jewish Law, which was present only as external commandments. Those before or outside of Christ are not capable of obeying God from the heart. So, for them, the Law is only a sign of death, not of life.[37] So, for Paul, it is the universal ethical commandments of the Law that the Christian now obeys from the heart through the indwelling presence of Christ. In common with other hellenized Jews, Paul identifies this universal ethical law with natural law and thus says that the Gentiles had this law given to them in the laws of conscience. But they, without the Power of Christ, could no more obey it from the heart than the Jews, who had the Law given them by God.[38]

It is not clear whether Paul regards the more particularistic commandments, such as circumcision, feasts and festivals, laws of purity and kosher, as abrogated by Christ for Jewish Christians. It is possible that Paul assumes that these Christians will continue to observe the whole law.[39] But Paul argues vehemently that those converted to Christ from gentile backgrounds do not need to come into the community of the new covenant through accepting the "yoke" of the Law, i.e., becoming Jewish proselytes. Baptism does not require circumcision. Christ has set the Christian free from the "slavery" of the Law.

Yet Paul was quite aware that his communities of Christians had not been transformed into saints through baptism. The power of the messianic age had dawned in the Church, which anticipates the redeemed age to come. But the present age of sin still reigns in the "world" and continues to lay hold of the minds and bodies of the baptized. So Paul must continue to exhort those who have been given the Spirit to "walk by the Spirit and do not gratify the desires of the flesh" (Gal. 5:16).

Paul habitually sets the new spiritual realities in Christ against their old territorial expression. In an exegesis of Genesis 21:10 on the two sons of Abraham, Paul says:

But the son of the slave was born according to the flesh, the son of the free woman through the promise. Now this is an allegory: these two women are two covenants. One is from Mount Sinai, bearing children for slavery. She is Hagar. Now Hagar is Mount Sinai in Arabia; she corresponds to the present Jerusalem, for she is in slavery with her children. But the Jerusalem above is free, and she is our mother. (Gal. 4:22–26)

Paul universalized the promise of progeny to Abraham by interpreting the people as numerous as the stars (Gen. 15:5) to be all the nations of the earth. This promise of numberless progeny precedes the command of circumcision of the first covenant. Paul understands this as an anticipation of the universal Christian people drawn from among all peoples who are heirs of the promise to Abraham by faith, apart from the Law (circumcision).

Several New Testament writers make use of cosmological and apocalyptic interpretations of the Temple. For Paul, it is the Christian community, with Christ indwelling in it, that is the true temple (1 Cor. 3:17, 2 Cor. 6:16). Each Christian's body is a temple of the Holy Spirit, which must be kept holy by avoiding sin (1 Cor. 6:19). The Book of Hebrews makes the most extensive use of the language of priesthood and sanctuary. Christ is the new high priest of the heavenly sanctuary not made with hands. The sacrifice of Christ in the heavenly sanctuary has replaced the sacrifices and priesthood of the historical Temple. These were merely an outward shadow of this higher spiritual reality. For the author of Hebrews, the new covenant not only fulfills but supersedes and annuls the old covenant. The old covenant, "becoming obsolete and growing old is ready to vanish away" (Heb. 8:13).

The four Gospels were given their final written form after C.E. 70, when the Temple had already been destroyed and Jerusalem ruined by the Romans. In various ways Jesus is made to predict this destruction as a punishment for the refusal of the Jewish leaders to accept his teachings as the culmination of the teachings of the prophets:

O Jerusalem, Jerusalem, killing the prophets and stoning those who are sent to you! How often would I have gathered your children together as a hen gathers her brood under her wings, but you would not! Behold, your house is forsaken and desolate. (Matt. 23:37–38)

Jesus' death and Resurrection are seen as an allegory of the destruction of the Temple and its replacement by an eschatological community that will spring from his risen body (Matt. 26:61; 27:40; Mark 15:58; 15:29; John 2:19).

The Gospels reveal their Jewish roots in their unquestioning assumption that the power of the messianic Spirit is revealed in Jerusalem. It is here that Jesus comes for the final confrontation with the powers of the "present age." It is here that he rises and here that the Spirit is poured out upon the messianic community of the last days. It is from Jerusalem that the gospel goes forth to the "ends of the earth." But there will be no messianic ingathering of the Gentiles to Jerusalem. This ingathering is already happening on a universal, spiritual plane with the conversion of the Gentiles into the Christian Church. This is the true ingathering of the nations to Zion:

> But you have come to Mount Zion and to the city of the living God, the heavenly Jerusalem, and to innumerable angels in festal gathering, and to the assembly of the first born who are enrolled in heaven . . . and to Jesus, the mediator of a new covenant. . . . (Heb. 12:22–24)

While Christians claim to supersede the material, historical realities with spiritual, eschatological ones, this does not allow them merely to cast off their ties with the Jews. The "old" covenant has been superseded, and yet, in some sense, the "old" Israel is still God's people. The Christian covenant is incomplete until the Jews enter it. Paul builds a bridge between his disappointment at the refusal of most Jews to convert to Christ and his faith that Israel is still God's people, who must finally be redeemed, by proposing a "mystery." God has a future timetable of redemption, according to Paul. The gospel must be proclaimed to the Gentiles until their "full number" is gathered in. Then Israel will turn and repent and enter the new covenant of Christ. There is one root of salvation, and this is God's election of Israel. Israel is the cultivated olive tree, and the Gentiles are merely "wild shoots" grafted into the tree. Some of the Jews are the branches that have been "broken off" to make way for these new branches. But eventually they may be "grafted in" again, in the one tree of God's planting (Rom. 11).

In the writings of the church fathers of the second to fifth centuries C.E., the relationship of "old" and "new" Israel becomes even more disjunctive than in the thought of Paul. The New Testament writers were still operating in an apocalyptic perspective that saw the Christian Church as part of the beginning of an eschatological "world to come." They believed that present world history was in its last days; it would soon be transformed by the completed manifestation of the age to come that had been begun in the risen Christ. Thus they could still see their "new covenant," in some sense, as the messianic covenant that fulfills the one covenant with Israel.

But this expected return of Christ failed to happen. As the Christian Church became more gentile and more institutionalized, it came to see itself more as a new elect *historical* community, superseding a morally and spiritually inferior historical community of the Jews. The church fathers typically read the relationship of the two covenants in this more disjunctive manner of historical superseding of one covenant by another in time. The two wives of Abraham, Sarah and Hagar, and their two sons, Isaac and Ishmael, and also the two wives of Jacob, Rachel and Leah, and the two sons of Isaac, Jacob and Esau, all provide metaphors for this relationship. The covenant with the Jews is always identified with the cast-off wife or son, while the Church is the offspring of the true bride.[40]

Some church fathers identify the people of the two covenants with Cain and Abel. This analogy yields the further thought that the Jew, like Cain, is a murderer of his brother. Just as Cain is condemned for this murder to be a homeless wanderer over the earth, so are the Jews. Circumcision is identified as the "mark" that God has given the Jews to identify them as a brother-murderer. Yet this mark protects the Jews from being exterminated themselves. In this way the church fathers suggest that the Jews must wander as a hated people throughout remaining history; they will never be restored to their homeland or be allowed to rebuild their Temple. Yet, though "marked" as a people under divine wrath, they must also be preserved, so that, in the last days, they can complete God's redemptive plan through conversion to Christ.[41]

Augustine integrates this view of the dispersion of the Jews and their final conversion into his interpretation of world history. Augustine believes that the Jews must be dispersed among all nations as a negative testimony of the election of the Church (*City of God* 18:46). But, in the last days, Elias will come and teach the Jews to interpret their own Scriptures spiritually, rather than "carnally." Then they will be able to understand their own Scriptures as predicting Christ. They will be converted and will be saved. This conversion of the Jews is understood by Augustine as a necessary preparation for the final return of Christ in the last judgment (*City of God* 20:29).

The church fathers understand the Christian Church as a spiritual, universal community gathered out of all nations. Thus the Church is not identified with any one culture, nation, or ethnic group. In the Christian Church, all divisions between nations have been overcome in a new universal people. Echoing the Pauline claim that the Christian community in Christ overcomes the division of Jew and Greek, early Christian apologists liked to speak of Christians as a spiritual "third race." They live in all cities but belong to none of them, for their true homeland is heaven. By being spread among all peoples, using the language and customs of all peoples, yet identifying exclusively with none, the Christian community sanctifies the whole world. Thus the author of the letter to Diogenes says:

The distinction between Christians and other men is neither in country nor language nor customs. For they do not dwell in cities in some place of their own, nor do they use any strange variety of dialect, nor practice an extraordinary kind of life. . . . Yet while living in Greek and Barbarian cities, . . . following the local customs both in food and clothing and in the rest of life, they show forth the wonderful and confessedly strange character of the constitution of their own citizenship. They dwell in their own fatherlands, but as if sojourners in them. They share all things as citizens, and suffer all things as strangers. Every foreign country is their fatherland and every fatherland is a foreign country . . . to put it shortly, what the soul is in the body, that the Christians are in the world. The soul is spread through all the members of the body, and the Christians through all the cities of the world. The soul dwells in the body, but is not of the body, and Christians dwell in the world, but are not of the world. . . . The soul dwells immortal in a mortal tabernacle, and Christians sojourn among corruptible things, waiting for the incorruptibility which is in heaven.[42]

As the Christian Church institutionalized itself in the sociopolitical patterns of the Greco-Roman world, and then was taken over by Constantine in the fourth century c.e. as the new imperial religion of a Christian Roman state, this vision of the Church as a sojourner community, in but not of all nations, was subtly transmuted. Christian universalism came to be identified with the universal *Pax Romana*. The Christian Roman emperor came to be seen as a reflection in the political cosmos of the reign of the cosmic Logos, Christ, over the natural cosmos.[43] This identification of Christian universalism with Roman imperial universalism created grave problems for those Christians who fell outside the boundaries of this empire, in Zoroastrian Persia and, later, in Islamic lands. Christians could be seen by those non-Christian empires as secret adherents to a foreign empire. This conflict caused many such Christians to stress hetero-dox creeds in order to make clear their difference from "orthodox" (i.e., imperial) Christians. Many such Christians would convert to Islam, thus leaving Christianity as a dwindling remnant outside the Greco-Roman orbit of culture.[44]

The union of Christian and Roman imperial universalism also heightened the triumphalism with which such Christians regarded the Jews. Christian political power was read as evidence of divine favor, while Jewish dispersion and political disenfranchisement were understood as proof of divine wrath upon the people of the "old" covenant who had failed to accept Jesus as their Messiah.[45] A Christianity now in power as the religion of Christian states believed its obligation was to reenforce the Jews' status of powerless-ness and ignominy. Christians passed civil and ecclesiastical laws that prevented the Jews from prospering economically, entering the public offices of the state, or having a secure foothold in Christian towns.[46] Prosperity and power among Jews thus was implicitly understood by Christians as an "affront" to their belief that they were God's new elect people, while the Jews were under divine wrath.

Christianity translated into legal, political, and social forms its belief that the Jews were to be a wandering and unfortunate people throughout the rest of world history. Yet Christianity also allowed the existence (both socially and religiously) of the Jews in what was otherwise a Christian state that exluded all other religious groups, whether pagans or heterodox Christians. This sufferance of the Jewish presence in an exclusivist Christian society expressed the Christian belief that the Jews must be preserved until they manifest the turning of the tide of history through their conversion to Christ. This connection of repression and preservation was to shape the fateful history of Jews in Christendom. While Jews were continually persecuted, they were also allowed minimal rights to live in Chris-tian lands.[47]

THE COMMUNITY OF ISLAM AND THE PEOPLES OF THE BOOK

Islam is the third great monotheistic religion of the Semitic world to arise out of a common stock of Hebrew Scripture. Created through the charisma and leadership of Muhammed, Islam had spread through the Arabian peninsula by the time of Muhammed's death in C.E. 632 and, by the end of the century, had conquered a vast empire that stretched from the Punjab to North Africa. Its rapid advance owed a great deal to the willingness of the Jewish and Christian populations to receive it as a welcome alternative to Christian Byzantine rule from Constantinople.[48]

Although Muhammed originally thought of his revelations as a special dispensation to the Arabs,[49] Islam quickly began to interpret itself as a universal faith for all tribes or nations of people. Muhammed was not only the final prophet, the seal of the prophets, completing the line of propets of the Jewish and Christian traditions; he was also seen as renewing the original, simple monotheistic faith of Abraham and Moses from its corruptions by Judaism and Christianity. Thus Islam adopted a strategy typical of a new religion: it claimed all that was authentic in its forebears. It saw itself as going beyond them, fulfilling and completing them, but also reaching back before them to the renewal of their original normative roots.

Muhammed drew on the Jewish Talmudic elaboration of the story of Ishmael, son of Abraham, as the father of the Arab people.[50] Abraham, he claimed, was neither a Jew nor a Christian, but a Muslim, the original monotheist who, together with his son Ishmael, overthrew idolatry and founded the monotheistic cult of the Ka'ba in Mecca.[51] Thus the central Islamic sanctuary in Mecca is the original Abrahamic shrine renewed and the restoration and completion of the authentic line of prophecy.

Say, O Muslims: We believe in Allah and that which is revealed unto us and that which was revealed unto Abraham and Ishmael and Isaac and Jacob and the tribes and that which Moses and Jesus received and that which the Prophets received from their Lord. We make no distinction between any of them and unto Him we have surrendered. (Sūra II:136)[52]

Islam is seen as representing the original unity of humanity, united in worship of the One God. But humanity had fallen from its original unity and righteousness into discord and evil. From this sinful discord arose the many nations of humanity, set against one another. God, through Abraham, the prophets, and Jesus, has continually sent revelations to restore humanity to unity and righteousness, culminating in the final prophet, Muhammed. This final revelation restores the original unity of humanity, breaking down all barriers of race and class. It brings together the partial insights of all true revelation of the past and prepares humans for the final day of judgment through the path of true righteousness and submission to the one God, freed from all superstition, miracles, and priestcraft. This is the basic vision of Islam.[53]

From the time of Muhammed, however, Islam was confronted with rejection by those religions it claimed to complete. From the time of Muhammed's ministry in Medina, he was faced with the stubborn refusal of the strong Jewish communities of that region to capitulate to the new religion. They even criticized and mocked his grasp of their ancient Scriptures, thus threatening his claims to prophetic status.[54] These conflicts with the Jews are the source of negative statements against them in the Qur'an. Borrowing anti-Judaic themes from Christianity, the Qur'an depicts the Jews as having received the covenant from God but as having lost it through their many backslidings. Their Scriptures are corrupted and do not represent the original revelations of Moses and the prophets, which have been restored by Muhammed.[55]

The Qur'an also criticizes Christianity. Christians also are said to have fallen away from the original revelations of Jesus into superstition. Perhaps following comparable Jewish critiques of Christianity, the Trinity and the worship of Jesus as God are attacked as idolatry.[56] Thus Islam, like Christianity, claims to incorporate and complete its predecessors but also sets itself against them as corrupted faiths that are no longer reliable guides.

As Islam spread during Muhammed's lifetime and that of his immediate followers, it encountered large Jewish and Christian groups that did not accept Islam. A pattern of treaties was developed between these Jewish and Christian communities and the Muslim rulers, who allowed them to retain their religion and communal self-government in exchange for submission to Muslim overlordship. The payment of the *djizya*, or poll tax, by these subject communities was the basic expression of this relationship between the Muslim rulers and the subject "peoples of the Book," guaranteeing them protection and the right of worship without being pressured to convert to Islam. In time, this status was extended to other religious groups in the territories conquered by Islam, such as Zoroastrians, Samaritans, and even Hindus.[57]

This became the origin of the *dhimma*, or subordinate but protected status of Jews and Christians and other peoples to whom this privilege was extended. It differentiated them from idolaters or polytheists, to whom Islam could offer only the alternative of conversion or the sword.[58] This status was based on Sūra IX:29:

Fight those who believe not in God nor the Last Day, nor hold that forbidden which has been forbidden by God and His apostle, nor acknowledge the Religion of truth (even if they are) people of the Book, until they pay the *djizya* with willing submission and feel themselves subdued.[59]

This practice is at the heart of the contradictory images of Islam in Western society: on the one hand, as the intolerant faith riding out in holy war, offering its conquered people the alternative of Islam or death; and on the other hand, as a tolerant religion where Jews, Christians, and other minority religions were allowed to keep their separate religious practices. Muslim scholars have often portrayed premodern Islamic society as an idyllic time when Jews, Christians, and Muslims lived in harmony and equality.

The reality lies somewhere between these two extremes. The choice of Islam or the sword was offered primarily to the polytheists of Arabia. As Islam encountered more organized religious groups with written Scriptures, it adapted itself to a policy of making treaties with these groups that allowed them to retain their religion in exchange for political submission. But the status of the *dhimma*, the tolerated and protected groups, was hardly one of perfect harmony and equality with the Muslims. A great deal has been written on the exact condition of Jews and Christians in Islam, often comparing it with the status of Jews in Christendom. Verdicts have varied from seeing it as as bad or worse, to much better than the record of the treatment of the Jews in Christian states.[60]

Any accurate comparison of the status of Jews in classical Christian and Islamic lands must cover a period of some fifteen centuries. It must also compare a wide range of different areas and regimes where these religious systems held sway. Such a comparison, even if the sources were available to do it justice, goes far beyond the scope of this brief survey. So we will confine ourselves to some impressionistic generalizations.

The Muslim myth of Jewish "failure" may have lent itself to far less visceral hatred of Jews than did the Christian myth. For the Muslim, the Jews were people who were in the line of true prophecy but who had failed to accept the final prophet. For Christians, the Jews were Christ-killers, deicides, and people whose conversion was demanded in order that redemption be fufilled. The Christian myth has lent itself to a combination of intense paranoia and demanding identification of Christians toward Jews. The Islamic myth suggested rather a somewhat detached contempt.[61] To the Muslims, the Jews were one people of the Book among others; their status was paralleled by that of Christians and other religious minorities. In Christendom, however, Jews were the only non-Christian group allowed to exist at all. Islam lacked the same intense focus on the Jews as a "problem."

The Jews, along with other protected minorities, expressed their submission primarily through the payment of a poll tax. This could be a considerable burden, especially for poorer Jews, but it also suggested a more regular, contractual relationship between the Jews and Muslim rulers. Overall, there was less vulnerability to sudden shifts from prosperity to persecution. Since Islam lacked the Christian myth that the Jews must be converted in order for the final messianic events to be fulfilled, there was not the same possibility of sudden persecutory demands for conversion, such as occurred in Christian lands, especially at times of insecurity and crisis that awakened expectations that the end was near.

At its height, during the tenth to thirteenth centuries, Islamdom allowed Jews not only to prosper as merchants and scholars but to develop a well-organized network of communications from Spain to the Punjab. Within this network, Jews moved freely, as merchants, as pilgrims, and as emissaries from the great seats of learning in Babylonia. The *Gaonim* delivered *responsa* to questions of local communities. Jewish communities throughout the Islamic Diaspora sent donations to support the exilarch (the head of the Jewish community in exile, believed to be a descendant of the royal house of David) and to the *Gaonim* or heads of the two Jewish academies, as well as other worldwide Jewish charities.

Although the status of the Jewish community declined in the thirteenth to fifteenth centuries, along with the general decline of Islamdom, the Jewish community again prospered during the first two centuries of Ottoman rule in the sixteenth and seventeenth centuries. Jews expelled from Spain were welcomed by the Ottomans.

These Jews flocked to the major capitals of the Ottomans, playing important roles in commerce and administration. The schools of Kabbalistic mysticism flourished in Safed in Palestine. Again, the security of the empire allowed Jewish merchants, pilgrims, and scholars to circulate freely from city to city, as part of a distinctively Jewish network of communication within the larger Muslim world.[62]

But there were also patterns of humiliation, occasional persecution, and erratic changes in Muslim relations to Jews, as well as to other minority communities. The Muslims exacted various outward symbols of humiliation, such as wearing distinctive dress. Originally this was done to tell each of the minority groups apart from each other and also from Muslims, but it soon came to be seen as a mark of degradation. There were also laws prescribing that Jews and other minorities should not ride quality steeds, should not wear fine clothes, should keep their houses and synagogues low and shabby, and should not make a display of religion in the streets in outdoor processions.[63] Such regulations often faded away in times of well-being, but they could be suddenly renewed by a zealous ruler who was anxious to renew the faith.

Also, as in Christendom, there was a popular feeling that Jews (and Christians) should "stay in their place," a place distinctly inferior to that of Muslims. So, if the Jewish (or Christian) community became too prosperous and some of its leaders too influential in government, this could bring popular riots and outbreaks of persecution. This resulted in a custom of Jews in Muslin lands wearing beggars' clothing in the streets and keeping the outsides of their houses very shabby, to avert the jealousy of their Muslim neighbors from their actual prosperity; this custom lasted into the twentieth century among some Sephardic Jews.[64] Persecution could also break out if the minority community was perceived as engaged in treasonous collaboration with the enemies of Islam, a charge that fell more frequently on Christians, as co-religionists with the Byzantines and Europeans.[65]

Most scholars have concluded that the status of the Jews was somewhat better in Islam than in Christianity. Jews under Islam suffered from less restriction in residential locations (although each group tended, voluntarily, to live in their own "quarters"). There was also less restriction in occupations, the main occupation closed to minority groups being the army. But humiliation, persecution, and expulsions also took place in the Islamic world, while Jews in

Christendom enjoyed periods of prosperity and near equality, as well as periods of repression, persecution, and expulsions. As S. D. Goitein put it in his classic study, *Jews and Arabs: Their Contacts Through the Ages:*

The position of the Jews inside Arab Muslim society was relatively better than that enjoyed by them in Medieval Europe. But only relatively. In principle, they and other non-Muslims were second-class citizens and consequently their position was always precarious, often actually dangerous. The moving plaints of the great Hebrew poet Yehuda Halevi (d. 1141), who had lived in Muslim and in Christian Spain, that the one was as bad as the other is an eloquent testimony to this state of affairs.[66]

Although Islam claimed to be a universal religion, renewing and completing all past revelations and reconstituting the original unity of humanity, in reality it soon established its own social and territorial limits. Its conception of equality was a patriarchal and ethnocentric one. In practice, the equality of "man" meant the brotherhood of free Muslim males. The subordination of women to men and of slaves to their masters was taken for granted as the natural and divinely given social order.[67] The superiority of the Arabic to the non-Arabic-speaking Muslim world, the identification of Africans with slaves, and the vehement, sectarian divisions within Islam also set up patterns of discrimination. But, most of all, Islam set up—precisely in its claims to universal finality—a rigid line of demarcation between Muslim and non-Muslim. The idolator or polytheist had no right to exist. Islam was called to conquer all nations for the one true and final revelation. This militant, imperialist universalism was modified, as we have seen, by the acceptance of religious toleration for peoples of the Book. But non-Muslims were still marked off in a permanent status of inferiority to Muslims.

Islamic religious and military conquest, which proceeded so rapidly in the first century of its existence, also set up a territorial division of the world. At the center was *Dar al-Islam*, the house of Islam, all those territories brought under submission to Allah and his Prophet. Outside this region lay *Dar al-Harb*, the house or realm of war, yet to be conquered by Islam. In theory, Islam commits itself to a permanent conflict with those regions, conflict that is to end in bringing the whole earth under Islam. In practice, certain limits were gradually established, particularly vis-à-vis the Christian realms of the West. These non-Muslim regions could come to be regarded as the *Dar al-Sulh*, or regions where treaty relations have been established between Islam and non-Muslim peoples, terminating the necessity of warfare.[68]

Since Islam thinks of religion as part of a total political and social order, the mere expanding presence of Muslims in Western Europe and America does not make these regions part of *Dar al-Islam*. This occurs only in those areas where Islam informs the reigning legal and cultural patterns of the society. Islam also generates a strong sense of the worldwide unity of the Muslim *umma* or community. Every male Muslim is committed to a pilgrimage to Mecca once in his lifetime. All Muslims, worldwide, follow the same patterns of prayer and fasting. All Muslims are to see themselves as knit together in one worldwide community across many nations.

How does this Islamic conception of *Dar al-Islam* affect the Muslim view of Palestine and Jerusalem? There is no response within the Qur'an or in classical Islam to Jewish claims to rule this region — probably because no such claims were operative during that period. The Qur'an mentions the giving of the land to the Jews as part of God's covenant.[69] But there is no attention to this idea as an ongoing claim. The covenant with the Jews is conceived of primarily as revealed commandments — commandments that the Jews have broken, thereby corrupting their Scriptures. Islam shared with Christianity and with much of Judaism at that time the interpretation of the future messianic kingdom as a heavenly realm, not an earthly restoration of the Jews to the land.

On the other hand, Muhammed and classical Islam have been very aware of Palestine and Jerusalem as a Holy Land and holy city for Jews and Christians. Muhammed, in his conflicts with the Jews of Medina, sought to supersede the claims of Jerusalem as the holy city by establishing a prior relationship of Abraham to Mecca, declaring that the Muslim should turn to Mecca, not to Jerusalem, to pray.[70] But the popular pull of Jerusalem was too strong to be negated. Within the first generation after his death, the tradition had been established that Jerusalem was the third holiest Islamic city, after Mecca and Medina, and the only other city to which the Muslim might make pilgrimage.[71]

The tradition was established that the night journey of Muhammed to the most distant sanctuary (*al-Masjid al-Aqsa*) was a journey to Jerusalem (Sūra 17:1). When the Muslims conquered the city (bloodlessly) in C.E. 638, the ancient temple mount was cleared to become a focus of Muslim pilgrimage to the site of what was regarded both as the rock of Abraham's averted sacrifice of Isaac and also the place where Muhammed ascended to heaven. The Islamic claims to the site were crowned by the building of the Dome of the Rock on this site by the Umayyad Caliph Abd al-Malik (C.E. 685–705). In the construction of this magnificent building, the caliph sought both to supersede in magnificence the Christian Church of the Holy Sepulchre and also to symbolize the fulfillment of the Jewish and Christian prophecies of a rebuilt Temple.[72]

Despite these Islamic claims to the city, the new Muslim rulers also recognized Jerusalem as a holy city for Jews and Christians. Jerusalem was an entirely Christian city in the seventh century. Jews had been forbidden to reside there after the defeats of the second Jewish rebellion against the Romans (C.E. 136). This tradition had been jealously guarded by the Christian control of the city from the time of Constantine (C.E. 325). After the Muslim takeover of Jerusalem, the Christian population was recognized as a protected minority, and its freedom of worship was established. But the new rulers also allowed the Jewish community to return and reestablish their presence there after more than five hundred years. The contrast between Christian exclusivism and Muslim relative pluralism is vividly illustrated in the treatment of Jerusalem by the two faiths. In C.E. 1099, when the city was captured by the Crusader armies, Jews and Muslims were massacred. Jerusalem again became an exclusively Christian city. But when Saladin retook the city in C.E. 1187, the Jewish presence was again allowed, along with the return of the mosques that had been made into Christian churches.[73]

Jerusalem and Palestine were seen as an integral part of *Dar al-Islam*, from the first decade after Muhammed's death. Not only Jerusalem, but also other sites in Palestine—such as the tomb of Moses in Jericho and the burial place of Abraham in Hebron—are sacred to Muslims and the focus of popular pilgrimage. Characteristically, Islam allows the two earlier monotheistic faiths to continue their devotion to their holy places in Palestine and Jerusalem, while incorporating into itself these past traditions.

For Islam, a fundamental difference exists between allowing Jews and Christians to reside in or make pilgrimage to Palestine and

Jerusalem as tolerated minorities and a takeover of the city and region as a Jewish or Christian state. The first has been operative policy in Islamic history. The second is regarded as an abomination, a just cause of holy war to regain the city and region for *Dar al-Islam*. Islam remembers a previous effort by Westerners, using the Christian Scriptures, to claim this region as their own. During the Crusader period, Christians expelled Jews and Muslims from the city and established an exclusively Christian state in the Holy Land. During the Muslim struggle to regain the city from the Crusaders, the *Fada'il al-Kuds*, a literature of praise and longing for Jerusalem, flourished.[74]

From the Islamic point of view, the Zionist state is a new effort, this time by Jews aided by Western Christians, to use the Bible to lay political claim to Palestine and Jerusalem. The widespread anger and resistance to this effort by the Islamic world expresses the modern developments of Arab nationalism and resistance to Western colonialism. But it also reflects deep emotions, rooted in thirteen centuries of Islamic identification with this region as an integral part of the House of Islam and as a Holy Land of the first and final prophets of Allah, Abraham, and Muhammed.

SUMMARY

All three monotheistic faiths have elements of religious exclusivism and self-centeredness that have been expressed in violent fanaticism toward religious rivals and internal dissenters, as well as elements of ethical humanitarianism. All three have typically negated the right of polytheist nature religions to exist and have believed that they had the right to exterminate those religions by force. They have seen themselves as superseding those religions, in having been called into a unique relation to the one true God. This election makes each of them the one true people of God.

None of the three monotheistic faiths have had a place in their classical theories for a new elect people arising after themselves. Thus Judaism did not recognize the legitimacy of Christianity or Islam to become a second or third covenant people, and Christianity has traditionally rejected the claims of Islam to be the higher and final revelation. Christianity and Islam have had ambivalent views of the covenant people(s) they regard as their religious ancestor(s).

Their traditional pattern has been to see them as having a partial legitimacy, but in an inferior relation to themselves. The earlier religions are seen as an anticipation and beginning of what is completed and fulfilled in themselves. The earlier religions are also seen as having failed, spiritually, by not recognizing and accepting the later revelation, which superseded them.

In contrast to their total intolerance of paganism or heresy, Christianity allowed Judaism, and Islam allowed Judaism and Christianity, the right to exist within the new religiopolitical order they established. But these ancestral faiths were allowed only an inferior status in this new order—an inferior status that often turned to persecution when the other groups were perceived as "getting out of their place." Each of the three religions has seen itself as the epicenter of a universal redemptive history. This redemptive history moves toward a triumphant culmination that will incorporate the whole of humanity, with all rival faiths being either vanquished and destroyed or converted into the one true people of God.[75]

Modern liberal movements in Judaism, in Christianity, and in Islam have suggested a more pluralist universalism that would allow for greater parity among the three monotheistic faiths (and perhaps other "great religions").[76] But such concepts of pluralist universalism are seen as infidelity by the orthodox. All three faiths have seen the revival of exclusivist fundamentalism in recent years, spurred by rivalry over possession of the Holy Land.[77] The following chapters of this book will trace the history of the conflict over the land created by modern Zionism. In the concluding chapter, the book will return to a reflection on what kinds of paradigm shifts in the self-understandings of the monotheistic faiths are demanded today, if the peoples of three faiths are to share the Holy Land in justice and peace.

PART 2.

HISTORICAL DEVELOPMENT OF THE ISRAEL-PALESTINIAN CONFLICT

2. Religious and Secular Roots of Zionism

Woe to you who desire the day of the Lord! Why would you have the day of the Lord? It is darkness and not light; as if a man fled from a lion, and a bear met him; or went into the house and leaned with his hand against the wall, and a serpent bit him. Is not the day of the Lord darkness, and not light, and gloom with no brightness in it? . . . Take away from me the noise of your songs; to the melody of your harps I will not listen. But let justice roll down like waters, and righteousness like an ever-flowing stream.

AMOS 5:18–20, 24

KABBALISTIC MESSIANISM AND THE RETURN TO THE HOLY LAND

As we have seen in the previous chapter, Jewish communal life had adapted itself to the Diaspora from the time of the Babylonian exile in the sixth century B.C.E. With the destruction of the Temple and the razing of Jerusalem after the Jewish Wars of C.E. 66–73 and 133–136, a new religious center was constituted by the rabbis at Yavneh. With their genius for creating myths of continuity in the midst of radical adaptation to new circumstances, the rabbis not only declared that prayer and observance of the Torah could replace the temple cult but also that the heads of rabbinic government, the exilarch of Babylonia and the *Nasi* of the Palestinian Jewish community were descendants of the royal line of David. Thus the rabbis replaced not only the ancient priests but also the ancient kings of Israel. Each Jewish community had its communal organization that claimed basic rights of self-government, such as taxation, legislation, and judiciary. Within larger imperial political systems, Jewish communities constituted a network of self-governing societies that sought to maintain links with each other through shared centers of leadership.[1]

Although the expectation of a return to Jerusalem, the restoration of the Temple, of the sacrificial cult, and of the Davidic monarchy was maintained; the restoration project was religiously sublimated and indefinitely postponed. Ordinary Jewish religious and political life went on through these substitutionary vehicles. It was at moments of crisis, when these vehicles of communal life broke down, that messianic fervor tended to arise. The two parallel streams of rabbinic thought, the rational and the mystical, might clash at such moments. Some rabbis sought to avert the feared fanaticism and the abandonment of rabbinic law that typically accompanied such messianic fervor by minimalizing the importance of belief in the coming of the Messiah or even denying that it was a necessary part of Jewish faith at all.

Moses Maimonides, the great medieval rationalist, declared that the only difference between present history and the messianic age would be that Israel would regain its sovereignty and be ruled by a restored Davidic king in Palestine. There was to be peace under his governance, but otherwise nature would continue its ordinary course.[2] Several Spanish rabbinic teachers, such as Hayyim ben Galipapa and Joseph Albo in the fourteenth and fifteenth centuries, taught that the messianic promises were already fulfilled at the time of the Maccabees or that messianic belief, while allowable, was not essential to Judaism.[3]

The mystical and ecstatic side of Judaism was expressed in the development of Kabbalah, which had its ancient roots in Jewish apocalyptic and Gnostic writings. Side by side with scholastic rationalism there arose, in the twelfth century, a new flowering of mysticism, expressed particularly in the Zohar, which appeared around C.E. 1300. The Zohar was compiled from various sources by Moses ben Shemtov de Leon of Granada (d. 1305). Kabbalistic thought is imbued with intense messianic longing; it views the created cosmos and all its creatures as engaged in a vast struggle to overcome an original cosmic fall into chaos and evil and to restore harmonious unity between God and Creation. This restoration, it was taught, will allow the power of divine blessing to flow freely and fully throughout the world.

Central to Kabbalistic mysticism is a belief that the human being can make a contribution, both personally and cosmically, to this healing of Creation. By ascetic practices, fasts and ablutions, by the study of Torah and Talmud, and by meditative practices (which involved esoteric knowledge of the links between the divine and the created), the mystic can hasten the healing of the brokenness of Creation. Individual Jews and the Jewish community collectively play the paradigmatic role in this cosmic drama. The dispersion of the Jews throughout the world is represented as the diffusion of divine light into the darkness of the impure souls of Gentiles. This impure world is thereby penetrated by divine light and drawn back to its God. In the time of final redemption, the Jewish community will be restored to its land in Palestine as the culmination of the healing of the whole cosmos. Through the restoration of Israel to its kingdom and Temple in Jerusalem, divine light will flow forth, suffusing the whole universe with God's blessing.

In the fifteenth century, Spanish Jewry experienced a continuous worsening of its situation as Catholic Spain completed the recon-quest from the Muslims, unifying the kingdoms of Castile and Ara-gon. The reforming zeal initiated by these events was directed at the purging of heretics and Jews from Spain. In 1492, the same year that Christopher Columbus would set sail for the "new world" and thus begin the saga of Spanish colonialism, the Jews of Spain were com-pelled either to convert to Roman Catholicism or to depart. Many Spanish Jews became *conversos*, real or apparent. Some 170,000 fled, some to Holland and England and others to North Africa, Egypt, and Turkey. This disaster was to have repercussions in Jewish reli-gious life for several centuries thereafter. Spanish Jews scattered, carrying their Kabbalistic literature and practices with them. Under the influence of its messianic teachings, they saw the disaster as the messianic woes that would precede redemption.

The conquest of Palestine by the Ottoman Turks in 1517 allowed some of these Spanish exiles to take up residence there. The town of Safed in northern Galilee became a new spiritual center of the kind of rabbinic learning, imbued with Kabbalistic mysticism, that produced such masters of Jewish mysticism as Moses Cordovero (d. 1570) and Isaac Luria (d. 1572). Kabbalistic learning spread from Safed to other Jewish centers in Palestine: Tiberias, Jerusalem, and Hebron, as well as into the Diaspora, both in the Muslim and Chris-tian worlds.

The popularizationof Kabbalah, despite its supposed secret and esoteric nature, sparked a number of messianic pretenders from the fourteenth to the seventeenth centuries. The most important of these was Sabbatai Sevi (1626–1676).

Sabbatai Sevi imbibed a Judaism already suffused with Lurianic mysticism in the schools of his home town of Smyrna; he pursued this path further through his studies in Saloniki, Constantinople, and Jerusalem. In his travels from Jerusalem to Egypt, he gained his primary disciple in Nathan of Gaza. He proclaimed openly his messianic identity in his home community of Smyrna on Rosh-ha-Shona in 1665. A wave of messianic excitement swept the Jewries of Eastern and Western Europe and the Middle East, only to be shocked in September of 1666 by Sabbatai Sevi's apostasy to Islam, following his imprisonment by the sultan in Constantinople.

This apostasy caused a crisis of faith in his followers. Most fell away in disappointment, but some turned themselves into messianic sects that followed the esoteric interpretation of Sevi's apostasy by Nathan of Gaza. Nathan interpreted Sevi's apostasy as a redemptive *kenosis*. He had descended into the darkness of the gentile world in order to redeem the sparks of light entrapped there. Sabbatian messianic sects spread in Turkey, Italy, Poland, and Germany and sparked various new messianic pretenders in the seventeenth and eighteenth centuries. Several of these movements inspired small migrations of believers to Palestine to await the coming redemption.

In the early eighteenth century a great movement for repentance, inspired by several Sabbatian teachers, swept Polish Jewry. Rabbi Judah Hasid gathered up about fifteen hundred of these Hasidim, through the course of his evangelistic tours through Europe, and brought them to Jerusalem in 1700.

These messianic movements of medieval and early modern Judaism, and the resultant small migrations to Palestine, were fundamentally different from Zionism. Although the reestablishment of Jewish sovereignty in the land might have been their goal, the means to this end were the religious practices of fasting, study, prayer, and observance of divine commandments.

These Jews believed that the way to transform the physical was through the spiritual. They did not negotiate with sultans and kings for political rights; nor did they found agricultural colonies. Rather, they thought of Palestine, and especially Jerusalem, as the mystical center of a spiritual cosmos upon which the physical cosmos depended. They came to the Holy Land to heal the cosmos and hasten the coming of the Messiah through their religious practices. Most of them remained miserably poor, dependent on shop-keeping relatives and the charity of Diaspora Jewries to support their spiritual redemptive work. Nevertheless, Kabbalistic messianism provided a religious vision upon which secular Zionists would draw. As we shall see, a later religious Zionism would seek to synthesize secular Zionism with these earlier Kabbalistic roots.

EUROPEAN NATIONALISM AND THE RISE OF ZIONISM

The eighteenth and nineteenth centuries saw a series of upheavals in European societies that would provide the impetus for the rise of Zionism. The old feudal corporate society, with its separate estates and self-governing communities, was in its final stages of collapse. In its place, the national state, under monarchs and their state bureaucracies, struggled with the demands of parliaments for popular representation in government. Revolutionary liberalism, exemplified in the American and French Revolutions, sought to replace kings and aristocracies with constitutional government. Instead of belonging to a particular estate or community with distinct privileges, all members of the society were to become citizens of the nation-state, with equal civil rights.

This new definition of membership in society had no place for the old Jewish *Kehillah*, or quasi-self-governing communal organization. Liberalism sought to dissolve the old disabilities that had kept Jews in the ghetto and had barred them from entrance into the political, economic, and educational institutions of Christian society. But the price for this emancipation was the dissolution of Jewish corporate self-government. In the debate over the emancipation of the Jews in the French Constituent Assembly in December, 1789, Count Clermont-Tonnerre summed up the liberal position: "Everything must be denied to the Jews as a nation and everything granted to them as individuals. They must not form either a political body or an order in the state; they must be individual citizens."[4]

A brief excursus on the terms 'race' and 'nation', 'racism' and 'nationalism' might be helpful at this point. In the nineteenth century the terms race and nation were closely associated. In a 1934 edition of Webster's *New Collegiate Dictionary* race is defined as "descendents of a common ancestor, a family, a people, a tribe or nation".

In the nineteenth century race-theory meant a belief that human groups could be ranked according to superior or inferior capacities and even as descendents from different primal ancestors. These different groups were seen as distinct sub-species. Racists regarded groups such as Germans and German Jews as distinct "races." Today anthropologists tend to make distinctions of race only between large groups that are physically distinct in a recognizable way, such as Caucasian, Negro, Polynesian or Oriental. All human beings are seen as one species and ranking of capacities between human groups is rejected.

Nineteenth century nationalism believed that each distinct ethnic-linguistic group should be a self-governing political entity. This was the meaning of the term 'nation-state.' Today nationality is used primarily to refer to the state where one holds citizenship, regardless of one's ethnicity of origin. Few, if any, states today have a homogeneous ethnic population. Thus the concept of the nation-state has proved unrealistic. Nationality and citizenship have become umbrella terms which encompass people of a plurality of ethnic and linguistic groups within one political community.

The emancipation of the Jews was one facet of the secularization of European society. The church lost its right to ban heretics or members of other religions from society, and its control over other public institutions, such as schools and hospitals, was loosened. Religion was defined as a private, voluntary choice, not established by the state. This shift in the public status of the church was deeply resented by much of the clergy and feared by conservative Christians. The nineteenth century saw a protracted struggle between conservative lay and clerical forces and liberalism. This included a debate over the emancipation of the Jews. All the old anti-Jewish canards of Christian culture about the supposed evil nature of the Jews, and the need to keep them in a state of misery and subjugation because of their guilt in the crucifixion of Christ, were revived in these arguments over Jewish emancipation.

In the process of this debate, the "Jewish problem" in European society was to become intensely exaggerated. Instead of seeing Jewish emancipation as one facet of larger shifts in society, Jews themselves came to be seen as the principal cause of these shifts. The cultural paranoia that Christian culture had harbored toward the Jews was given new power as the Christians imagined that the Jews were a secret cabal plotting the disintegration of the old values of Christian feudal corporate society. Modern reforming and revolutionary movements, such as liberalism and socialism, were seen as movements created and dominated by Jews, rather than movements to which some emancipated Jews were attracted.

In this struggle between conservativism and liberalism, new racial theories were born. European nationalities, themselves the product of a mixture of migrating peoples over several millenia, began to imagine that each belonged to a distinct organic community, tied together by biological bonds of common blood and rooted in a common national land. This nationalist racial theory, in turn, defined the Jews, no longer as adherents of an alien religion, but now as an alien race, foreign and unassimilable to European peoples. The term *anti-Semitism* was coined in 1879 to name this new anti-Jewish racism. Anti-Semitic parties arose in Europe, using the Jews as scapegoats for a variety of changes brought by secularizing and industrializing developments. In spite of this new anti-Semitism, the emancipation of the Jews gradually won in Western Europe in the second half of the nineteenth century, although many disabilities in housing, education, and professions continued to linger.

In Eastern Europe a much different history unfolded. Toward the end of the eighteenth century, some one million Jews lived in Poland. Between 1772 and 1795 Poland was subdivided three times, in 1795 disappearing into the surrounding monarchies of Russia, Prussia, and the Austro-Hungarian empire. All three of these monarchies, where previously few Jews (or, in the case of Russia, no Jews) had lived, now acquired large and growing Jewish populations. Eastern European Jewry would grow to 5.5 million by 1900 and 7 million by 1930, despite large-scale emigration, particularly to the United States. The great majority of Eastern European Jewry was in Russia and in Russian-controlled Poland. The Czarist empire especially pursued repressive policies toward the Jews, trying to persuade them to assimilate and to convert to Christianity. Those who refused to convert were isolated by limiting their numbers, places of residency, occupations, and educational opportunities.[5]

In Russia, the most backward of the three monarchies, during the first half of the nineteenth century, laws were enacted that abolished the authority of the Jewish *Kehillah* and expelled Jews from the villages. Compulsory twenty-five-year military service was required of Jewish youths from their teens, with the intention of forcing them to lose their Jewish identity and convert to Christianity. As a result, Jews crowded into urban areas, particularly in the Pale of Settlement (formerly Poland). The reign of Czar Alexander II (1855–81) brought liberal reforms that allowed some Jews more educational and professional rights.

Jews were caught between various tensions in society. Partially emancipated Jews were attracted to the revolutionary movements for democratic and socialist reforms against the autocratic regime. During this period serfdom was abolished, but the serfs were not given land on which to make a living on their own. Restive and impoverished peasants were encouraged by the government to direct their anger against the relatively more prosperous Jews. Rising nationalism of subjugated ethnic groups, such as Poles and Ukranians, often cast Jews as beneficiaries of the dominant regime and as the enemies of such national aspirations.

In 1881 Alexander II was assassinated by young revolutionaries. The Jews became the scapegoats of revolutionary tensions, and a series of government-promoted pogroms (organized massacres) was directed against them in the late nineteenth and early twentieth centuries. Jews responded to these tensions and assaults in various ways; many simply tried to continue their traditional way of life. For millions, the solution was immigration to America or Western Europe. Many joined movements for democratic and socialist revolution.

Those joining revolutionary parties were divided between nationalists and universalists. Universalist socialists wanted to join with other workers to create a workers' movement in which differences of nationality would be dissolved in a common international socialist struggle. Other Jewish socialists argued that Jews, like Ukrainians and Poles, were a distinct nationality and needed to organize workers along national lines. These nationalist Jewish socialists, in turn, were differentiated between those who wanted to remain in Europe and be recognized as a distinct national group and those who sought to immigrate to a Jewish homeland and build a new Jewish society in a land of their own. Those in the second group were later called Zionists. The Zionist option grew particularly rapidly after the 1881 pogroms convinced many Jews that the virulence of anti-Semitism made it impossible for them to be accepted as equals in Europe, either as individuals or as a national community.

A few isolated voices had advocated Zionism before 1881. One of these was Moses Hess, a former univeralist socialist who collaborated with Karl Marx in founding the First International. In the middle of the nineteenth century, Hess was influenced by rising movements for national emancipation, especially by the Italian national unification movement led by Mazzini, to reidentify with his Jewish roots by defining Jews as a nation. In 1862 Hess published his Zionist manifesto, *Rome and Jerusalem*. Here he argued against Enlightenment universalism and declared the futility of Jewish efforts to disassociate themselves from their ethnic culture in order to become acceptable, as democrats or socialists, in secular states. He also rejected the efforts of Reform Judaism to refashion Judaism as a private religion, shorn of many of its public, collective features.

Hess argued that individuals have identities and rights only as part of a national community and that the Jews need to return to themselves as a nation, refounded on their ancient homeland in Palestine. He saw this renationalization as particularly necessary for the downtrodden Eastern European Jews, although he conceded that assimilation might be possible for bourgeois Western Jews. He envisioned the refounded Jewish nation as a model of ethical socialism for all other nations. True universal humanity, Hess believed, can exist only as an international community of nations, each accepting the other's national rights.[6]

In contrast to Hess's secular socialist Zionism were other forerunners, such as Yehudah Alkalai and Zvi Hirsch Kalisher, who sought to combine nationalist ideas of return to Palestine with the religious tradition of messianic hope.[7] Rather than returning to the land only for prayer and study, they argued that Jews oppressed elsewhere should buy land and start colonies. Although redemption is still in the hands of God, the coming of the Messiah could be hastened by these more secular types of human effort.

VARIETIES OF ZIONISM

PRACTICAL ZIONISM

In 1882, Leo Pinsker, a secularized Russian Jewish physician, horrified by the 1881 pogroms, wrote *Auto-Emancipation*. He argued that Jews, instead of being the objects of assimilation projects within majority cultures, must become the subjects of their own emancipation. Jews, he declared, are essentially a nation, not a religious community. But they lack the key elements of a nation: a national language and a national homeland. Without a land to embody their nationhood, they are like ghosts floating around in other people's homes. Pinsker even attributed anti-Semitism to a phobia evoked in other people by this ghostlike existence of the Jews. The only way to cure anti-Semitism, he argued, was for Jews to claim their national identity, in the process rejecting the passivity inculcated into them by their religious traditions. Jews should organize a national fund to buy land for a national homeland. For Pinsker this could be any freely available land, not necessarily in Palestine.[8]

Pinsker's book caused a sensation when it was published (originally anonymously). It was denounced by the religiously orthodox as heresy and by the liberals as loss of faith in the promise of emancipation in secular democratic states. But it was adopted as the manifesto of Jewish cultural nationalist groups that had arisen in Odessa and elsewhere in Russia. Calling themselves *Hovevei Zion* (Lovers of Zion), these groups were interested in revival and transformation of Jewish identity, including the recreation of Hebrew as a national language, rather than only as a language for prayer and religious study. They sought to create schools for modern Hebrew education.

Unlike Hess or Pinsker, the Jews of *Hovevei Zion* were close to Jewish communal and religious roots. Typically, they had been raised in Orthodox homes and given traditional religious education but had revolted as youths against the narrowness of this religious culture by reading the new literature of the Enlightenment. They were now seeking a way to integrate their religious roots with their new Enlightenment ideas. The call to build the Jewish nation brought together their new secular faith with the older visions of messianic redemption. While a thoroughly secularized man such as Pinsker might contemplate a Jewish national homeland in Argentina, for them there could be only one place where such a homeland could be built. That was *Eretz Israel*, the ancient biblical homeland.

Inspired by these visions, the first wave of colonists set out for Palestine in the 1880s to found agricultural colonies. But they had difficulty financing their ventures. So a delegation led by Yosef Feinberg, together with Pinsker, visited Baron Edmond de Rothschild, the Jewish banking aristocrat, to ask for his help. Rothschild agreed to subsidize the colonies and spent some 1.4 million pounds sterling on these over the next twenty years. This led to one of the foundational disputes of early Zionism. The *Hovevei Zion* settlers saw their colonies as utopian socialist communities where class divisions between owners and workers would be overcome. They imagined that, through agricultural labor, the Jew, so long confined to an alienated urban life, would be transformed into a full-bodied "natural" person, in touch with the soil and with the bodily world.

Rothschild, by contrast, viewed the colonies as a colonial commercial venture that would be profitable, as well as providing a living for destitute Jews of Eastern Europe. He wanted them to specialize in viniculture, since he was involved in the wine trade in Europe. While the *Hovevei Zionists* wanted a diversified agriculture that would create self-sufficiency for an egalitarian society, Rothschild saw the colonies as private enterprise. He also assumed that the colonists would use Arab labor for the manual work; this collided with the colonists' vision of a homogeneous, Hebrew-speaking community. In order to supervise such labor, the colonists would have to spend most of their time speaking Arabic, not Hebrew.

The question of Arab labor was to be an explosive one in the first three decades of the twentieth century, as Zionist colonists, inspired by utopian socialist ideas, planted the foundations of the *kibbutzim* and *moshavot* colonies (the former have a totally collective life, while the latter allow for separate family ownership within a shared enterprise). The use of Arab labor was in conflict with the nationalist and socialist ideals of these settlers. As articulated by spokespersons such as Aaron David Gordon (who joined a *Hovevei Zion* agricultural colony at the relatively advanced age of forty-eight, after a previous life as a business manager), direct agricultural labor was endowed with mystical powers to redeem the Jews from the personal and social alienations that had been generated by the ghetto. The ghetto, to which the Jews had been confined in European Christendom, was seen as having stunted their existence. Cut off from nature and from manual labor, they had been forced to live primarily by their intelligence. Confined to a narrow spectrum of marginal professions, most commonly as moneylenders and tax collectors, the Jews had been forced socially into a class antagonism against those who worked with their hands, agricultural laborers and urban workers.

Labor-Zionists called this effort to create a Jewish working people "the conquest of labor." Agricultural labor was seen as transforming all these internal and social alienations. The antagonism between managers and workers would be overcome in workers' self-managed cooperatives. Through bodily labor, Jews would get back in touch with their vital energies as embodied beings. There lingered in Gordon's Labor-Zionist thought an emotional sense of the mystical qualities ascribed by the Jewish religious traditions to the land and soil of the Holy Land, now translated into the language of romantic nationalism. Getting back in touch with the holy soil of the land of Israel, Jews would return to their own fullness of being. Gordon's romantic nationalism, which linked the Jewish spirit with its national homeland, is evident in this extract from a 1920 writing:

There is a cosmic element in nationality which is its basic ingredient. That cosmic element may best be described as the blending of the natural landscape of the Homeland with the spirit of the people inhabiting it. This is the mainspring of a people's vitality and creativity, of its spiritual and cultural values. Any conglomeration of individuals may form a society in the mechanical sense, one that moves and acts, but only the presence of the cosmic element makes for an organic national entity with creative vitality. . . .

Jewish life in the Diaspora lacks this cosmic element of national identity; it is sustained by the historic element alone, which keeps us alive and will not let us die, but cannot provide us with a full national life. What we have come to find in Palestine is the cosmic element. . . . It is life we want, no more and no less than that, our own life feeding on our own vital resources, in the field and under the skies of our Homeland, a life based on our own physical and mental labors; we want vital energy and spiritual richness from this living source. We come to our Homeland in order to be planted in our natural soil from which we have been uprooted, to strike our roots deep in its life-giving substances, and to stretch our branches in the sustaining and creating air and sunlight of our Homeland.[9]

While Gordon focused on communion with the land, other cultural nationalists, such as Asher Ginsberg (whose pen name was Ahad Ha'am), concentrated on the recovery of the Hebrew language and its transformation from a sacred to a national language, as the key element in Jewish national redemption. Brought up in an Orthodox household in the Russian Ukraine, Ginsberg lost his religious faith by reading forbidden Enlightenment literature. His literary work can be seen as a lifelong effort to replace that religious faith with a new secular spirituality. He became the gadfly of political Zionists who thought of Zionism primarily in terms of diplomacy with imperial powers. But he was also deeply angered by some of the *Hovevei Zion* agricultural colonists whose sense of cultural superiority to the local Arab population, as well as their methods of acquiring land, led to demeaning and violent relations with their Arab neighbors.

Ginsberg was an early voice warning against these anti-Arab attitudes of the Zionists; he emphasized the need to find ways of settlement that would build mutual respect.

One thing we certainly should have learned from our past and present history, and that is not to create anger among the local population against us.... We have to treat the local population with love and respect, justly and rightly. And what do our brethren in the Land of Israel do? Exactly the opposite! Slaves they were in their country of exile, and suddenly they find themselves in a boundless and anarchic freedom, as is always the case with a slave that has become king, and they behave toward the Arabs with hostility and cruelty, infringe upon their boundaries, hit them shamefully without reason, and even brag about it. Our brethren are right when they say that the Arab honours only those who show valour and fortitude, but this is the case only when he feels that the other side has justice on his side. It is very different in a case when [the Arab] thinks that his opponent's actions are iniquitous and unlawful; in that case he may keep his anger to himself for a long time, but it will dwell in his heart and in the long run he will prove himself to be vengeful and full of retribution.[10]

Despite the idealistic beliefs of socialist Zionists that, through communal institutions and Jewish labor, they would avoid setting up a new class hierarchy, it is evident that the Arabs in Palestine experienced the Zionist settlements as a threatening form of Western colonialism. Not only did the Zionists buy up land from Arab landlords, creating economic prosperity for Arab elites (while displacing Arab tenants who previously were tillers or animal herders on the land), but the settlers refused to allow those former tenants to regain employment by working as hired laborers in the very fields from which they had been displaced. This refusal took the form of an economic vigilantism on the part of Zionist militants, who drove Arab laborers out of fields where they had been employed by less ideological Jewish farmers, or who boycotted the agricultural produce that the Arabs sought to peddle to their Jewish neighbors.[11]

The Palestinian Arabs experienced the Zionists as planting exclusivist institutions, setting up a total way of life, culturally and economically, that eliminated interchange between Arab and Jew. These Zionists were different from the Jews who had previously lived in Palestine; their concerns had been primarily religious. Most of them, especially the Sephardim, had spoken Arabic as the language of daily life because Hebrew was a sacred language, restricted to religiously educated men.[12]

POLITICAL ZIONISM

The founding of Zionism as a political movement, seeking national sovereignty over Palestine as a Jewish state, begins with Theodor Herzl. Herzl was a secularized westernized Jew, born in Budapest, the only son of a wealthy merchant. The family moved to Vienna when he was eighteen. Herzl studied law but found more congenial employment as a journalist; in 1891 he was sent to Paris by his newspaper to be its resident correspondent. A brilliantly creative author of theatre plays, Herzl's hopes for acceptance in European society were repeatedly shocked by incidents of rising anti-Semitism, both as a social theory among intellectuals, such as in Edouard Drumont's book, *La France Juive* (1856), and in popular outbreaks, particularly the prolonged struggle in French society over the Dreyfus case. Captain Dreyfus, a French-Alsatian Jew with the French army general staff, was used as a scapegoat by the French military for the sale of French military secrets to the Germans. Herzl was present at the École Militaire when Dreyfus was publicly humiliated, stripped of his epaulets, and sent off to prison on Devil's Island, while the crowd howled "*à bas les Juifs.*"

These experiences made Herzl believe that assimilation into European society was impossible for the majority of Jews. He became convinced, instead, that Jews should seek support from world political leaders and their own wealthy philanthropists to found and finance a state of their own. The majority of the Jewish population of Western and Eastern Europe could then be removed to this state, thereby solving at the same time the problems of Jewish alienation and European anti-Semitism. Herzl expected European political leaders would want to support this program, since they would have a stake in solving the problem of anti-Semitism in their societies by getting rid of most of their Jews.

Herzl thought of the Jewish state as a solution to anti-Semitism, but he also expected to use anti-Semitism as a means to this end.[13]

to

This notion that Zionists could look to anti-Semites as allies in founding a Jewish state, thus using the desire of anti-Semites to rid their societies of Jews, was to be a fateful combination in Zionist history. It would mean that political Zionists would have very little interest in ameliorating anti-Semitism in European societies, or in opening up other opportunities for Jewish migration, since they would see the victims of anti-Semitism as the potential immigrants who would build the Jewish state.

In the second half of the nineteenth century, several leading Jewish philanthropists, including Britain's Sir Moses Montefiore and the Franco-German barons Maurice de Hirsch and Edmond de Rothschild, had funded Jewish colonies in Palestine and also in other areas, such as Argentina. These philanthropists had no interest in Jewish nationalism; their projects were aimed (particularly in Montefiore's case) at ameliorating the poverty of Palestine Jewry, who traditionally were dependent on Western Jewish charity, as well as siphoning off the destitute Jews who were pouring into Western Europe from Eastern Europe. They sought to make the position of successful Jews, such as themselves, more secure in Western nations by removing poor, unassimilated Jews who might stir up the antagonism of their gentile neighbors. These Jewish philanthropists prided themselves on being Jews but also on being leading citizens of England and France.

Shocked by his experiences with the Dreyfus case, Herzl sought to interest Hirsch and Rothschild in his project of a Jewish state. In the process he wrote his manifesto, *The Jewish State* (1896), as a way of presenting his plan to these philanthropists, but he was rebuffed by both of them. He found more support from Eastern European practical Zionists and began to look to them as the base of his movement. In 1897 more than two hundred delegates answered his call to come together in Basel, Switzerland, to found the World Zionist Organization. Still Herzl did not give up his hopes of finding a world power that would provide the political charter for national sovereignty for a Jewish state. He met with such world leaders as the sultan of Turkey, Germany's Kaiser Wilhelm, the king of Italy, Pope Pius X, the grand duke of Baden, and the British colonial secretary, seeking his national charter but was disappointed by each.[14]

Herzl was a highly theatrical personality, and it was due to his extraordinary charisma that he was able to be received by these leaders at all. Almost by the force of his own personality, he put Zionism on the map of world politics. Under his leadership, Zionism became a political movement with a world organization that could represent the "national will" of Jews as a nation and that would eventually succeed in winning from the British the national charter that Herzl had failed to secure in his own lifetime; he died in 1904 at the age of forty-four. Herzl's concept of seeking a national charter from a world power bore the fateful consequence of attaching Zionism to the patronage of Western colonialism — German, British, and, later, American.

Herzl, as a secular Jew, had little understanding of the religiously rooted emotions for the Jewish homeland and for the Hebrew language that pulsated in Eastern European Zionism. He was quite willing to entertain a proposal by the British for a territory in Eastern Africa (Uganda) for the Jewish state. His vision of the ideal community that Jews would found was the epitome of European literary sophistication: there Jews would be masters of the major European languages, not creators of a Hebrew-speaking national culture.[15] In *The Jewish State*, Herzl lays out the dilemmas of anti-Semitism for Jews and Gentiles and how the Jewish state would solve them. He also sketches the organization of the agencies that would found the Jewish state.

Herzl envisioned a Jewish Company as a chartered joint stock company under British jurisdiction, similar to the British East India Company that laid the basis for the British colonial occupation of India. This Jewish Company would convert the property of departing Jews into capital; it would purchase land in the territory to be acquired for the Jewish state and would then lease or sell land to the settlers. Herzl envisioned enormous profits accruing to this Jewish Company through land speculation, both in the lands from which Jews were emigrating and in the one to which they were to migrate; these profits were to provide a sound financial base for the enterprise. The Jewish Company would assist gentile nations in facilitating Jewish emigration and would also organize the settlement of Jews in their new land.

There would also be a Jewish Society that would represent the international arm of Jews themselves engaged in this project, in interlocking relationship with the Jewish Company.[16] In this manifesto, Herzl envisioned a pattern that would largely come to pass in the basic organization of Zionism: the World Zionist Organization, the Jewish Agency for Palestine, and the Jewish National Fund. These organizations would not only shape the securing of land and the fundraising and political negotiations of world Zionism but would also continue to shape the actual organization of the State of Israel.

In the subsequent meetings of the international congresses of the World Zionist Organization during the first three decades of the twentieth century, fierce arguments raged over the divergent approaches of Eastern European practical Zionism and Western political Zionism. Eastern Zionism decided the issues over where the Jewish state must be (Palestine) and its national language (Hebrew). Yet arguments continued over whether the Jewish state should be founded by a gradual process of migration, land purchase, and settlement, seeking only afterwards the political charter for national sovereignty, or, as Herzl had thought, by seeking the national charter from a world power first and then arranging rapid mass migration of Jews. The changing configuration of these arguments is too complex to trace here, affected as it was not only by the ideological differences among Zionists but also by changing international political realities.

In retrospect, the two approaches proved complementary, rather than mutually exclusive. When the final political charter sought by Zionism was granted by the United Nations in 1947, it was evident that Jews could gain international recognition only from Western, but not from Arab and Third World, nations and only for those areas that the Jews had partially colonized already, not areas to which they laid theoretical claims but had not managed to settle, such as the West and East banks of the Jordan. Even those territories where they had settled contained a majority of Arab residents—a basic problem for the definition of a Jewish state that will be spelled out in greater detail in a later chapter.

In the early twentieth century there arose other variants of Zionism: Orthodox religious Zionism and Revisionism. Each would contribute in decisive ways to the shaping of the state that would become Israel in 1948.

ZIONISM AND JUDAISM

Zionism had a religious background in Jewish messianism. In the nineteenth century, some Orthodox religious Jews began to translate messianism into practical plans for colonization. But most religious Jews, both Reform and Orthodox, remained basically hostile to Zionism until the Second World War. For Orthodox Jews, Zionism was a secular messianic heresy, an effort to do by human means what could be accomplished only by God. Although settlement in Palestine remained a sacred obligation for them, this was for the purpose of more effective prayer in the Holy Land. The return of Jewish political sovereignty over the land promised them by God could be accomplished only by the Messiah.

Eastern European (Ashkenazi) Orthodox Jews also were offended by Zionist efforts to transform Hebrew into a modern secular language. To them, this was a profanation of the sacred and reminded them of the efforts of forced secularization that enlightened despots had tried to foist upon Jews in Russia. Zionists themselves, as secular Jews who no longer observed the ceremonial and ritual commandments of Torah, were deemed non-observant, if not apostate; they were therefore unfit for the holy task of building Zion in anticipation of the Messiah's arrival.

Orthodox opponents of Zionism particularly cited a portion of the Babylonian Talmud, where the community of Israel was said to have sworn three sacred oaths to God at the beginning of the Exile. These three oaths were to (1) refrain from "forcing the end," i.e., trying to hasten the promised restoration of the land; (2) abjure any rebellion against the peoples of the world; and (3) abjure any attempt at regaining possession of the Holy Land. Orthodox Jews in Palestine also opposed Zionism. Rabbi Joseph Hayyim Sonnenfeldt, writing from Jerusalem in 1898, declared that "Doctor Herzl comes, not from the Lord, but from the side of pollution."[17]

Reform Jews, on the other hand, saw Zionists as apostates, not so much from Judaism, as from the promise of the Enlightenment. Reform Judaism was developed by emancipated German Jews in the early and midnineteenth century and became the predominant form of worship and theology in American Judaism. In America, Reform Judaism reshaped Judaism as a religion so that it would be more easily compatible with secular democratic nation-states, such as the United States, in which religion was separate from state. Many cultic laws, requiring kosher and a separate way of life for Jews, were dropped by Reform Judaism.

Judaism was reconstructed on what was regarded as its essence, namely its ethical and monotheistic core.[18] The Reform temples became like Unitarian churches, with organ music, mixed gender choirs, benevolent societies, and family-centered activities. Rabbis became more like liberal Protestant ministers in their functions. In America, Judaism thus could be seen as the Jewish religious option; it stood side by side with a variety of other voluntary religious or nonreligious options for personal life for people who then came together politically in a common secular nationalism.

In America, Reform Jews were committed to the fulfillment of the promise of secular democracy. They sought to integrate Judaism as one of the civic religions in American public life. Some also sought to eradicate racism, so that peoples of all religions and races could become fully equal as citizens. They believed that Jews could be assimilated politically and culturally and remain Jews religiously. Zionists represented an antagonistic challenge to this project, because Zionists claimed that such states, where Jews would be accepted fully as fellow citizens with their gentile neighbors, could never happen. It was the very nature of the nation-state to be ethnically particularistic. For Zionists, Jews were essentially a nation and must seek their own nation-state. Judaism as a religion was ancillary to their national identity.

In this conflict of Zionists against Reform and secular non-Zionist Jews, there can be seen a fundamental conflict between two views of the state: one pluralist and universalist view and the other racial-ethnic and particularist. For the pluralist-universalist, the state becomes a political framework in which people of many religions, ethnicities, and races are to live together. This perception begs the question of how such a state is a "nation" at all. What holds the state together as a cultural community? Is there to be one national language? Whose language will it be? Can there be a nation without some cultural commonalities?

The particularistic view, by contrast, defines each ethnic group as a biological, cultural entity that should possess its own national land, language, and sovereignty. This is the view that animated European nationalists of the late nineteenth and early twentieth centuries and that shaped Zionism, as well as European racism. It is the view that lay behind a variety of other nationalist movements, such as Irish nationalism and Ukranian, Polish, and other Eastern European nationalist movements. The treaty settlements in Europe after World War I expressed this principle by attempting to accord national sovereignty to various ethnic groups that had been submerged in the Austro-Hungarian and Russian empires.[19]

Yet this belief that each ethnicity should have its own sovereign state has also proved contradictory. Wars and migrations have created too many mixtures of ethnic groups, languages, and cultures for these to be neatly separated in distinct political communities. Some acceptance of ethnic, religious, and even linguistic plurality has become necessary for the modern state in order to ameliorate the conflicts between different religions and ethnic communities within its borders. This, in essence, is the dilemma confronted today by the State of Israel with its racial, ethnic, and Orthodox-religious definition of itself as a Jewish state. It is ironic that most American Jews, who are strongly committed to the view of the secular, pluralistic state in the United States, support an ethnically and religiously exclusivist Jewish state in Israel.

During the first decades of the twentieth century, Abraham Isaac Kook, (1864–1935) Ashkenazi chief rabbi of Palestine under the British Mandate, sought to reconcile secular Zionism with Orthodox Judaism by stretching the interpretation of traditional Kabbalistic messianism. The Kabbalists had taught that pious Jews could hasten the arrival of the Messiah by their religious labors. Kook extended this idea to say that the secular Zionists were also hastening the coming of the Messiah through their agricultural labor. (The Hebrew word for worship, *avodah*, is the same as that for labor.)[20] The fact that the Zionists were motivated by secular goals and were religiously nonobservant did not prevent them from being an expression of the divine will. In God's providential plan for redemption, they were laying the foundation for a return to Zion that would then, at a later stage, flower into a revival of religious piety. The Spirit of God and the Spirit of Israel being identical, Zionists, in their nationalist return to collective peoplehood, were acting through the Spirit of God, even if unknowingly.[21]

Kook's thought is replete with a mystical view of the properties of the land and soil of Eretz Israel. That land lies at the center of

Creation and is closer to God and less in exile from God than the rest of the earth. The land itself is holy, and life in it becomes holy and purified by being closer to the Source of Creation. For Kook, it was impossible to live a full Jewish religious life in the Diaspora. The gentile world is unholy, and Jewish life there is polluted. Only in the land of Israel can the commandments be fulfilled with full efficacy. Kook believed there was a cosmic redemptive mystery at work in the return of Jews to the Holy Land. This, for Kook, must eventually be a return to the land of Israel for *all* Jews. As Jews gather into their land, the whole cosmos will be restored to its authentic center. The whole of Creation will be redeemed through the resto-ration of the people of Israel to its land.

Eretz Israel is not something apart from the soul of the Jewish people; it is no mere national possession.... Eretz Israel is part of the very essence of our nationhood, it is bound organically to its very life and inner being.... Jewish original creativity, whether in the realm of ideas or in the arena of daily life and action, is impossible except in Eretz Israel. On the other hand, whatever the Jewish people creates in Eretz Israel assimilates the universal into characteristic and unique Jewish form, to the great benefit of the Jewish people and of the world. The very sins which are the cause of our exile also pollute the pristine wellspring of our being, so that the water is impure at its source....

Revelations of the Holy, of whatever degree, are relatively pure in Eretz Israel; outside it, they are mixed with dross and much impurity.... In the Holy Land man's imagination is lucid and clear, clean and pure, capable of receiving the revelations of Divine Truth and of expressing in life the sub-lime meaning of the ideal of the sovereignty of holiness; there the mind is prepared to understand the light of prophecy and to be illumined by the radiance of the Holy Spirit. In the gentile lands the imagination is dim, clouded with darkness and shadowed with unholiness, and it cannot serve as the vessel for the outpouring of the Divine Light, as it raises itself beyond the lowness and narrowness of the universe.[22]

For Kook, however, the almost two millenia of Jewish Diaspora were not just an expression of sin and exile from God; the Dias-pora also was part of the divine plan of redemption. Since the souls of the Jewish people carry the divine light with them, through their dispersion, they were scattering contact with the divine throughout the gentile world. During the time of the Dias-pora, the very land of Israel grew barren and desolate as the light that poured forth from God was carried far from its center into the impure realm. Thus the return of the Jews to their land was also to be a redemption and restoration of the land itself. The ingathering of the Jews to their land, itself the cosmic center of Creation, would unite a gentile world, renewed by the effluence of the divine through the Jewish presence in their midst, with its own divine center as well.[23]

The fact that the Jews were without national sovereignty during the Diaspora meant that they could carry the divine message to the Gentiles untarnished by the corruption of political power. However, the restoration of the people of Israel to their land and the restoration of national sovereignty must also point to a transformation of politics. Both in the land of Israel and among the nations, political power must be subordinated to the ethical concerns for justice and peace among all peoples.

Thus Kook's vision of redemption had a universal periphery, with Israel as land and people as its paradigmatic center. But it also contained a warning: If the regaining of political power by the Jews in the national homeland was not part of a transformation of the political into a redemptive ethic, then it would not signify the restoration and healing of universal alienation.[24] Although Kook might see secular Zionists as building the foundations for a messianic eschatology, there still remained an unfulfilled dimension of the messianic transformation. It was still necessary to remake the human soul and bring about a community of nations, united through the divine spirit and at peace with one another.

ZIONIST REVISIONISM AND THE JEWISH STATE

Over against, and in stark contrast to, Rabbi Kook's vision of Zionism as the prelude to a time of universal peace among nations, where all use of violence and brute force had been overcome, is the perspective of Vladimir Jabotinsky, founder of Zionist Revisionism. Jabotinsky was born in 1880 in Odessa, which was then a very cosmopolitan city; he grew up with an Orthodox religious Hebrew education on the elementary level. He early displayed a talent for languages and, like Herzl, became a journalist, traveling to Bern and to Rome as a foreign correspondent for his newspapers. Particularly formative were the three years he spent in Italy, until 1901. He would later speak of Italy as his spiritual homeland. But the Italy that began to fascinate him was not only the Italy of art and song but also the Italy of militant nationalism and emerging fascism. This new Italy was to be, in Jabotinsky's words,

the land of industry and cars and electricity, it is not just the promenade for international do-nothings who look for aesthetic recreation. The New Italian is organized and orderly, meticulous in his accounts — a builder and a conqueror, obstinate and cruel. This is the first origin of fascism.[25]

Jabotinsky admired those who could use power without ethical reservations, confident of their own racial superiority. He admired this quality in British imperialism and sought to attach Zionism to British imperial interests, although he also foresaw the need to fight the British to establish the Jewish state. Jewish military self-defense absorbed him from his earliest days. In his early twenties he organized a Jewish self-defense militia to defend the Jews of Odessa against pogroms. He persuaded the British to accept three Jewish battalions in the First World War. One such battalion fought with Allenby in the campaign in Palestine in 1918. Jabotinsky himself enlisted in the British army, where he was commissioned an officer and highly decorated.

During the communal riots in Palestine in 1920 Jabotinsky expanded the *Haganah* as a self-defense corps in Jerusalem. He was sentenced by the British to fifteen years of hard labor but soon thereafter pardoned. Jabotinsky himself died in 1940 at Camp Betar, New York. Those who claimed to be his heirs, such as Menachem Begin, David Raziel, and Avraham Stern, would organize the *Irgun* and the "Stern Gang" as paramilitary terrorist organizations to fight the British and force them to withdraw, leaving Palestine to the Zionists.

Jabotinsky rejected the socialism of the Labor-Zionist tradition and sought to discredit its institutions. His idea of the state seems inspired by a fascist concept of corporate state capitalism. The working class was to have no autonomous right to strike or otherwise assert "class conflict" with the rulers of the state. All institutions of the state must be united as part of one state corporation, subordinate to the "national will." In this ideal state the individual would be strictly subordinate to the collective will of the nation, in militaristic discipline. In the style of 1930s fascism, Jabotinsky's paramilitary organization, *Betar*, emulated parades and military uniforms as expressions of this subordination of the individual to the corporate unity. In Jabotinsky's words:

Betar is structured around the principle of discipline. Its aim is to turn Betar into such a world organism that would be able, at a command from the center, to carry out at the same moment, through the scores of its limbs, the same action in every city and every state. The opponents of Betar maintain that this does not accord with the dignity of free men and it entails becoming a machine. I suggest not to be ashamed and respond with pride. Yes, a machine. Because it is the highest achievement of a multitude of free human beings to be able to act together with the absolute precision of a machine.[26]

For Jabotinsky, the law of nature was the right of the stronger. It was also part of nature that there are stronger races or nations who have a right to conquer the weaker races or nations. The characteristic of these superior races was their self-confident use of power and their strict refusal to assimilate with or imbibe the cultural expressions of inferior races. Jabotinsky thought of the Jews as such a superior race, but his views reflected a certain ambivalence. He also spoke of them as a "nasty people" and professed an understanding of European nationalists who wanted to get rid of them.[27] Like Herzl, Jabotinsky was ready to collaborate with even the most rabid anti-Semitic nationalists. When condemned for his efforts to ally himself with the Ukrainian pogromist, Semyon Petlyura, he declared that "in working for Palestine, I would even ally myself with the devil."[28]

Yet it would not be Jabotinsky's Revisionists, but the Labor Zionists, led by David Ben-Gurion, who would engage in the boldest collaboration with the anti-Semites, in the form of the rising Nazi regime, during the 1930s. In the spring of 1933, Hitler's intentions to destroy Jewish life in Germany were already evident. But the German economy was still wracked by the Depression. A world boycott of German goods had emerged spontaneously, despite the unwillingness of the major Jewish organization leaders to endorse it. Many European and American Christians, out of humanitarian or self-interested motives, were ready to collaborate with the boycott. Had the world Jewish organizations, Zionist and non-Zionist, chosen to combine their efforts in order to create a massive unification of the boycott, some believe that the Germany economy might have cracked and Hitler's regime toppled.[29]

However, a network of Zionist leaders in Palestine conceived of an alternative plan. They saw the opportunity to bring out a portion of the wealth of German Jewry to build the economy of Palestine. During the spring and summer of 1933 they negotiated a transfer agreement with the Third Reich. This transfer agreement (*Ha'avara*) would allow the frozen bank accounts of German Jews who wanted to leave Germany to be used to buy German goods. The proceeds from the sale of these goods in Palestine would then be used to provide these immigrants with land, equipment, and funds to start a new life in Palestine. Most of the proceeds, however, would find their way into the Jewish National Fund to build the state for other immigrants as well.

This transfer agreement was quickly expanded into a variety of trade agreements between the Jewish organizations in Palestine and the Third Reich to trade food stuffs, such as oranges, for German manufactured goods. This German-Palestine trade outgrew the Jewish community itself and was passed on in trade agreements negotiated by the Jewish *Yishuv* and Germany with the Arab world. The result was that the world boycott against Nazi Germany failed.[30] Hitler remained very much in power, rearmed Germany, and embarked on the conquest of Europe. By late 1941, Hitler turned from expulsion to physical extermination of the Jews as the "final solution" to the Jewish question. The economy of Jewish Palestine thrived, building the infrastructures of the future Jewish state, while European Jewry was being murdered.

Jabotinsky's Revisionists fiercely opposed the transfer agreement and sought to champion the world boycott against Nazi Germany in the early thirties. During the Second World War, however, his heirs, the *Irgun*, attempted their own alliance with the Nazis against the British.[31] This *Realpolitik* of political Zionists toward European anti-Semitism was also matched by racist hostility to the Arabs. Here again, Jabotinsky and the Revisionists have been characterized as the exceptional "bad examples" of Zionist anti-Arab racism. In fact, the views that Jabotinsky and the Revisionists stated out loud were not much different from those held in private by the centrist Zionist leaders, such as Chaim Weizmann and David Ben-Gurion.

Weizman and Ben-Gurion shared basic common assumptions with Jabotinsky, despite differences in style and strategy. All three negated the existence of the Palestinians as a national group. For all three, the Palestinians were a fragment of the Arab nation that accidentally happened to be living in Palestine but with no intrinsic roots there. They assumed that this group of "Arabs" could be easily uprooted from their lands and villages and attached to some surrounding Arab state, Transjordan, (Jordan), or Syria, either by economic inducements or by force.[32] These Arabs would soon forget their former homes and identify with other Arab regions. This notion of Palestinians as "anonymous Arabs" without any real identity in Palestine continues to be official Israeli dogma.

This view of Palestinians connects with views of Arabs in general that reveal a European sense of superiority toward "Orientals," who are seen as lacking the same level of moral sensitivity. Arabs are thought of as both impulsively violent and cowardly. "They only understand force," is the Zionist assumption that continues to echo from Israeli soldiers in the Occupied Territories during the 1980s. It was assumed already by Ben-Gurion that, once Arabs had been thoroughly beaten and humiliated, they would retreat and accept the "facts" of Zionist political claims. Arabs were also typically seen as lazy and backward. Zionist leaders assumed that they would be grateful to Zionism for the great economic development the State of Israel would bring to the region. A major part of the noncommunication between Israelis and Arabs lies in this inability to recognize Arabs as proud and sensitive human beings and to perceive the offensiveness of these Western attitudes toward Arabs. Jabotinsky boldly stated a Western colonialist view of Arabs shared by much of Zionism when he wrote:

We, the Jews . . . have no connection with that "Orient," perhaps even less than other European people. . . . [W]e are one of the peoples who have created European culture — and we are one of the most important creators of that culture. . . . And in Palestine this creativity will continue. As Nordau has put it so well, we come to the land of Israel in order to push the moral frontiers of Europe up the Euphrates.[33]

Jabotinsky is typically characterized as the "maximalist" Zionist who believed the Jews had a right to the "whole" of the land within what was construed to be its biblical borders, i.e., from the Litani River in southern Lebanon to the Negev and inclusive of both sides of the Jordan. However, Weizmann and Ben-Gurion were also maximalists who saw as their goal a Jewish state in this whole area, but to be achieved "step by step" rather than all at once. This goal of a Jewish state meant a state of and for Jews. Although in the early thirties Ben-Gurion endorsed the idea of "parity" with the Arabs in Palestine, the Jews were then but a distinct minority. He abandoned parity when the possibility of a Jewish majority in some part of the land became possible.[34]

Herzl in his *Diaries* already suggested that building a Jewish state would entail "spiriting" the Arabs across the border.[35] The Peel Commission in 1937 recommended the partition of Palestine into a Jewish and an Arab state, with the removal of Arabs from the Jewish state, an idea readily endorsed by Ben-Gurion.[36] Thus, despite misleading appearances, Ben-Gurion never endorsed binationalism, but he sought an expanding and exclusively Jewish state from which the Palestinian Arabs would be removed, and then attached, not to a national state of their own, but to some other Arab state, most likely Jordan.

It was David Ben-Gurion—a soldier in one of the Jewish battalions under General Allenby in 1918, one of the founders and general secretary of the *Histadrut* (the Congress of Labor Unions) from 1921 to 1935, chairperson of the executive of the Jewish Agency from 1935 to 1948, and commander of the armed forces and first prime minister in 1948—who can be seen as welding together the practical Labor-Zionist tradition with the political Zionism of Herzl. Ben-Gurion also integrated the militaristic and statist tradition of the Revisionists into the *Haganah* (the Jewish Defense Force), elevating it to be the dominant ethos of the new state.[37]

Ben-Gurion also brought the clerical religious parties into the first cabinet of the State of Israel by acceding to their demands that Orthodox religious law dictate key areas of public culture. His failure to promulgate a civil constitution left open the possibility of realizing the dream of Rabbi Kook and other Orthodox religious Zionists that the Torah (as they interpreted it) would become the law of Israel.

DISSENTING VOICES: BINATIONALIST ZIONISTS

The process of the emergence of the Jewish state through the creation of a Jewish majority and the removal of Palestinians from the territory did not lack for some dissenting voices. Already in the early decades of Zionist settlement, thinkers such as Ahad Ha'am, who sought to build a homeland that would be the center of a moral and spiritual renewal of the Jewish people, began to fear the consequences of an arrogant view toward the Arabs. In the 1920s, the Brith Shalom (Covenant of Peace) group promoted the idea of a binational state. Many of the leaders of this group were practical Zionists, engaged in building up settlements, but who also believed that this must be done in a way that would be sympathetic to Arab culture and of mutual benefit to both the Jews and to their neighboring Arab villagers. Some important voices in this group were Oriental Jews familiar with Arab culture. One of these was Dr. Nissim Malul, son of a Tunisian Jewish family, who was born in Safed and who then studied and taught in Cairo. Malul promoted the vision of a joint Hebrew-Arabic renaissance that would ally the Jewish people with the revival of the Arab world and against Western colonialism.[38]

A group of pacifist Zionists, led by intellectuals such as the philosopher Martin Buber and Judah L. Magnes, an American Reform rabbi who became the first president of Hebrew University, also promoted binationalism in the 1920s. Magnes envisioned the Jewish homeland as a center of moral and spiritual renewal of world Jewry. But he also saw it as serving a world Jewry, most of whom would remain citizens of their own countries. Such a homeland, for him, did not require the establishment of a Jewish state. Indeed, the moral purpose of this homeland would be vitiated by the emergence of a state built on military conquest and on the oppression of its Arabs. In 1930 he wrote:

The Dispersion and Palestine are both required for the fullest development of the Jewish people.... [A]n intensive center and a great periphery.... Palestine can help this people perform its great ethical mission as a national-international entity. But this eternal and far-flung people does not need a Jewish state for the purpose of maintaining its existence.

Much of the theory of Zionism has been concerned with making the Jews into a normal nation in Palestine like the gentiles of the lands and the families of the earth. The desire for power and conquest seems to be normal to many human beings and groups and we, being ruled everywhere, must here rule; being the minority everywhere, we must here be in the majority. There is the *Wille zur Macht*, the state, the army, the frontiers. We have been in exile; now we are to be masters of our own Home.... We are told that when we become the majority we shall then show how just and generous a people in power can be. That is like the man who says he will do anything and everything to get rich, so that he can do good with the money thus accumulated.

We the great democrats of the world are trying to find every kind of reason to justify the denial of even the beginnings of democracy to ourselves

and others. I am afraid of this demoralization. . . . What I am driving at is
to distinguish between two policies. The one maintains that we can establish a Jewish Home here through the suppression of the political aspirations of the Arabs, and therefore a Home necessarily established on
bayonets over a long period—a policy which I think bound to fail because
of the violence against us it would occasion. . . . The other policy holds that
we can establish a Home here only if we are true to ourselves as democrats
and internationalists, thus being just and helpful to others, and that we ask
for the protection of life and property the while we are eagerly and intelli-
gently and sincerely at work fo find a *modus vivendi et operandi* with our
neighbors. [We] should not either will or believe in or want a Jewish Home
that can be maintained in the long run only against the violent opposition
of the Arab and Moslem peoples.[39]

In 1942 the Zionist leaders openly declared their intention to found
a state in Palestine and demanded that the Jewish Agency for Palestine be vested with control over immigration and with authority to
establish the state.[40] It also became evident that the victory of the Allies
over the Axis powers would not assure such a state and that the
Zionists would have to go to war for it. It was in this context that
Magnes, Buber, and other Zionist pacifists and binationalists formed
the *Ihud* (Union) to put forth an alternative position. In 1947 their
proposal of a binational state was submitted to the Anglo-American
Committee of Inquiry, which sought to find a political settlement that
would be acceptable to Palestinian Arabs and Jews.

Ihud leaders insisted that Palestine could be neither a Jewish state
nor an Arab one, that there existed in Palestine two national communities that each had equally valid claims to it, the Jews on the
basis of their ancient historical roots and recent settlements and
the Palestinians on the basis of their long residence there. Moreover, as the meeting place of three world religions, Judaism, Christianity, and Islam, it was inappropriate to establish a state in which
one of these traditions would dominate over the other two. The *Ihud*
also rejected partition into two states. They sought a binational
state that would recognize within it both national identities. Jewish
immigration would be limited to the number that would bring Jews
into parity with Palestinians but not create a Jewish majority.

The *Ihud* leaders knew that most of the Palestinians were not yet
ready to accede to such a state. They envisioned a gradual process of
developing a binational state and building cooperation between the

two peoples. A legislature would be set up with equal representation of both communities. This would be based on dividing the territory into cantons or counties, some of which would have an Arab majority, some a Jewish majority, and some mixed. Many of the governmental functions would be carried out on this cantonal level, creating practical experience of self-government and cooperation. They wanted this government to be put into place by the British colonial authorities and then handed over to a cooperative process of the Jewish Agency and the Arab League. The last step would be the proclamation of an autonomous Palestinian Arab-Jewish binational state.

In contrast to Western Zionists, who thought of the Jewish homeland as an outpost of European culture, *Ihud* envisioned the Palestinian state as a part of the Arab world. It supported the emergence of autonomous Arab states, gathered into the Arab League, and expected the Palestinian binational state to become a member of this Arab union of states. Buber and Magnes concluded their testimony before the Anglo-American Committee with this desperate plea:

What a boon to mankind it would be if the Jews and the Arabs of Palestine were to strive together to make their Holy Land into a thriving, peaceful Switzerland situated at the heart of this ancient highway between East and West. A Palestinian Solution is required for the Palestinian problem. This would have an incalculable political and spiritual influence in all the Middle East and far beyond. A binational Palestine could become a beacon of peace in the world.[41]

SUMMARY

The development of Zionism has been discussed as a movement built on great idealism that drew on ancient religious visions of a messianic return to the biblical homeland and modern revolutionary ideals of democracy, socialism, and romantic utopianism. But it was also a movement deeply flawed by ethnocentric nationalism and Western colonialist views of the Arab world. The Zionist belief that the Jews were a separate nation that could never successfully integrate into other national communities, and that must expect new waves of anti-Semitism designed to attempt to expel them, led its leaders to be less than concerned about the civil rights of Jews who chose to remain in other lands. They expected and even welcomed the eternal persistence of anti-Semitism in the Diaspora.

World Jewry was, too often, regarded as a material resource of wealth and population to be exploited to build the Jewish state. Ruthless alliances with anti-Semites, such as the transfer agreement, were allowable if they served that end and led to Jewish migration to *Eretz Israel.*

Zionist ethocentrism was also directed toward the Arab world. Viewing the Arabs as intrinsically and culturally inferior to themselves, Zionists sought to separate themselves from the Arab world and to prevent "Levantinization," that is, the merger between Jewish national and Arab culture. Even the Arab Jews, who migrated to the state in large numbers in the 1950s, were seen as inferior because of their Arab culture. The Israeli government integrated them into the state by seeking to divest them of their Arab linguistic and cultural heritage and to Westernize them. Thus, despite idealistic views of an egalitarian community without class hierarchy, Israel has succeeded in duplicating typical colonialist attitudes and exploitative economic relationships toward Arabs and even toward Oriental Jews.

These flaws, of course, are not unique to Zionism, but they are flaws that it shares with the Western nationalisms and colonialisms that shaped Zionism. The highly idealistic assertions of its spokepersons, who claim the Jewish religious and secular heritages, and Zionism's need to present itself to world Jewry and to the Christian world as the redemption of the Jews from past victimization, created an official culture of extreme duplicity. Many of the basic facts about how the State of Israel was built are shrouded in secrecy. Not only Western Jews and Christians but also most of the Israelis grow up with a series of elaborate falsifications about the foundations of the state.[42] The need for these falsifications conceals a profound fear of illegitimacy that lurks under constant demands that the nations, especially the Arab ones, recognize Israel's "right to exist."

This sense of illegitimacy can never be overcome by lies or by force. It can be overcome only by risking truth and by openness to justice in the relationship between Israelis and Palestinians. The Jewish prophetic and ethical traditions provide standards of justice between peoples. The humanistic Zionist traditions of Buber and Magnes sought, not only an egalitarian society for Jews, but one that would live in mutual affirmation with its Palestinian neighbors. These are resources for an alternative future.

3. Christianity and Zionism: The Making of an Alliance

Thus says Cyrus King of Persia, "The Lord, the God of Heaven, has given me all the Kingdoms of the earth, and he has charged me to build him a house at Jerusalem, which is in Judah. Whoever is among you of all his people, may the Lord his God be with him. Let him go up."

2 CHRON. 36:23

This chapter will survey the most important elements in the complex history of Christian relationship to Zionism. Protestant Christians began to advocate a return of the Jews to Palestine, and a restored Jewish state there, long before there was an organized Jewish Zionist movement. This idea of Jewish "restoration" was an integral part of revived Protestant millennialism. The idea of Jewish restoration began to be translated into political terms in the nineteenth century, as England and France began to compete for the Middle Eastern spoils of a disintegrating Ottoman empire. The mingling of religious and political motivations for Jewish restoration played key roles in both the British decision to support a Jewish homeland in the Balfour Declaration of 1917 and the American advocacy of the State of Israel in the crucial UN vote of 1947.

THE REFORMATION ERA AND THE RESTORATION OF THE JEWS

The patristic view of the Church as the new universal Israel, and the belief that the Jews were to be exiles until the end of history, continued to be normative for medieval Christianity. In this view, the Jews were assumed to be under divine reprobation for their failure to accept Jesus as their promised Messiah. In the last days they would convert, but this final conversion was not linked to any restoration to the land. For medieval Christianity the messianic Promised Land was understood to be heaven, the realm of eschatological redemption. The biblical land was seen, not as the land of Israel, but as the Christian "Holy Land."

Already in the time of the Constantinian establishment of the church in the fourth century, Palestine became a Christian land of pilgrimage. Medieval Christianity launched a series of military adventures called the Crusades to reclaim this Holy Land from the Muslims. But, for the medieval Crusader, the Jews in Europe or in the cities along the way to Palestine were as much "infidels" as the Muslims. The Crusaders generated pogroms, or sackings and massacres, of Jews in Jewish quarters along the routes of the Crusader armies.

The sixteenth century saw a series of shifts of attitude of Christians about their own identity that would also reshape views of the relationship of the Christian new covenant to Israel. The emergence of militant nations, centered in their national monarchies in Spain, Portugal and France, Holland and England, made the nation, rather than a universal European Christian community, the new focus of European identity. These Christian nations were engaged in wars with each other that mingled religious rivalry (created by the Reformation) with competition for the commercial trade routes being opened up by colonialism in Africa, Asia, and the Americas. The idea of the "New Israel" was shifted from a universal religious community, the Christian Church, to the nation as an "elect people," commissioned by God to defend the true faith (whether Catholic or Protestant) and evangelise the "heathen."

This nationalizing of the New Israel as elect nation was aided by the new biblical scholarship of the Renaissance and the Reformation. Allegorical interpretation was rejected in favor of literal, historical interpretation. Bible reading in the vernacular, among Protestants, created a new identification with the people of Hebrew Scripture. The prophets and heroes of Hebrew Scripture replaced the Catholic saints as the figures of Christian story and self-identification. The Promised Land of the Hebrew Bible was understood as the actual historical land of Palestine, not as an allegory for a transcendent realm. Jews came to be seen less as a rival religion and more as another nation vis-à-vis the European nations.

An important impetus to this racializing of the Jews in European thought was created by the Spanish expulsion of the Jews in 1492.

The Spanish, having completed their reconquest of the peninsula from the Muslims, ordered all Jews to convert or get out of Spain. Although many fled, many others stayed and accepted baptism. This meant that the old laws restricting the Jews in Spanish society were rescinded for these new Christians, for those laws had been based on religion. New Christians soon began to enter the highest places of Spanish society. To prevent this, the Spanish passed new restrictions against these converted Jews, called the "laws of pure blood."

For the first time, Jews were defined, not as a religious group whose identity was changeable by conversion, but as a biological group whose identity was permanently fixed by "blood."[1] The pope protested these laws of pure blood as contrary to Catholic tradition, according to which there should be no discrimination among Christians based on race.[2] But it was the Spanish king, not the pope, who was in control of the Spanish Inquisition. These events expressed a new ambivalence toward Jewish identity—whether to see them as a religious or as a racial group—that would continue its tangled variants down to the present day.

In the countries influenced by the Protestant Reformation, particularly among Calvinists, the new identification with the Hebrew Bible created a more positive relationship between the biblical Israel and the Christian national New Israel. Jews fleeing from Spain and Portugal were welcomed in the Protestant commercial cities of Amsterdam and Hamburg. Such Protestants came to look on such Jews as living descendants of the ancient biblical heroes, rather than as despised members of a superseded covenant.

The conversion of the Jews was still expected. Indeed, there was a new emphasis on this hope for Jewish conversion as part of a millennial transformation of the world. Protestants tended to assume that their purification of Christianity from Catholic "errors" would facilitate this conversion. The Renaissance and Reformation established Hebrew as one of the needed scholarly languages for the study of the Old Testament in the original. This study of Hebrew further deepened the affinity between Jews and biblical Protestants.

Protestants of the Reformed tradition saw the Hebrew Bible as a source of all truth, including political truth. The covenant of God with Israel was regarded as a model for the Christian commonwealth. The Law given at Sinai was the basis for the law code of a Christian nation.[3] Some radical Puritan theorists believed that such covenants or social contracts of the people under God could bypass and eliminate national kings: God alone was to be king in the Christian theocratic commonwealth. Such ideas would be secularized by Puritan political thinkers such as John Locke and were to become a basis of modern theories of democratic government.[4]

In the sixteenth and seventeenth centuries, though, the idea of the New Israel as a political government, established by a new covenant with God, mingled with millennarian expectations that the present world of sin was about to be overcome by the Second Coming of Christ who would establish his direct reign over the nations of the earth. This millennarian expectation flourished under the pressure of social upheaval caused by the wars of religion in the late sixteenth and seventeenth centuries, especially during the Thirty Years' War in Europe (1611–48) and the English Civil War and the Protectorate (1640–60).

Christian millennialism was influenced by the revival of messianism among Jews after the expulsion from Spain. As we have seen in chapter 2, Kabbalistic thought had developed among Spanish Jews from Gnostic systems going back to the second century C.E. In the fifty years after the expulsion of the Jews from Spain in 1492, these mystical doctrines of cosmic redemption were interpreted in terms of expectations of imminent messianic deliverance. One messianic Kabbalist, Abraham ben Eliezer, living in Jerusalem in the sixteenth century, interpreted the expulsion from Spain as the "travail of the Messiah" that is ushering in the coming of the Messiah. For such Jewish messianists, the glorious restoration of the Davidic kingdom in the Promised Land was an integral part of redemption from the *galuth*, or exile.[5]

Christian Renaissance Hebraists were eager students of Jewish Kabbalistic writings. One such Christian humanist scholar was Johannes Reuchlin, who expounded Kabbalistic writings in his books *De Verbo Mirifico* (1494) and *De Arte Cabbalistica* (1517). Reuchlin's Hebrew lexicon and grammar put the study of Hebrew on a new scientific footing for Christian scholars. The reading of the books of Jewish mystical messianism, plus their own literal reading of Scripture, shaped a new interpretation of "last things" that characterized Protestants of the Puritan and Pietist traditions.

These Protestants read the disasters of war, famine, and social upheaval in Europe as signs that history was entering its final period of catastrophic turmoil from which redemption would emerge. To the Augustinian notion that the conversion of the Jews would signal the last days before the return of Christ, these Christian millennialists added the idea that the Jews would be restored to the biblical land. Some Christians believed that this restoration would take place after the Jews were converted; but some believed that the Jews should be gathered into their Promised Land first and, after their return, they would be converted to Christ.[6]

Ideas of Jewish restoration to the land were proposed by a few maverick thinkers in the sixteenth century, such as Servetus and Frances Kett,[7] both martyred for their dissenting ideas. Thomas Brightman, in 1600, in his tract *Apocalypsis Apocalypseos*, argued that the Jews should return to their land so that they would not "strive any longer as strangers and inmates with forraine nations."[8] One member of Parliament, Sir Henry Finch, took up Brightman's ideas and proposed that biblical prophecy entailed the collective restoration of the Jews to their own country. He explicitly rejected the traditional allegorical interpretation of these ideas of Jewish restoration as references to Christ, choosing instead a literal interpretation, referring to the Jews as a nation.[9]

Such ideas were still regarded as dangerous and heretical in the sixteenth century, even by mainline Protestant thinkers. But, in the seventeenth century, they became much more general, although still linked primarily with millennialist thinkers. During the English Civil War they became widespread among all the Puritan parties, from Cromwell to radical groups such as the Levellers. Popular prophets and prophetesses poured out tracts, inspired by the books of Daniel and Revelation, in which they charted the final messianic travails and coming deliverance into the events of English conflict. The restoration of the Jews to their land was a stock feature of such English Civil War millenialism.

One such millenialist seer was the English prophetess Mary Cary, later Mrs. Mary Rande, who wrote her apocalyptic interpretation of British political history in the 1640s and 1650s. One writing was titled *The Little Horns Doom and Downfall*; it contains a section called "A New and More Exact Mappe of New Jerusalem's Glory" (1651).[10] Cary envisioned a coming rule of Christ and his saints over the whole earth. Included among these saints will be converted Jews. The Jews have been kept from seeing the truth of Christ by the evils of Roman Catholicism, but the purification of Christianity by the Puritans will overcome their unbelief. They will convert, and then the promises made to them in Scripture will be fulfilled. The ten tribes will be gathered together out of their exile among the nations and joined to the two tribes, and they will be restored to their land as an eternal possession: "Here are clear promises that they should be brought out of Egypt and Assyria whither they had been carried and brought to their own land again. . . . They will possess their own land, even the land given to their fathers to possess."[11] Cary also believed that the heathen who refuse to convert (in which she includes Christians of other persuasions) will be subdued by the sword wielded by the righteous army of the saints. This millennial warfare she calculated as taking place between 1656 and 1701. After this would come the thousand-year reign of the saints over the earth, which would include the resurrection of past saints and the thousand-year binding of Satan. Cary imagined this millennium in very material terms. The saints would enjoy good weather. They would have nice houses and gardens, and their barns would be filled with wheat. Humanity and the earth would be restored to pristine goodness, so there would be no danger that the saints would be corrupted by that material abundance.

English men and women in this period had little acquaintance with actual Jews, as the Jews had been expelled from England by the Crusader king Edward I in 1290. Among English Puritans, the ideal Jew of the Bible mingled in their imagination with contemporary Jews. During the Protectorate, the debate over readmission of the Jews came to a head, led by the Lord Protector Oliver Cromwell. Cromwell saw concrete commercial advantages to such a readmission of Jews to England. England's neighbor and rival, Holland, was prospering and expanding her trade contacts in the Middle and Far East. Cromwell believed that a Jewish presence would help England rival such Dutch trade.

But, for Cromwell, and for other theologians and jurists who gathered at Whitehall in December, 1655, to discuss the legal and religious basis for the readmission of the Jews, the fulfillment of prophecy was always the uppermost theme. It was believed that the Jews must be dispersed in all lands before their ingathering into the

Promised Land.[12] England's lack of Jews was seen as an obstacle to these redemptive events, so the Jews needed to be readmitted to England, there presumably to be converted to Christianity by the good example of English Puritans. Then the final events of redemption, including Jewish restoration to the land, could be accomplished. In this way the decision to readmit Jews to England became interconnected, in contemporary English thought, with their ingathering into Palestine. The chief rabbi of Amsterdam, Menasseh ben Israel, was present at these discussions at Whitehall. His book *Spes Israel*, which had been translated into English in 1655 and widely read, similarly linked readmission of Jews to England with their restoration to Palestine.[13]

Although English Puritans of the seventeenth century are a major source of such millennialist ideas of Jewish restoration, they are by no means the only Protestants of the period to espouse such ideas. Beliefs that Jewish restoration to the land will be an integral part of the final redemptive events are found among Dutch Calvinist writers and French Huguenots, as well. One French Huguenot, Pierre Jurieu, in his tract *L'Accomplissement de Propheties*, predicted that this restoration and the establishment of a Jewish kingdom in Palestine would be accomplished by the end of the seventeenth century.[14] Similar ideas also spread among pietists in Germany, particularly in Hamburg, and from there to Denmark. One Danish thinker, Holder Paulli, even suggested that the European Christian nations should undertake a new crusade to free the biblical land from the Muslims so that it could be given to its rightful owners, the Jews. Paulli submitted this plan to the Dutch king William III, who had been established on the English throne in 1689. Paulli addressed the king as a new Cyrus who, like the Cyrus of Scripture (2 Chron. 36:22–23), would be the divine instrument for effecting this return of the Jews from exile.[15]

CHRISTIAN ZIONISM AND EUROPEAN EMPIRE

In the nineteenth century the Ottoman empire, which since the sixteenth century had ruled a vast domain stretching from the Balkans across the Middle East and North Africa, was disintegrating. Russia was expanding into the Crimea to win a warm-water port through the Black Sea to the Mediterranean. The French were eyeing the coast of North Africa. The Balkans and Egypt were in revolt.

The British became the protectors of the Ottomans to prevent further Russian expansion into Turkey.

In 1798–99, Napoleon made a lightning expedition into the Middle East and succeeded in occupying Egypt. He was marching through Palestine when he was defeated by a combined British-Turkish army at Acre. Before this battle, while anticipating a victorious entrance into Jerusalem, Napoleon had offered to the Jews a restored state in Palestine. Although Napoleon was hardly religious, nevertheless, biblical history was not absent from his thinking. For Napoleon, biblical history was part of a story of ancient empire. He imagined himself a new Persian emperor offering to the Jews a restored homeland within his empire and thereby winning Jewish support throughout Europe. Addressing the Jews as the "rightful heirs of Palestine," he declared:

Israelites, arise! Ye exiled, arise! Hasten! Now is the moment, which may not return for thousands of years, to claim the restoration of civic rights among the populations of the universe which have been shamefully withheld from you for thousands of years, to claim your political existence as a nation among nations, and the unlimited right to worship Jehovah in accordance with your faith, publicly and most probably forever.[16]

Although Napoleon's advance was thrown back, his announcement of a restored Jewish nation in Palestine set a precedent that would be followed 118 years later, as the British, under General Allenby, were poised to complete their conquest of Palestine with a triumphal entrance into Jerusalem. It was at this moment that the British government issued the Balfour Declaration, declaring:

His Majesty's government view with favour the establishment in Palestine of a national home for the Jewish people and will use their best endeavours to facilitate the achievement of this object, it being clearly understood that nothing shall be done which may prejudice the civil and religious rights of existing non-Jewish communities in Palestine or the rights and political status enjoyed by Jews in any other country.[17]

For the British, too, the primary motive for this declaration was their expanding imperial interests. They saw Palestine as the key buffer state that guarded the Suez Canal and the route to India, the crown jewel of the British empire. But biblical history was not absent from their thinking. Again, the question was not one of religious faith in biblical prophecy and the return of Christ, such as motivated Christian evangelicals. Rather, Jerusalem and Palestine figured as glorious names in an ancient history of empire that they sought to emulate. As classicists, they imagined themselves new Alexanders and Caesars. But as Christians, steeped in biblical history, they saw themselves as gracious and righteous emperors, offering to those whom they saw as the contemporary descendants of the ancient Jews, their ancient homeland.

As Barbara Tuchman has pointed out, in her history of the self-identification of the British with the Israelites over fifteen hundred years, the gesture was aimed as much at the British conscience itself as it was at the Jews.[18] The name of Jerusalem was too weighty in ancient symbolism to be a mere part of a British land grab; it must be invested with a high tone of *noblesse oblige*. Restoring it to the Jews fulfilled that function. One should not see this as a consciously hypocritical garb covering crass imperial interests. The British, like the Americans, have a moralistic culture that demands that their imperial power be interpreted in their own eyes as a noble service to the best interests of humanity. Imperial self-interest and moral righteousness mingle as two inseparable parts of the same personality. By offering Palestine to the Jews as a restored homeland, the British saw themselves as engaging in a grand deed of historic justice to the heirs of those who had originally owned the land. They were paying a debt to the people who had bequeathed biblical religion to Christianity and at the same time patronizing the establishment of a nation that would become dependent on them and that would permanently represent British interests in the region.

To understand the Balfour Declaration, therefore, one must see the coincidence of two realities: a political and economic reality of advancing British imperialism, with Palestine as a key strategic region, and a Christian religious culture that had long believed, not only that modern Jews represent the ancient Hebrews of the Bible, but also that their restoration as a nation in Palestine is integral to the establishment of a future reign of peace and righteousness on earth. This latter idea had its roots in Puritan theology in the seventeenth century, as we have seen. It faded from the stage but never entirely disappeared from British and French evangelical thought in the eighteenth century. The nineteenth century saw a major resurgence of evangelical piety in Britain, stunned by the dangerous effects of rationalism in the French Revolution.

New evangelical sects, such as the Christadelphians and the Plymouth Brethren, led by John Nelson Darby, arose in the middle of the century, teaching a premillennial, dispensational theology. According to this view, the promises to the Jews—including restoration to Palestine and rebuilding the Temple—must take place first, and then the promises to the Christian Church—the return of Christ and the conversion of the whole world—would follow. The influence of Darby and others of this tradition would spread to the United States, where it would reinforce similar American evangelical thinking.

Not only was evangelical thinking of this type found in the sects, but it also shaped an evangelical party in the Anglican church. The most important representative of evangelical piety in the established church was Lord Anthony Ashley Cooper, seventh Earl of Shaftesbury. Shaftesbury was an earnest believer in the interpretation of biblical prophecy, in which the restoration of the Jews was the prerequisite for the return of Christ and the establishment of the millennium on earth. He worked all his life, from the 1830s to his death in 1885, for this great event. But he was also intimately connected with the major British political leaders of the day and frequently conveyed his enthusiasm for Jewish restoration in terms intended to recommend the project for its political and economic advantages to British interests. In 1840 he influenced Lord Palmerston, British foreign secretary, to write to the British ambassador in Istanbul, recommending that the sultan encourage Jewish settlement in Palestine.[19]

Shaftesbury was also a leading influence in the decision of the Church of England to establish an Anglican bishopric of Jerusalem. Shaftesbury, as a leader in the London Society for Promoting Christianity among the Jews, envisioned a vast redemptive project in which unconverted Jews would return to Palestine and then be converted to Christianity (Anglican, of course); these two events would prepare the way for the Second Advent. The first incumbent of this Anglican See of Jerusalem was a converted Jew, the Reverend Dr. Michael Solomon Alexander, professor of Hebrew and Arabic at Kings College.

In Shaftesbury's vision of the future age of redemption, Christ would reign from a restored Jewish nation of Anglican Israelites.[20] The "Jews Society," as it was called, had the restoration of the Jews to their national existence in Palestine as an integral part of their purpose. Lord Shaftesbury also opposed the civil and political emancipation of Jews in England. He opposed the Emancipation Bill that would have removed the disabilities of Jews from full participation in English political and cultural life. Thus, like many an evangelical restorationist, his enthusiasm for the return of the Jews to Palestine went hand in hand with his refusal to accept their full equality as citizens of his own nation.

British Christian Zionism was also expressed through the work of the Palestine Exploration Fund to promote biblical archaeology. In a manner anticipative of the role of archaeology in Israel today, the Palestine Fund mingled antiquarian interest in exploring the ancient sites of the Bible with military interest in securing accurate surveys and maps of the country. Much of the biblical archaeology sponsored by the fund was carried out by army officers designated by the War Office: men such as Colonel Claude Condor, author of *Tent Work in Palestine* (1878), who combined dedication to biblical archaeology with the role of mapping Palestine for the British army.[21]

Although British Jews as a whole were cool to restorationist ideas, seeing them as a threat to hard-won civil rights in England and possibly as a preparation for deportation, several prominent British Jews played key roles in the mingling of Jewish restoration and advancing British imperial interests. One of these was the wealthy philanthropist Sir Moses Montefiore, who sponsored building and agricultural projects to alleviate the poverty of Jews in Jerusalem.[22] Another was Benjamin Disraeli, who would become prime minister of England in 1865 and who would use a loan guarantee from prominent British Jew, Lord Lionel Rothschild, to purchase the Suez Canal for the British.[23] From a converted Jewish family, Disraeli had, in his youth, written a novel, *Alroy*, which described a revived kingdom of Israel. Although his energies turned to British rather than to Jewish politics, he was a key figure in the acquisition of Egypt as a buffer state to the Suez Canal route to India. These acquisitions suggested the need for a parallel control of Palestine.

By the end of the nineteenth century an organized Zionist movement had arisen. Now there were groups of Jews, mainly Eastern European, who wanted to colonize Palestine, to interact with British religious and political visions of a restored Jewish state as a means, at once, of redemptive hopes and imperial interests. British control of India, Burma, Afghanistan, Egypt, and the Transvaal progressed rapidly in the last quarter of the century. But still the British posed as protectors, not liquidators, of the Ottomans.

Theodor Herzl, hammering on British doors in 1903, received the offer not of Palestine but of Uganda, from the head of the Colonial Office, Neville Chamberlain, an offer that was indignantly turned down by a vocal minority of the delegates of the Sixth Zionist Congress. This event was sufficiently intriguing to the new prime minister, Lord Arthur Balfour, to cause him to seek a meeting with Chaim Weizmann, the new leader of the world Zionist movement. Balfour was deeply impressed by Weizmann's impassioned explanations of why the Zionists could accept no other homeland than their ancient land of Palestine.[24]

This relationship of Balfour and Weizmann would bear fruit ten years later, when the embattled Ottomans allied with Germany in the First World War against their erstwhile protectors, the British. The defeat of the Axis thus paved the way for the Allies, the French and British, to replace the Ottomans with their own imperial control. The intricate machinations of French and British secret agreements with opposing parties, particularly with the Arabs, who hoped to win national self-determination from the war, will be discussed in a later chapter. Suffice it to say here that the decision (on the eve of General Allenby's entrance into Jerusalem) to offer to the Zionists a "Jewish homeland" under the British Mandate was the culmination of a long history in which biblical nostalgia and imperial interests mingled.

Although the decision undoubtedly gained something from the enthusiam of the moment, it was by no means intended as a ploy. It was regarded by its author, Lord Balfour, and also by Herbert Samuel, the future first high commissioner of Palestine, and by David Lloyd George, the prime minister, as a firm commitment.[25] The declaration was, in turn, incorporated into the laws of the British Mandate for Palestine, approved by the League of Nations in 1922, and thus assumed the legal status of a treaty. The preamble to the Mandatory declares the Mandate government

to be responsible for putting into effect the Declaration originally made on 2nd November, 1917 by the government of His Britannic Majesty and adopted by the said (Principal Allied) Powers in favor of the establishment in Palestine of a national home for the Jewish people.[26]

In defending these decisions in the House of Lords in 1922, Balfour made clear the mingling of practical and religious motivations that guided it:

I hold ... that the policy we initiated is likely to prove a successful policy. But we have never pretended that it was purely from these materialist considerations that the declaration originally sprang. ... [S]urely it is in order that we may send a message to every land where the Jewish race has been scattered, a message that will tell them that Christendom is not oblivious of their faith, is not unmindful of the service they have rendered to the religions of the world, and most of all to the religion that the majority of Your Lordships' house profess, and that we desire to the best of our ability to give them that opportunity of developing, in peace and quietness under British rule, those great gifts which hitherto they have been compelled to bring to fruition in countries that know not their language and belong not to their race? That is the ideal which I desire to see accomplished, that is the aim which lay at the root of the policy I am trying to defend, and though it is defensible indeed on every ground, that is the ground that chiefly moves me.[27]

AMERICAN CHRISTIAN ZIONISM AND THE FOUNDATION OF ISRAEL

As the Second World War and its aftermath rent the fabric of the British empire, it would be the United States of America that would step into its place as the leading Western power and chief guarantor of the emerging State of Israel. Again, as in Britain, it was evangelicals, with their visions of millennial glory, who prepared the soil for American support of Israel. But the decisions that pushed forward the final 1947 United Nations vote that established the Jewish state, as part of a partition of Palestine, were carried out by practical politicians.

In these politicians, too, though, we catch glimpses of biblical nostalgia mingled with their political strategizing. In 1947, the grandiose vision of becoming a new Cyrus to restore the Jews to their homeland was mixed with the horror of the revelations of the Nazi death camps and with pity for the remnants of those camps who lingered in European displaced persons' camps. American religious and political statements sought to "do something" for the Jews to make up for the terrible losses they had sustained in the Nazi extermination project (although neither the Americans nor the British had been willing to divert any of the resources from the war effort to rescue some of those Jews while extermination was actually going on).[28]

American identification with Jewish nationalism is deeply rooted in its history. The English colonists in America brought with them from their homeland an identification between England and Israel as God's elect people. This was reinforced for the Puritan settlers who saw their exodus from England in the mirror of the story of the Exodus of the Jews from Egypt to the Promised Land. The Native Americans were seen as Canaanites whose idolatry merited their displacement from the land in favor of God's elect. As relations between the colonists and Indians worsened, the Indians were even dubbed the Amalekites who deserved to be utterly exterminated (1 Sam. 15:18).[29] Thus, America as the new Zion was an idea firmly fixed in American national mythology from the seventeenth century.[30]

In the last decades of the nineteenth century, as millions of Jews fleeing from pogroms in Russia found refuge and a chance for equality of opportunity in America, Jews also came to see America as their "Zion." A committed Zionist such as Judge Louis Brandeis assumed that the Jewish settlement in Palestine was primarily for impoverished Jews from Eastern Europe, while most American Jews would stay in America as supporters of the Jewish state. Brandeis linked Zionism with the American Puritan heritage and saw, in this American identity, a historic affinity with Jewish nationalism.[31] So, as America emerged as the primary Western superpower, it is not surprising that it also became the prime supporter for the State of Israel, committing almost a third of its foreign aid to this tiny state since 1948.[32] Israel is seen by many Americans as a kind of "double" for America in the Middle East.

The idea that Christians should support the restoration of the Jews in their ancient homeland was also a recurring theme in the American Christian tradition. English Puritans carried to America the idea that Jewish restoration was a key event leading to the Second Advent of Christ. Several seventeenth- and eighteenth-century American religious leaders speculated that America would have a key role in this restoration.[33] Millennial impulses were renewed in America in the evangelical crusades of the First (1738–50) and Second (1800–1835) Great Awakenings. The Millerite movement of the

1840s split American millennarianism by its premature announce-ment of the date of the Second Advent.

After the Millerite debacle, conflicting views of the millennium developed among American Protestants. Amillennialists con-tinued the Augustinian tradition that there would be no earthly millennium; they believed that this idea referred to the ingathering of souls for Christ. Postmillennialists married millennialism with progressivism and believed that the seeds of redemption were already planted through the democratic revolution. The Kingdom of God was to be built on earth through cooperation between humans and the divine Spirit within history.

Premillennialists rejected this optimistic view. For them, history was going downhill toward a final cataclysmic denouement; Christ will return and inaugurate the millennium or the thousand-year reign of the righteous on earth, only after the battle of Armageddon defeats the powers of evil, both human and demonic. These premillennialists included the doctrine of restoration of the Jews to the biblical homeland in their schema of the "last things."

In 1878, premillennialists convened the first International Bible Prophecy conference to explore these views. Successive interna-tional conferences took place in 1886, 1895, 1901, 1914, and 1918. The conferences featured interchange between British and American premillennialists, including leading Christian restorationists such as Lord Shaftesbury.[34] The typical scenario that became fixed in this tradition of the "last things" went as follows: First, the Jews would be restored to their land in an unconverted (non-Christian) state. They would rebuild the Temple on its former site and restore the ancient sacrificial cult. Then there would be a period of tribulation in which an Antichrist and False Prophet would mislead the Jews and the world. This would lead to the return of Christ as conquering Messiah, to the conversion of the Jews, to the defeat of the Anti-christ, and to the establishment of the millennium in which the righteous (Gentile and converted Jewish "true Christians") would reign with Christ for a thousand years. After this, there would be a final period of tribulation, the final defeat of evil and the creation of an eternal heaven and earth.[35]

This premillennialist scenario was propagated not only by prophecy conferences but also by educational institutions such as the Moody Bible Institute in Chicago, popular publications and, later, radio and television shows. Its penetration to grassroots, Bible-reading Americans can be credited especially to the Scofield Reference Bible, the most popularly read Bible in America. The scenario described above is basically derived from a synthesis of the Old Testament Book of Daniel and the New Testament Revelation. But it lends itself to a continual updating of the "signs of the times," such as interpreting World War I and then World War II as the "tribulation." The actual beginnings of Jewish colonization of Palestine in the Zionist movement were hailed immediately by these Christians as an indication of the restoration. When the State of Israel was founded in 1948, heirs of this premillennialist theology saw their beliefs in prophecy as fulfilled.

This viewpoint, however, is by no means limited to premillennialist fundamentalists but is widely held by American Christians, both Protestant and Catholic. It is deeply embedded in popular American Christian culture. According to a study published in 1987, 57 percent of American Protestants and 35 percent of American Catholics responded positively to the statement that the founding of the State of Israel in 1948 was the fulfillment of the biblical prophecy that the Jews should be restored to their own land.[36]

Already in the 1890s, American Christian evangelicals sought to translate the idea of a millennial restoration of the Jews to their land into practical politics. William Blackstone, the author of a popular apocalyptic book, *Jesus Is Coming* (1878), organized the Blackstone Memorial in 1891. This was a petition addressed to President Harrison to support a restored Jewish state in Palestine. Harrison and his secretary of state, James Blaine, were urged "to consider the situation of the Israelites and their claims to Palestine as their ancient home." It was suggested that President Harrison might be the modern-day Cyrus who would return the Jews from Exile.

The Blackstone Memorial gained attention, although no action, because it was signed by 413 leading Americans, including John D. Rockefeller, Cyrus McCormick, J. Pierpont Morgan, the Chief Justice of the Supreme Court, and the Speaker of the House of Representatives, as well as senators, clergy, and newspaper editors. Blackstone and many of the clergy may have been motivated by biblical ideas, but many of the other signers saw this appeal as an effort to divert the flood of Jewish refugees streaming into America in the 1890s from the pogroms in Russia. The petition had been prompted by the pogroms and by nativist American Protestants' fears of Jewish immigration.[37]

The American Jewish community, dominated by Reform Judaism, responded with outrage to these Christian restorationists' efforts in the late nineteenth and early twentieth centuries. The 1885 Pittsburgh Conference of Reform Rabbis stated unequivocally: "We consider ourselves no longer a nation but a religious community, and therefore expect neither a return to Palestine nor a sacrificial worship under the sons of Aaron nor the restoration of any of the laws concerning the Jewish state."[38] In response to Christian fundamentalist insistence that Palestine was given to the Jews and only to the Jews, the *American Israelite*, the periodical of Reform Judaism, stated bluntly: "Palestine is no longer our land."[39] Such American Jews saw in Christian restorationism a scheme for deportation that threatened their status as American citizens. But they also reflected the Reform Jewish understanding that Judaism had transcended nationalism, with the rabbinic teachings of the second century C.E., and that Judaism was to be understood as a universal religion of Jews who belonged to many nations. Reform Judaism even deleted the prayers for a messianic restoration to Jerusalem from their prayer book.[40]

By the 1920s, American Jewish views of Zionism were beginning to shift. Although Zionism was still a minority movement,[41] the identification with Zionism by leading American Jews, such as Supreme Court justice Louis Brandeis, made it socially respectable and compatible with American patriotism. The events of Nazi persecution and then the revelations of mass exterminations of European Jews turned the tide. By 1948 about 50 percent of American Jews would see themselves as supporters of a Jewish state, although few American Jews intended to immigrate there. Leading American Christians such as Reinhold Niebuhr, Paul Tillich, Daniel Poling, and William Albright organized the Christian Council on Palestine in 1942 to promote immigration of Jewish refugees to Palestine. These Christians were motivated by humanitarian concerns, rather than by millennial visions. But it is notable that they followed the American Zionist lead in making immigration to Palestine, not expanded immigration to America, the solution to this problem of Jewish persecution.[42]

The roles of President Roosevelt in the fate of European Jewry under Hitler and of President Truman in the UN vote for the partition that established the Jewish state in 1947 have been exhaustively canvased in other books and will not be treated in detail here. Suffice it to say that although both men were practical politicians, both had, in different ways, strong socialization in biblical Christianity that disposed them to give special attention to the establishment of a Jewish state. Roosevelt has been vilified for his inaction toward Jewish refugees during the war, and Truman has been praised for his support of the UN vote. But, as Peter Grose has shown in his detailed study of both men, it was actually Roosevelt who was the more unequivocal supporter of a Jewish state. He emphatically believed that Palestine belonged by right to the Jews and only to the Jews. He imagined that, after the war, he would devote himself, not only to securing this area for the Jews, but also to seeing to it that the native Arabs were removed. He confidently believed that he could, with American money and patronage, accomplish these goals through adroit negotiations with Arab leaders.[43]

Truman, by contrast, was motivated primarily by humanitarian concerns for the Jewish refugees in European displaced persons' camps and by his personal relations with Jewish friends. But he was plagued with doubts about a Jewish state and suspected that the Jews, once installed in their land, would prove as great tyrants over others as their former oppressors. His final acquiescence in the vote was secured only by enormous organized Zionist pressure on himself and his administration.[44] Yet, when the state was finally secured, following not only the UN vote, but the 1948 war, Truman was capable of lapsing into traditional biblical metaphor and exclaiming, in astonished delight, "I am Cyrus, I am Cyrus."[45]

4. The Emergence and Survival of Palestinian Nationalism

> And behold, one of those who were with Jesus stretched out his hand and drew his sword, and struck the slave of the High Priest, and cut off his ear. Then Jesus said to him, "Put your sword back in its place; for all who take the sword will perish by the sword."
>
> MATT. 26:51–52

The story of Palestinian nationalism from the First World War to the late 1980s is preeminently a story of survival against extraordinary odds. It is a testimony to the tenacity of a Palestinian national consciousness and community, buffeted by the conflicting forces of the disintegrating Ottoman empire, the emergence of Arab nationalisms and of Arab nation-states, Zionism, and Western Imperialism. Zionism has been the major antagonist to Palestinian nationalism, but Western imperial powers and Arab states have been unreliable friends and sometimes open enemies of Palestinian national self-determination. While Palestinian nationalists at various times have sought sympathetic allies in all three of these camps, especially from the Arab states, they have had increasingly to stand alone and to insist that only representative Palestinian national institutions speak for Palestinians. They have done so since 1948 under conditions of statelessness and increasing landlessness.

The turns and twists of this history are complex, and often disputed by the parties in conflict. It is beyond the scope of this chapter to tell this story in detail, a task that has already been the subject of many excellent studies. Rather, this chapter attempts to sketch the general configuration of this struggle for survival in order that the questions of truth and justice can be more correctly posed.

Although there have been endless shifts in the debate over Palestine since 1917, there are also remarkable continuities that have persisted in the struggle of Palestinian survival vis-à-vis Zionism, Western imperialism, and the Arab states. Certain patterns of relationship were set during the period 1908–22 with the disintegration of the Ottoman empire, the emergence of Arab nationalism, and its frustration by the Western imperial presence (in the form of the mandatory powers and the support for Zionism) that continue to shape the framework of the struggle. This chapter will begin by summarizing this framework; the relationships will then be fleshed out in further detail.

Zionism has been the major antagonist of Palestinian nationalism, because the Zionist ambition to plant a Jewish state in Palestine demanded that a rival Palestinian nationalism be liquidated. There has been a long line of Zionist moderates who have recognized and, in various ways, sought to support a sharing of Palestine between the two national movements. But these moderates have never predominated; they have been minority voices with little influence. The main line of Zionist leadership, from Weizmann and Ben-Gurion to Meir, Begin, Shamir, Peres, and Rabin, has believed that there was room for only one national movement, the Jewish national movement, in Palestine. These leaders have rejected both binationalism and a two-state solution.[1] They have sought to prevent a Palestinian state from emerging in any part of Palestine west of the Jordan, hoping to expand into most of this area themselves and to attach any residue of land in Palestine that they could not control to another Arab state, specifically to Jordan. Moreover, they have hoped that most of the Palestinian people could also be removed from the territory of the Jewish state and attached to Jordan or some other Arab state, thus disappearing as a national community.

The second important force in this conflict has been Western imperialism — that of Britain, France, and the United States. British imperial ambitions played a role in encouraging Arab nationalism against a disintegrating Ottoman empire in the pre–World War I period. But they frustrated the hopes of Arab nationalism for a unified Arab state that would include the Arab heartland from the Hejaz to the Persian border on the east to the Mediterranean coast on the west. Instead, the British betrayed their agreements with Arab leaders and, with the French, fragmented the region into mandatory entities that, in turn, became the states of Lebanon, Syria, Iraq, and Jordan, and the State of Israel, which emerged from the promises of the British Mandate for Palestine to the Zionists.

British imperialism sought control of this region, as well as of Egypt, in uneasy compromise with French claims. British and American interests, seeking control of the region, have always had a geopolitical context. Specifically, they have sought to deny influence in the region to their global rivals, the Germans and the Russians. A Zionist state was supported by Britain, and then by America, primarily as a surrogate state to protect their interests. But both have sought to balance this support of a Zionist state with the creation of allies docile to their interests among the Arab states. Both Britain and the United States have ignored Palestinians or, when noticing them at all, have sought to merge them with other border states allied to the West, particularly Jordan. Only in an extreme moment, when Western control of the region was in jeopardy from a rival geopolitical power, Nazi Germany, forcing Britain to tilt toward their Arab allies, did Britain consider real support for a Palestinian state.

The Arab states, specifically Syria, Iraq, Egypt, and Saudi Arabia, have been the chief ideological allies of Palestinian nationalism; but this ideological support has in practice been highly ambivalent because of numerous internal conflicts within each of these states and vis-à-vis one another. (For purposes of simplification of an already very complex story, the roles of the North African Muslim states of Morocco, Algeria, Libya, and Tunisia will not be considered here.)

The term *Arab* is a cultural-linguistic term. It means Arabic-speaking people. This has included Arabic-speaking Christians, Muslims, and Jews. However, the state of Israel has created a separation of Jewish identity from Arab identity. Arabic-speaking Christians, by contrast, have claimed Arab identity as a way of overcoming religious divisions. The term Arab does not include Iranians or other non-Arabic-speaking people of the larger Muslim world.

Syria, Iraq, Jordan, and Lebanon have each had difficulties in establishing legitimacy as national governments. This is due to their mandatory origins, conflicting religious and ethnic minorities, and stresses of modernization, over against traditional ideals of Muslim unity and way of life. "Moderate" Arab leaders have made compromises with modern secular culture, as well as with Western and Zionist presences in the region; such compromises have continually generated threats of explosions against these leaders by traditional and populist Muslim elements.

Muslim radical and traditionalist elements have been the guardians of a complex array of Arab aspirations: Muslim unity against fragmentation of the Arab world; Muslim traditional way of life against Western secular life styles; and economic justice for the whole community over against corruption and a growing gap between rich and poor, signaled by the dependency of Arab elites on Western capitalism. This complex and by no means coherent combination of traditional and future ideals of a just, powerful, and religiously obedient Muslim world, against a Christian and secular West, can be summed up as Arab identity, self-esteem, and well-being. Internal secularism, corruption, and injustice, as well as defeats and humiliation by the West and its surrogate, Israel, are seen as parts of one dilemma. For radical and traditionalist forces of the Arab world, this dilemma is summed up in its most extreme form as a battle of good against evil, Allah against Satan.[2]

Arab national leaders since the 1930s have walked a tightrope between *Realpolitik*, which dictates compromises with Western imperialist and Zionist interests, and these explosive radical and traditionalist forces. The shadow of assassination dogs every Arab national leader should he fail to uphold this agenda of Arab identity and self-esteem by showing himself corrupt and unjust at home or weak and compromising vis-à-vis the West and Israel. A long line of assassinated Arab leaders in the twentieth century, such as Abdullah, King of Jordan (1951) and Anwar Sadat of Egypt (1982), testifies to the reality of this danger of loss of legitimacy. Sometimes these acts have been packaged in the language of *jihad*, or holy war, against Arab leaders whose failures and weaknesses have made them the objects of crusades by radical factions of the Arab world. Such radical factions regard the assassination of such "traitors" as the purging of an instrument of Satan — not just a political necessity, but a holy duty.[3]

For the national leaders of Egypt, Iraq, Syria, Saudi Arabia, and, to a lesser extent, Lebanon and Jordan, anti-Zionist rhetoric is a requisite for Arab and Muslim identity and legitimacy. This rhetoric (the word *rhetoric* is used here, not in the sense of insincerity, but in the sense of public speech for the rehearsal of communal identity) is demanded both by pan-Islamist and by pan-Arabist worldviews. In the pan-Islamist worldview, Palestine is an integral part of *Dar-al Islam*, the realm conquered by the true religion of Allah and rescued from the forces of idolatry and infidelity. In the pan-Arabist world-view, Palestine is an integral part of Arab culture and communal life. Although these worldviews would say that Jews can live and always have lived in this region as minority communities, a Jewish state created by Western colonialism is anathema.

In the context of these worldviews, support for Palestinian national self-determination is an ideological necessity for any legitimate Arab leader. To affirm Palestinian rights is to deny Zionist claims to a Jewish state created by Western colonialism. Yet this ideological necessity to support Palestinian nationalism has hardly been matched by deeds. There are several reasons for this. First, the internal and interstate conflicts of Arab nations have not given them the economic power or the political cohesion to deny Israeli ambitions, either on the battlefield or in geopolitical diplomacy.

Second, Arab leaders (including Palestinian leaders) have, again and again, been unable to take advantage of the timely moment when compromise with Israel and with the West might have won part of their demands, for at the moment when compromise was possible, it appeared illegitimate to make such compromises. Then the moment was overtaken by new "facts" of Israeli expansion, and the Arabs were faced with new demands for compromise. Thus the Arab world experiences itself as having been pushed back, step by step, by new "facts" of Israeli expansion that immediately become a new nonnegotiable "status quo." Arab leaders, caught in the bind of domestic militancy and Israeli opportunism, have typically sought to placate domestic anti-Zionist feeling with militant rhetoric against Israel, while seeking more moderate compromises with the Israelis and the West in private conversations. But this effort to find a basis for negotiation has been met by an Israeli intransigence whose basic agenda is an expanded, and dominantly Jewish, state.[4]

Efforts of Arabs to communicate with the West have been hampered by deep anti-Arab racism in Western culture. Stereotypical hostility to Arabs is pervasive among Western Europeans and Americans. The Arab effort to present its case to the West is also hampered by differences of culture that make Arabs very inept at organizing mass communication for the Western mass democratic culture. Precisely in this area of mass communication to the Western world, however, Jews have excelled. Vehement Arab anti-

Zionist (sometimes anti-Jewish) rhetoric has been exploited by world Zionism to convince Jews and Christians that Arabs are irrationally violent, in contrast to Israeli "reasonableness."

While Arab leaders tend to be militant in rhetoric but conservative and often indecisive in practice, Israeli leaders are usually carefully moderate in public rhetoric but decisively opportunistic in diplomatic and military action. They have typically concealed the continually expansionist nature of their project from their Western sponsors and pursued a "step by step" process toward these goals. While pointing to militant Arab rhetoric to frighten Jews and convince them that the Arab world is genocidal toward Jews and that no peace is possible with them, Israeli leaders have been quite aware of the actual inability of the Arab world to deliver on this militant rhetoric. But they have preferred to cultivate the militant, rather than the moderate, side of the Arab world, in order to avoid responses from Jews and Western sponsor governments that might force them to limit their expansionist ambitions.[5]

The inability of the Arab states to deliver on their promises to defend Palestinian nationalism has been partly due to economic and military weakness and diplomatic ineptitude. But it has also been caused by the fact that several of the key Arab states have had their own nationalist ambitions vis-à-vis Palestine. Jordan, Syria, and Lebanon, and even Iraq, are all haunted by the ghost of "greater Syria." This was the idea of a unified Arab state in the Arab heartland that was the Arab nationalist goal after the First World War.[6] For each of these states, Palestine continues to be seen as a potential province within this Greater Syrian state. These Arab states' support of Palestinian national self-determination is often qualified by a desire to co-opt the Palestinian cause into their own nationalist agendas. This has been particularly true of Jordan, which was created by Britain's splitting off part of the British Mandate for Palestine and which attempted to lay claim to the West Bank, during the 1948 war, as part of its expanded national territory.

Saudi Arabia and Egypt have generally seen themselves as mandated to check these ambitions of Jordan and Syria to become the representative pan-Arab state. Their interventions, ostensibly on behalf of Palestinian national rights, have often been geared to checking Jordanian or Syrian expansion. Thus the Palestinians, in looking to the Arab world for support in their struggle against

Israel, have often found themselves caught in internecine conflicts within or between Arab states.

Having sketched this general framework of the dilemma of Palestinian nationalism as caught between the ambitions of Zionism, Western imperialism, and Arab nationalisms, this chapter will outline the historical stages of this dilemma: (1) The beginnings of Arab nationalism and its betrayal by Western imperialism, 1900–1920; (2) Palestinian nationalism during the mandatory period, 1920–48; (3) the suppression and resurrection of the Palestinian national movement, 1948–75; and (4) the period from the Lebanese conflict to the uprising in the Occupied Territories, 1975–88. A concluding section will summarize the development of Palestinian nationalist ideology in relation to Zionism.

THE BEGINNINGS OF ARAB NATIONALISM AND ITS BETRAYAL BY WESTERN IMPERIALISM

At the end of the nineteenth century the Ottoman empire was called the "sick man of Europe." The Greeks had won their independence from it in 1829, and the Balkan states were struggling to free themselves from it. The Western European powers, at the time engaged in dividing Africa among themselves, were also each vying for their piece of the Ottoman empire. Britain had established its control over Egypt in 1882, which retained nominal allegiance to the Ottoman government in Istanbul. Italy eyed Libya, while France was establishing its influence in Algeria, Syria, and Lebanon. The British sought to secure access to the Suez and the Persian Gulf for themselves.

In 1908 the Young Turks began a military revolution against the oppressive rule of the sultan, Abdul-Hamid, promising a democratic constitutional government. But it soon became clear that they intended to continue Turkish centralized control over the non-Turkish areas, rather than allowing equal representation for the Arabs. In the wake of these disappointments, Arab nationalist societies such as *al-Fatat* and *al-'Ahd* began among Arab intellectuals and military officers, particularly from the areas of Syria, the Lebanon, and Palestine.[7]

With the outbreak of World War I, the Turkish empire cast its lot with the Central Powers of Germany and the Austro-Hungarian empire. The Turkish sultan and Ottoman Muslim religious leaders called for *jihad*, or holy war, of all Muslims against the Entente powers of Russia, France, Italy, and Britain.[8] This call was not actually heeded by Arab or Indian Muslims, but the British feared the possible rise of a united Muslim world against the Allies. British authorities in Cairo put out feelers to Husain ibn 'Ali (who had been appointed by the Young Turks as grand sharif of Mecca) in an attempt to splinter Turkish unity by creating a British alliance with the Arabs.

In the correspondence that took place between Sharif Husain and Sir Henry McMahon, high commissioner for Egypt and the Sudan, between July 1915 and January 1916, McMahon promised the sharif an independent Arab state in exchange for an Arab alliance against the Turkish-German power. In his correspondence, the sharif defined the Arab state in terms that coincided with the plan developed by the Arab nationalist societies *al-Fatat* and *al-'Ahd* in their Damascus Protocol of May 1915. This state was envisioned as including a territory west from the Mediterranean along the thirty-seventh parallel, south along the Persian border and the Arabian peninsula, and north along the Mediterranean coast. McMahon, in his letter of October 24, 1915, agreed to support such an Arab state, with the exception of coastal areas west of Damascus and north along the coast to port cities on the southern coast of Asia Minor. No mention was made of excluding Palestine, although, in 1922, the British would insist that this area was also excluded in the correspondence.[9]

On the basis of this correspondence, which the sharif understood as a firm agreement, the Arab revolt against the Turkish and German armies began in June 1916. The Arab armies, with the assistance from daring British officers such as T. E. Lawrence, captured the Arab peninsula to the Gulf of Aqaba and then, in coordination with Allenby's army, drove north and west to capture the areas of the Arab region to the thirty-seventh parallel.

Meanwhile, however, the British foreign office, represented by Sir Mark Sykes and Lord Balfour, entered into conflicting agreements with France and Russia and with the Zionists. In April and May of 1916, Sykes worked out a secret agreement with the French consul general of Beirut, Georges-Picot, to divide up this Arab region into five parts. One part, corresponding to the coastal regions from Tyre to Alexandretta and southern Anatolia, would be under direct French administration. Another area of the Tigris-Euphrates valley from the Persian Gulf beyond Baghdad would be under direct British administration. A third large area, forming a triangle from Damascus north to Aleppo and west to Rowanduz, would be under French "sphere of influence," and a fourth large area of the Fertile Crescent, from Gaza and Aqaba in the west to the Persian border and south to the Persian Gulf, would be the British sphere. A fifth area of Palestine was reserved as an international zone under the three Allied powers (Britain, France, and Russia). The largely undeveloped Arab Peninsula was left to a self-governing Arab state.

When this agreement was leaked to the Arabs from the revolutionary Bolshevik government in December 1917, the Arab leaders were outraged.[10] Shortly before, they had learned of yet a third agreement, between Lord Balfour and the Zionists, promising a homeland for the Jewish people in Palestine. The French had not been informed of the correspondence with Husain; nor did the Zionists know of the other two agreements at the time they were negotiating with the British.

In the following months, the British would seek to cover these contradictions and placate Arab outrage. On June 16, 1918, the British Foreign Office issued a declaration to the Arab leaders in which it affirmed its support for independence and self-government for all the Arab territories liberated by the Arab and British armies.[11] This was followed by an Anglo-French declaration in November 1918 in which the two powers promised to follow the principle of self-determination and consent of the governed for the territories liberated from Turkish rule in the war.[12]

However, when Amir Faisal, son of Sharif Husain and chief military leader of the Arab revolt, arrived in Paris in January 1919 for the Versailles Peace Conference, he found himself disregarded by the French, who were pressing for the observance of the Sykes-Picot agreement. Although there was more personal sympathy for the Arab cause among some British leaders, in practice the British were pressing to enlarge their sphere of influence at the expense of French demands. The British sought to expand into the oil-rich Mosul region and also to claim exclusive control over Palestine, rather than establishing Palestine as the international zone envisioned by the Sykes-Picot agreement. By recognizing French rights in Lebanon and the northern interior of Syria, the British also gained control of the southern region of the Transjordan.

Arab nationalist leaders in these regions did not passively wait for the decisions of the peace conference, however, but moved ahead rapidly to try to secure their demands for a unified state. Al-Fatat transformed itself into the Arab Independence Party and held elections in these territories under discussion. Meeting in assembly in Damascus in July 1919, they called for an independent Syrian state, including Palestine, under Faisal. However, this clear expression of Arab demands for unity and independence was disregarded by the European powers.[13] In the San Remo agreement of April 25, 1920, the Allied powers agreed to divide up the area occupied by their armies into British and French "Mandates." The French would receive control over Lebanon, the northern coastal areas to Alexandretta, and the interior of north Syria. The British would receive two Mandate areas: Iraq (including the Mosul) and Palestine, as well as the attached Transjordan area (see map 1).[14]

Thus were the hopes of the Arab nationalist movement for a unified Arab state (originally for a state that would unite the whole Arab world, and then for a Syrian state) frustrated by the imposition of colonial rule. The northern Arab region was fragmented into separate zones of rival European power. Local antagonisms would be exacerbated, and there would emerge from the mandatory period a series of small Arab states and one Jewish state, each bearing, in various degrees, an onus of illegitimacy in the eyes of the Arab world, due to their origins as the creations of arbitrary colonial power amid Arab humiliation and betrayal.

PALESTINIAN NATIONALISM DURING THE MANDATORY PERIOD

The news of the San Remo decisions evoked widespread uprisings in the Arab world. The Arab peninsula, which had been left as an independent area, but under several different tribal authorities, saw a rapid movement of unification, led by Sultan ibn Saud and his fundamentalist Wahhabi army. Between 1919 and 1926 ibn Saud had absorbed the northern areas of the peninsula to the borders of Iraq and Transjordan. He also conquered the Hejaz, evicting Sharif Husain from his control over the holy cities of Mecca and Medina and sending him into ignominious exile. Except for coastal areas such as Yemen, all the Arab peninsula was transformed into a single Saudi Arabian kingdom.[15]

In Iraq, a violent uprising exploded against the British in 1920. After prolonged fighting that cost thousands of lives and millions of British pounds, the British conceded to transform Iraq into a quasi-independent kingdom under Amir Faisal. British tutelage remained for another eleven years until independence was granted in 1932.

Revolt also broke out in Syria against French rule. The French responded by marching their troops on Damascus, expelling Faisal, and imposing a harsh military dictatorship. Lebanese territory was expanded at the expense of Syria, incorporating the northern coastal area to Tripoli and the Biqa' valley. This brought an almost equal number of Muslims into what had been a predominantly Christian territory, laying the foundations both for future communal conflicts between Christians and Muslims and for territorial conflicts with Syria. The northern coast to Alexandretta was also fragmented by the French into two separate regions, cutting Syria off from coastal ports. French language and culture were promoted at the expense of Arab culture and institutions.

These French actions led to a rebellion in Syria in 1925–26 that was savagely repressed.[16] Continuing unrest, including a six-week general strike, led to the French concession of independence to the Syrians, granted in 1941 and implemented in 1944. A southern region of Syria, detached by the British from the French zone and attached to their Mandate for Palestine, became the Hashemite Kingdom of Jordan in 1921. In 1920, Amir 'Abdullah, brother of Faisal and third son of Sharif Husain, had brought his troops to Transjordan to assist his brother, who was embattled by the French in Syria. Winston Churchill, secretary of state for the colonies, sought to pacify the brothers by separating Transjordan from the Palestine Mandate and granting it to 'Abdullah, while sending Faisal to become king of Iraq.

The most intractable legacy of the mandatory period, however, would arise from the British handling of Palestine. This area had been designated by the Balfour Declaration as the region for a Jewish homeland. The British Mandate period would see, not only the expansion of the Jewish *Yishuv* in Palestine, but also the emergence of a Palestinian national consciousness and movement.

It has been often claimed by Zionists that Palestinians did not exist before this period. This has been taken to mean that the area was largely uninhabited by Arabs prior to the Jewish settlements—an assertion the next chapter will show to be false. It has also been taken to mean that the Arabs who lived in the region had no sense of belonging to a Palestinian nation.[17] This claim fails to recognize that, prior to the Mandate period, there was also no Syrian, Jordanian, Saudi Arabian, or Iraqi nationalism. These particular Arab nationalisms emerged out of the colonial fragmentation of the region. Moreover, nationalism itself was a Western, not an Arab idea, imported to the region in the late nineteenth century.

But this does not mean that the peoples of these regions did not have distinct regional identities within the larger contexts of Arab identity, the Ottoman empire, and the Muslim *umma* (community). Palestinians particularly were aware of belonging to a distinct historical region. The word *Palestine* goes back to the Philistines, the people who lived in the coastal region in the second millennium B.C.E. The Romans used the term *Palaestina* to refer to a large administrative district divided into three regions: Judaea and Samaria; the Jordan Valley and eastern and central Galilee; and the third region, Palaestina Tertia, covering the southern Transjordan, the Negev, and the Sinai.

From the fourth century to the present, the Greek Orthodox patriarchate preserved this Roman administrative unit of all three parts of Palestine in its jurisdiction. The Latin patriarchate, established in 1841, followed the same lines. The Roman divisions were also preserved in the administrative units set up after the Muslim conquest. Until the thirteenth century, the Muslims used the name *Filastin* to refer to Judaea and Samaria and the adjacent coastal regions. Both Christian and Muslim Arabs also had a distinct sense of this region as the Holy Land of both their Scriptures and traditions.[18]

The Zionist settlements of the late nineteenth century became the goad for a new development of Palestinian identity. From 1900, in protest literature against Zionist settlement, the term *Filastin* appears as the way to identify the local Arab community, both Christian and Muslim.[19] The Balfour Declaration and British Mandate crystallized this nascent sense of Palestinian national identity. The Mandate made the region a political unit, with Jerusalem as its capital. This created the context in which Palestinian national identity would be shaped for the next thirty years, both in protest against Zionist settlement and in appeals for self-determination.

The Balfour Declaration, which received international legal status with the acceptance of the British Mandate for Palestine by the League of Nations in 1923, did not recognize the existence of a Palestinian Arab national community at all. The Palestinians were referred to only as "existing non-Jewish communities" whose civil and religious (not economic and political) rights were to be safeguarded. The Mandate thus committed the British to building up a Jewish community through immigration and land sales until it was ready for independence.

The Palestinian community reacted to this Zionist commitment with protests on the first anniversary of the Balfour Declaration (1918), a huge demonstration after the San Remo conference in 1920, and street protests in 1920 and 1921.[20] The first Palestinian nationalist organizations were the local Muslim-Christian associations of this period.[21] At the third Palestinian Arab Congress of 1920 an Arab executive committee was formed to speak for the national movement. It argued for the creation of a national government of the Arabic-speaking people living in Palestine in 1914 (which would have included traditionalist Sephardic Jews). It rested its case on the McMahon pledges to Husain in 1915, the natural rights of the long-standing possession of the region by the Palestinian Arabs (since the seventh century), and the Wilsonian principle of self-determination.

Some Palestinians claimed earlier ancestry, going back to the ancient Canaanites who had founded the civilization in the region several millennia "before our Father Abraham arrived in the region." Jews, they said, had only had a state for a few hundred years and had not been a major presence for over eighteen hundred years. They argued that people long absent from a region do not have rights to return and prevail over the present residents. They asked, What if all people would claim the right to return to areas where they had once lived—for example, the Muslims in Spain?[22]

These arguments and protests began to make it clear to the British Mandate authorities that the Palestinians must be taken into consideration as a national community. Between 1922 and 1930 the British shifted to a new definition of its Mandate as one that sought to balance dual obligations to a Jewish national home in Palestine and to Palestinian national rights. Several attempts were made to set up a binational legislative council, with both Jewish and Arab representatives, to prepare Palestine for some kind of independence as a binational state. The Arabs boycotted the effort in 1920, and, when they were more ready to accept it in 1929, it was shelved because of the riots that broke out in that year.[23] Since the Arabs refused to accept any claim of the Jews to *national* rights, while the Jews sought to prevent any situation where they would become a minority in an Arab state, no satisfactory basis for collaboration could be found.

During the 1920s Palestinian parties were being formed, but they tended to represent powerful clans, with their familial and economic interests. The most important of these was the Palestinian Arab Party, dominated by the Husseini clan. In 1920 the British had helped to install an ambitious leader of the clan, al-Hajj Muhammed Amin al-Husseini, as head of the Supreme Muslim Council, the body that not only represented the majority of Muslims but also controlled the income from its substantial properties.[24] Al-Hajj Amin used this position as mufti of Jerusalem and head of the Supreme Muslim Council to build up a commanding political base and to sabotage any rivals to his leadership.

For the next thirty years the mufti would play the leading role in Palestinian nationalist politics, standing for intransigent maximalism against all compromises with Zionism and subverting the emergence of any alternative leadership. The failures of the Palestinian national movement to sieze its opportunities, as the British made successive retreats from its commitments to the Zionists, is largely the fault of his leadership.[25] The British, however, also bear a responsibility for having failed to support alternative leadership and to help develop a Palestinian political infrastructure for self-government.

The chief rival of the Husseini party was the National Defense Party, led by the Nashashibi clan, which represented large citrus growers and the majority of Arab mayors, and which was more willing to consider the various compromise proposals offered by the British. The *Istiqlal* or Independence Party sought the incorporation of Palestine into a pan-Arab state. These three parties, together with three other smaller parties, were able to create a loose alliance after the 1929 riots and come together as the Arab Higher Committee in 1936.[26] But this unity was based on acceptance of the predominance of the mufti and thus only papered over the actual factionalism, bordering on blood feud, between the Husseinis and their chief rivals.

In 1936, with unprecedented Jewish immigration flowing in from Europe under the pressure of rising Nazi anti-Semitism, the Palestinians were faced with the possibility that they might become a minority in their own land. At the same time, anti-British and anti-Jewish propaganda was flowing into the Arab world, as the Italians and Germans sought to woo the Arab nationalist leaders to their side in the coming contest against the British and French.[27] Palestinian protests broke out against increased Jewish immigration and land purchase. In 1936 the Arab Higher Committee (AHC) responded by calling for a boycott of the Jewish *Yishuv*. This boycott, however, had a far more drastic effect on the Arab than on the Jewish community. In fact, it allowed the Jews to consolidate the economic separatism that labor Zionists had long advocated, employing only Jews in place of Arab workers who now absented themselves from Jewish plantations and industries.[28] By October the AHC was forced to call off the boycott, partly due to pressure from the Arab states.

By this time the protest was passing out of the hands of the AHC into a popular revolt that the AHC no longer controlled. The British, mistakenly seeking to repress the revolt by suppressing its leaders, banned the AHC and the local party councils and arrested their leaders. The mufti was able to escape, and from 1937 until 1946 he controlled his party from various places of exile. This had the unfortunate effect of elevating him to the position of a national martyr and hero, while removing from immediate view the actual defects of his leadership.

The British sought to repress the rising revolt by full-scale martial law, massive arrests, and collective punishment. Thousands of Palestinians died in the guerrilla fighting of 1937–38; thousands more were wounded or imprisoned.[29] The British found themselves having to commit a large number of troops and massive expenditures to contain the Palestinian revolt, at a time when war with Germany and Italy was on the horizon and a very real danger existed that the Axis powers would succeed in winning the dissident Arabs to their side. As in the period before the First World War, the British moved to conciliate the Arabs in order to prevent them from allying with Britain's European enemies.

In the first stage of the revolt in 1936, a royal commission was formed to investigate the situation. Its report, released in July 1937, declared the Mandate to be unworkable and recommended the partition of Palestine into a small Jewish state (20 percent) and a larger Arab state that would be joined to Jordan. The British would retain control of the Jerusalem-Bethlehem area and a corridor to the sea, as well as key ports, railways, and airfields. Since the Jewish state would still contain some 300,000 Arabs, the Peel Commission report suggested that they might be transferred to the Arab state.[30] This report was rejected by the Palestinian parties, especially the Husseinis, who pointed out that the Jewish state would contain the richest agricultural land in the country where Arabs held four-fifths of the land and seven-tenths of the citrus groves.[31] Although the left and right Zionist parties rejected partition, Wiezmann and Ben-Gurion argued for its acceptance on the grounds that it affirmed the principle of a Jewish state, even though they did not accept the limited land base of the proposed state.[32]

In 1939, under the guns of impending war, Britain made a further retreat from its commitments to the Zionists. In the 1939 white paper issued unilaterally by the British, when neither the Arab Higher Committee nor the Zionists would accept it, the British virtually abandoned a commitment to a Jewish homeland. They committed themselves to strict limitation of Jewish land purchase and immigration (75,000 over five years) and the creation of a Palestinian state where Jews and Arabs would share government.[33] However, the mufti and his party, insisting on the full claims of the Palestinian National Pact (restriction of all land sales and immigration of Jews, immediate creation of an independent state) rejected the 1939 white paper.[34] It was also angrily repudiated by the Zionists, as a final betrayal of British commitments to them — and at the worst possible moment, when Nazi persecution was driving Jews from Europe and all other doors were shut against them.[35] From 1939 to 1948 the British would rule Palestine without the cooperation of Arabs or Jews. Jewish terrorist organizations (the *Irgun* and the Stern Gang) began to turn their guns on the British.

From 1939 to 1942 the Axis powers were in the ascendancy, and several Arab opposition nationalist leaders in Egypt, Iraq, Syria, and Lebanon cast their lots with the Italians and Germans, in hopes of being swept into power in independent Arab states by victory over the British. During this period, the mufti left his exile in Lebanon and made his way to Iraq where he became a virtual kingmaker in Arab politics, bolstered by generous funds from the Arab and

Axis states. In October 1941, with the failure of an Iraqi coup against the British, the mufti fled to Italy and then to Germany, where he cooperated with the Nazis for the rest of the war in beaming anti-Jewish propaganda to the Arab world and recruiting Muslims from the Balkans for the Axis armies. He imagined that the Axis would repay him for these services by sweeping the Jews out of Palestine and installing him as leader of a pan-Arab state that would include the entire Arab Middle East.[36]

Pro-Nazi sentiments in the Arab world were not confined to the mufti. Several Middle Eastern leaders, including Reza Shah of Iran, Rashid 'Ali Gilani of Iraq, and 'Aziz al Masri and his Brown Shirts in Egypt, sought to imitate fascist nationalism in the Arab states. We have seen that elements of Zionism were also not immune to this attraction, and the *Irgun* sought an alliance with the Nazis in the same period. But the primary reason for these Arab (and Zionist) leanings toward the Nazis was anti-British colonial politics. The political principle that "our enemy's enemy might be our friend" disposed some Arabs to think that they might make common cause with Germany against their enemies, the British and also the Jews.[37]

By the time the mufti had installed himself in Germany, however, the tide of war had turned in the Middle East. The German advance in the Balkans and across North Africa was beaten back. Arab national leaders began to cast their lot with what was likely to be an Allied victory. They hoped to be able to strike a better deal at the peace table than they had gotten after the First World War. By this time several Arab states had won their independence and were recognized members of the League of Nations. In 1945, seven of these states banded together to form the Arab League to represent Arab interests in international negotiations.

During this period—from the British suppression of the Arab Higher Committee and the arrest or flight of its leaders until the European powers again addressed the Palestine issue in the Anglo-American Committee of Inquiry in 1946—the Palestinian national movement remained quiescent and in disarray. The opposition rivals, the Nashashibi National Defense Party, had declared their willingness to accept the white paper of 1939 and to work with the British on that basis. But the British largely ignored them, while the remaining Husseini partisans left in Palestine sabotaged any possibility that they would be able to gather their forces into an alternative representative body.[38] For the majority of Palestinians, who had come to idealize the mufti and excuse his faults because of his status as an exiled martyr, and also for much of the Arab world, the mufti was able to retain his status as the leader of the Palestinian national movement, despite his wartime activities. In 1946 he managed to escape from France and make his way to Cairo where, under the patronage of the Arab League, he was again recognized as the spokesperson for the Palestinian cause.[39]

However, although publicly supported, in fact he was generally distrusted in the Palestinian and Arab world. Moderate Palestinians had no desire to see him installed as national leader of an independent state. There were widespread reservations among leaders of other Arab states as well, especially on the part of Abdullah, the king of Jordan, who was determined to prevent any Palestinian state from being formed with the mufti as its head. Even the Egyptians, who officially endorsed and protected him, did not trust him.[40] Thus the Palestinians entered their critical contest with the Zionists in the 1947–48 period with the contradictory onus of a national leader whom they could neither jettison nor entrust with any power. This situation was not unpleasing to the Zionists. Already in the late 1930s Ben-Gurion coined the phrase "rely on the mufti," meaning that the mufti could be counted on to prevent the Palestinians from making the realistic compromises that might have won their goals of an independent Palestinian state.[41]

THE SUPPRESSION AND RESURRECTION OF THE PALESTINIAN NATIONAL MOVEMENT

The 1948 war for Palestine has achieved a legendary status among Israelis as the war of national survival. It is typically presented as a war in which a small community of Jews, recently emerged from the Nazi genocide campaign, were able to win against the overwhelming odds of the combined armies of five Arab states. The Zionists, it is said, did not want war. They had accepted the UN partition of November 1947 and were ready for peace. It was the Arabs who rejected the partition and declared a war intended to exterminate the Jewish community in Palestine.[42]

Although superficially that account appears correct, the more one looks beneath the surface, the more strikingly different realities appear. Although the Zionists did accept that part of the partition plan that endorsed a Jewish state, in fact they did not accept either the territorial limits of that state or the parallel Palestinian state envisioned in that resolution. They saw the partition as a base for further goals that they expected to win through war.

The two national leaders most anxious to go to war were Ben-Gurion and Abdullah of Jordan. And yet, ironically, these two states were close to a secret agreement with each other over their mutual war aims when war broke out. Abdullah wanted to prevent an independent Palestinian state under the mufti from being created in the area designated by the UN for an Arab state; he had determined to annex this area to Jordan. During 1947 and early 1948 he held a number of secret meetings with British and Zionist representatives in an effort to gain an agreement to use his army only to occupy this Arab territory and to leave the Jewish area alone. But a final agreement was never concluded with the Israeli leaders, partly because each hoped to gain more territory.[43]

The Israelis were determined to expand their boundaries into the area designated as the Arab state. Abdullah occasionally imagined that he might succeed, with his British-trained Arab Legion, in occupying the whole of Palestine and annexing it to Jordan, in partial fulfillment of the ancient Hashemite hopes of creating a Greater Syrian state. Egypt, Syria, and Saudi Arabia, by contrast, suspected and were determined to thwart these Jordanian expansionist designs.[44] Abdullah constantly announced in public his championship of a Palestinian state in all Palestine in order to cover his negotiations and to prevent himself from being declared a traitor to the Palestinian cause by those rival Arab states.

Egypt, which would put the largest Arab army into the war, was the least anxious to go to war. Well into April 1948, it still had made no plans to go to war and hoped to avoid war by diplomatic negotiations in the United Nations that might create a retreat from partition and a UN trusteeship that would lay the basis of a binational state, a solution that key elements in the American State Department also favored.[45] But the Egyptian leaders were in danger from populist Muslim groups, who were enthusiastically recruiting volunteers from what they saw as a holy crusade against the Zionists.[46] Egyptian leaders had real reason to fear that the guns of this popular army would be turned against themselves in a coup, if they revealed their doubts about victory. Consequently they publicly poured forth a barrage of militant anti-Zionist rhetoric and premature claims of easy victory.

The period when the Zionists were in some real danger was before the Mandate formally ended on May 15, 1948 and the armies of the Arab states entered the field. During the period from November 1947 to April 1948, a Palestinian guerrilla army under the mufti's popular cousin Abdul Qadir al-Husseini, and the Arab Liberation Army (mainly supplied from Syria) under the leadership of Fawzi al-Kaukjii, the failed guerrilla leader of the 1937 revolt, attempted to secure Jerusalem and the Galilee.[47] During this period the British continued to prevent arms or immigrants from landing to supply the Zionist side. However, by late April this tense period for the Jews was largely over; they had created their own munitions factories and large shipments of arms and volunteer forces were ready to land.[48] They had secured their own settlements within the area designated for the Jewish state and had succeeded in terrorizing much of the Arab population in villages in this area, as well as the major cities of Haifa and Jaffa, into leaving. Abdul Qadir had died in the effort of the Palestinian popular militia to prevent Jewish control of the access route to Jerusalem.

The Israelis were never outnumbered by the combined Arab armies. Under the British, the Jewish *Yishuv* had built up an extensive militia (*Haganah*), ostensibly for self-defense, while the British had followed a rigid policy of disarming the local Arabs after the 1936 revolt.[49] The combined rifle strength of the various town and rural militias of the Palestinians was less than 2,000, while the volunteers who entered Palestine as the Arab Liberation Army from January to May 1948 were less than 4,000. The combined armies of the five Arab League states from Syria, Iraq, Jordan, Egypt, and Lebanon were about 14,000, giving a combined strength of all the Arab armies of less than 20,000 troops who were poorly armed, trained, and coordinated. The Israelis had by mid-May a well-organized army of 30,000, with another 32,000 in reserves who were not yet fully armed but soon to become so.[50] The Israel Defense Forces were highly motivated and coordinated, while the Arab armies were working largely at cross-purposes with one another.[51]

From mid-May the Israel Defense Forces were on the offensive, expanding into the territory designated for the Arab states. Much of the major Israeli expansion took place in surprise offensives under the cover of official truces. From October 1948 to March 1949, Israel secured much additional territory in western Galilee, the Negev to the Gulf of Aqaba, and the Etzion Triangle west of Jerusalem.[52] Methods of evicting the Palestinian residents became even more direct and brutal as Arabs became aware that, if they fled their homes, the Israelis would not allow them to return.[53]

After the war, the Arab leaders would pay for their vehement rhetoric and optimistic claims of easy victory. As the magnitude of the debacle became evident to the Arab peoples, they would explode in anger against their leaders. Egyptian prime minister Mahmud al-Nuqrashi, Syria's Husni al-Zaim, and Lebanon's Riyad al-Sulh would be assassinated. In 1952 the monarchy of King Farouk was overthrown by officers led by Colonel Nasser. Antigovernment protests led to a military coup in Syria in 1949. In July 1951, King Abdullah of Jordan would die of a bullet fired by a Palestinian refugee on the steps of the al-Asqa mosque, for what was seen as his betrayal of the Palestinian cause.[54]

In 1949 Palestinians seemed to have disappeared as a national movement. If they were remembered at all, it was as anonymous "Arab" refugees in camps in the West Bank, annexed to Jordan, in the Gaza Strip (which remained occupied by Egypt), in Syria, and in southern Lebanon. In 1949, 1,000,000 Palestinians were registered for relief under the United Nations Relief and Works Agency for Palestine Refugees in the Near East (UNRWA). This refugee population has grown in the subsequent decades to two million in 1982. The continued existence of refugees is due both to the failure of the original refugees and their descendants to be repatriated by Israel or assimilated into the various host Arab states and also to the continuous creation of new refugees by wars and by Israeli retaliatory raids into the border areas of surrounding states where camps are located. For example, the 1967 war caused not only 16,000 Palestinians but also 100,000 Syrians to be displaced from the Golan Heights and 300,000 Egyptians to be moved further west from the border areas.[55]

It is inappropriate for Israelis to claim that the Arab states have created this refugee problem and have the responsibility to solve it by assimilating the refugees. United Nations resolutions since 1948 have put the international community on record as supporting the principle that those refugees wishing to return to their homes in Palestine and live at peace should be permitted to do so and that compensation should be paid for the property of those not choosing to return — principles that Israel has repeatedly refused to accept.

Several Arab states did put forward plans for resettlement of the refugees as part of a comprehensive peace plan — plans that Israel rejected.[56] The Arab states have held to the basic principle that the refugees deserve repatriation or compensation. They have had limited resources to resettle the refugees, especially when they are coping with many refugee nationals of their own. Finally, however, the nonassimilation of the Palestinians into other Arab states reflects the Palestinians' own national consciousness, one that has grown rather than diminished over the last forty years.[57]

The first generation of adults displaced into the refugee camps in 1948–49 had been mainly self-employed peasants. Without land, they remained unemployed the rest of their lives. Education became the primary means of Palestinian upward mobility. Through UNRWA and Christian mission schools and self-help networks that sent Palestinian young people to universities throughout the Arab and Western world, Palestinians became one of the most highly educated populations in the Middle East, other than Israelis. Yet they have typically refused to give up their claims to the camps and thus to their rights to repatriation. As educated sons were able to earn high wages in the Gulf states, elderly family members remained in the camps, with financial help flowing back for their support, as well as for the education of younger family members.

It is the extended family that is, finally, the base of Palestinian survival — an extended family that both supports one another and links its members to the Palestinian community and its historical memory and identity. That memory and identity have been assiduously passed down from generation to generation. Young people whose ancestral villages disappeared under Israeli bulldozers forty years ago know exactly what village they came from and even where their family house was located in that village. Although UN funds have preserved a refugee population, and Arab funds have financed Palestinians' national organizations and institutions, to see these as the "causes" of a Palestinian national movement is to miss the more fundamental reality without which Arab funds would have had little effect. The Palestinians have remained agents of their own survival.[58] Their struggle has been to emerge from the tutelage of others and to assert and gain recognition of their autonomous self-determination.

Particularly for the Palestinians in the camps, the Arab states were as much at fault for their situation as Israel. Both Israel and the Arab states seemed equally determined that the Palestinians disappear as a national community. Pan-Arabism was a reigning Arab ideology in the 1950s and early 1960s. In this context, Palestinians were supposed to join themselves to some united Arab state that might be sponsored by Egypt, Syria, Iraq, or Jordan, not to become a self-determining movement calling for a Palestinian state. Each of these Arab claimants, competing to be the center of a pan-Arab state, wanted to control the Palestinians and use the Palestinian issue to further their own claims. Palestinian autonomy was seen as schismatic. Moreover, the Arab states bordering on Israel kept a heavy hand of repression on Palestinian activism within their own countries, both in fear of Israeli retaliation against their territory and because of the potentially revolutionary impact a conscious Palestinian movement might have on their own domestic affairs. It is in this context of near oblivion that an organized Palestinian national movement reemerged in the mid-1960s.

By the end of the 1960s, the Palestine Liberation Organization (PLO) emerged as the vehicle recognized by Palestinians as representing their national movement. This organization has a dual origin, from movements emerging among the Palestinian people themselves and from an organization created by the Arab states. In the early 1950s, Palestinian university students in Cairo, whose families had become refugees in Gaza, began to organize around a basic agenda of Palestinian nationalism. A core of these students, including Yasir Arafat and Saleh Khalef, came into contact with other Palestinian activists, such as Khaled al-Hassan and Khalil al-Wazir, in the Gulf states. Between 1959 and 1962 this group created *Fateh* around the basic concepts of the liberation of all Palestine through armed struggle.[59]

Fateh sought friendly Arab and international support, but itself was based on Palestinian self-organization. *Fateh's* basic ideology insisted that all factional disputes must be subordinated to Palestinian national self-determination. Thus *Fateh* determined to avoid intervention in political disputes within host Arab countries. It also sought to avoid ideological disputes over pan-Arabism versus separate Arab nationalisms, Marxism versus capitalism, or Islamic versus secular state goals. It sought to neutralize these disputes and create a unified movement focused on the goal of Palestinian national self-determination.[60]

In 1964, President Nasser of Egypt gathered the first Arab summit in Cairo. At the meeting the foundation of a Palestine Liberation Organization (PLO) was mandated. The bombastic but ineffective Palestinian diplomat Ahmed Shuqairy was named to head it. In May a founding conference was held in East Jerusalem, where the new organization was given a national charter and constitution.[61] But the PLO was a shadow movement for the next four years. During the 1967 war, in which Israel had occupied East Jerusalem, the Golan Heights, the West Bank, Gaza, and the Sinai, *Fateh* emerged as a major guerrrilla organization that attempted to raise a rebellion of the West Bank population. After the war, Arafat and the other leaders of *Fateh* decided to take over the PLO in order that the commando groups could operate with the legitimacy of the organization mandated by the Arab states.

During the period 1964–68 several other commando groups emerged. One was the Popular Front for the Liberation of Palestine (PFLP), which rose as the militant Palestinian branch of the Arab national movement and which was headed by George Habash, a Greek Orthodox Christian from Lydda. The PFLP split into bitter factional war, from which emerged the Democratic Front for the Liberation of Palestine (DFLP) and the Popular Front for the Liberation of Palestine, General Command (PFLP, GC). All shared a pan-Arab orientation, but the PFLP, GC did not share the Marxist orientation of the other two groups.[62] Another commando group was al-Saiqa, the Palestinian branch of the pro-Syrian Baath party.[63]

Arafat determined to try to create as broad a base as possible for the Palestine Liberation Organization by bringing all these commando groups with him into the PLO. This was a fateful decision. If *Fateh* had determined in 1968 to take over the PLO alone, and not include the other commando groups, much factional infighting in the PLO might have been eliminated.[64] *Fateh* itself has had a strongly cohesive leadership and is still governed collectively by its founding generation. But the other groups have not been committed to the *Fateh* principle of putting Palestinian nationalism above faction-prone ideology, pan-Arab or Marxist. They have tended to be tied to sponsoring Arab regimes, especially Syria and, more recently, Libya, and have helped drag the PLO into political factionalism within the host Arab states. This has brought the repressive wrath of the governments of those states down upon the whole *fedayeen* (commando) movement.

The organization that was developed for the PLO was designed to give representation to the whole Palestinian national community, within Israel and the Occupied Territories, the refugee communities in the neighboring Arab states, and the increasingly far-flung Palestinian Diaspora. The Palestinian National Council (PNC), which met eighteen times from 1964 to 1987, was designed to be a parliament in exile. At its sixteenth meeting in Algiers in 1983 it had 384 delegates. Another 120 delegates were unable to attend because they lived under Israeli control that denied them the right to travel to the meeting. Of the 384 seats, 92 went to commando groups, with *Fateh* holding 36 of these. Palestinian mass organizations for students, workers, women, professionals, and writers held another 63 seats. The Higher Military Council, linking the commando groups, had 24 seats, and the remaining 206 seats were allocated to different refugee communities and geographical areas. Since many delegates from the mass organizations and geographical communities were linked to one or another of the commando groups, these have operated as the major "parties" in the PLO, with *Fateh* holding the commanding majority.

Between meetings of the PNC two elected bodies, the Central Council (75 members) and the Executive Committee (15 members) operate as the ongoing government in exile. Members of the Executive Committee each hold various ministerial portfolios, such as information, military, and foreign diplomacy. Each of the commando groups has a parallel apparatus, which these PLO ministries seek to coordinate. Funding for the PLO comes mainly from direct grants from the Arab states, under provisions of successive Arab summit meetings, but funds also come from an income tax from Palestinians in the Diaspora.[65]

The PLO has also created a number of civilian institutions that connect to many aspects of Palestinian life. The Palestinian Red Crescent Society has built a number of modern hospitals in Lebanon (most of them bombed by the Israelis in 1982) and runs clinics in the camps. *Samed*, which started as an orphan aid program, has created a network of factories and economic self-help projects. Many of these were also destroyed by the Israelis in the 1982 invasion. The Palestinian Research Center sponsored political research, and several other political planning groups sought to develop the political, educational, and social welfare infrastructure for a future Palestinian state. The Research Center in Beirut was leveled by a car bomb in 1983, thus destroying much valuable research and information, including accumulated data on land ownership in Palestine before the 1948 war.

During 1968 to 1970, *Fateh* and other commando groups mounted raids mainly into the West Bank from bases in Jordan. Israel, in response, stepped up what had already been its policy of retaliatory raids and bombings, intended to take such a toll, not only of the refugee community but also of the population and resources of the host Arab community, that its government would crack down on the *fedayeen* in the camps. The retaliatory raids killed or wounded scores and sometimes hundreds in mainly civilian populations. The *fedayeen* themselves were seldom killed by such raids. The *fedayeen* raids into Israel and the Occupied Territories, and their organization of the refugee communities to resist retaliatory raids, stirred the imagination of a dispirited people and caused thousands of young Palestinians to flock into the commando groups. One major Israeli raid against the village of Karameh, inside Jordan, in March 1968 pitted 300 *Fateh* guerrilla fighters against 15,000 Israeli troops. Their spirited resistance inspired some 5,000 new recruits to join *Fateh* in the next two days. In 1970 some 50,000 *fedayeen* were in training camps in Jordan.[66]

Between 1968 and 1970, the PLO, against the better judgment of *Fateh*, decided to widen the struggle by hijacking El-Al planes. These "external operations" led to a diluting of the focus of the Palestinian issue and an increasing hostility to Palestinians as terrorists. Most Western media failed to distinguish between *Fateh* and dissident groups or renegade groups that were outside of and hostile to the PLO as a whole. Tightened security around Israeli planes led the PFLP to hijack planes from other nations deemed friendly to Israel. Actions were taken to secure the release of Palestinians imprisoned in Europe rather than in Israel. On September 6, 1970, three planes hijacked by the PFLP were landed on an airstrip in Jordan and blown up, after negotiations that led to the release of passengers. The main issues of Palestinian statelessness and the plight of the refugees tended to become lost in world response to these operations.

Such events, plus the growing presence of armed *fedayeen* and the devastating effects of Israeli retaliations, led King Hussein to decide to expel the *fedayeen* from Jordan. The majority of Jordanian citizens are Palestinians, and for them the Hashemite monarch there has questionable legitimacy. There was a real possibility that the monarchy might be overthrown and replaced by a Palestinian popular government. In coordination with the Israelis as well as with the United States, Hussein threw his army against the *fedayeen* in the camps around Amman and also beat back a brief intervention from Syria. By July 1971, several camps had been reduced to rubble, some 3,000 Palestinians (military and civilian) had been killed, and the *fedayeen* had been largely expelled from Jordan.[67] This left only Lebanon as the major base of *fedayeen* operations, since Syria had been careful to prevent any Palestinian armed movement that was not an extension of its own national policies.

The blow to Palestinian operations in Jordan led to a widening of external operations under the Black September movement, with which parts of *Fateh* cooperated. The most notorious act of this movement was the seizure of eleven Israeli athletes in the September 1972 Olympic Games at Munich. The eight Septembrists and all the athletes were killed, mainly by the German police. Israel retaliated with raids against refugee camps and border villages in Lebanon. Increasingly, Israeli retaliatory raids were being carried out, not in response to events from border Arab states, but in response to international activities of the Palestinians. This included diplomatic victories as well as terrorist actions.[68]

The Munich events caused *Fateh* to reject the Black September operations and to expel from its ranks two members who were associated with it. One of these, Ahmed Abdel-Gaffer, defected to Libya and was later assassinated while on a visit to Beirut. The other, Sabri al-Banna (Abu Nidal) defected to Iraq where he became the head of a renegade terrorist group operating not only against Israel and its allies internationally, but also against the *Fateh* leadership itself. As the PLO moved increasingly away from military operations toward diplomacy and possible compromises with Israel, Abu Nidal,

funded by the Iraqi intelligence service opposed to these developments, assassinated almost a dozen of the best PLO information
officers stationed in European capital cities between 1978 and 1982.
One of these, Said Hammami, PLO representative in London, had
spearheaded PLO contacts with Jewish and Israeli peace groups.[69]
Abu Nidal is a shadowy figure who may no longer be alive. Since
1982 it has been suggested that the Abu Nidal group has actually
become a front for the Mossad (Israeli Intelligence).

Although *Fateh* never believed that the Palestinian commandos
could win back their homeland solely through a military struggle
with Israel, it has seen "armed struggle" as a key way to awaken hope
and build a movement for national self-determination among dispirited Palestinian youth. These "exemplary actions" were designed
to attract more general Arab support and, eventually, to lead to a
solution negotiated by the international community through the
United Nations. After 1973, *Fateh* determined to concentrate less on
armed struggle and more on building international political support. Ties had been created with China in the mid-1960s. Ties were
made to the Soviet Union in the early 1970s.

The Soviets influenced the PLO to abandon its claim to the liberation of all Palestine and to accept a Palestinian state on the West
Bank and Gaza, a position that was partially endorsed at the twelfth
PNC meeting in June and July, 1974. In November 1974, Arafat
addressed the United Nations. Following his address, the UN
passed Resolution No. 3236, which extended earlier UN resolutions
(in favor of the rights of Palestinians to return or receive compensation) to the right of national self-determination, independence,
and sovereignty. The PLO was granted observer status at the UN.[70]

The period from 1974 to 1982 also saw the PLO gaining increasing
international respectability as the legitimate representative of
Palestinian national rights, not only among Communist-aligned
countries, but also in Africa and among the Third World nona-
ligned states and in Western Europe.[71] The UN vote in favor of the
rights of Palestinians to national self-determination and sovereignty (#3236) was passed by a vote of 89–7. However, the United
States, the key international power to any effective diplomatic settlement, was persuaded by Israel in 1975 to officially boycott any
direct relations to the PLO.[72] The labeling of the PLO solely as a "terrorist" group, rather than as the legitimate representative of the

Palestinian people, who must be included in any international settlement, became an increasingly isolated view. This view is presently endorsed principally by the United States, Israel, and South Africa. Washington's refusal to recognize the PLO has become a key factor in the blocking of the Geneva peace conference, which, from the mid-1970s, had been proposed as the means to a political settlement between Israel and the Palestinians.[73]

Not all *fedayeen* groups were willing to accept the idea of a ministate within the West Bank and the Gaza Strip, since this implied an acceptance of partition and a recognition of the State of Israel within the 1948 boundaries. For Palestinians whose family homes and lands had been within those 1948 borders, this implied relinquishing their historical claims and forgetting the injustice of Israeli expulsion of their families and confiscation of their property. In October 1974 a delegation representing the PFLP, the PFLP, GC, the Palestinian Popular Struggle Front, and the Iraqi-sponsored Arab Liberation Front traveled to Iraq. Together with their Iraqi hosts, the National Command of the ruling Baath party, they issued a rejection of a "surrenderist solutions"— that is, they rejected a mini-Palestinian state. This Rejectionist Front sought to rival the *Fateh*-controlled PLO for leadership of the Palestinian people.[74]

However, the forces of the Rejectionist Front soon found themselves devastated in the 1975–76 Lebanese civil war, where they took the side of the Lebanese Left against the Christian Phalangists. They were also weakened by internecine warfare with each other. By 1977 the challenge of the Rejectionist Front to the *Fateh* leadership of the PLO was effectively over. The 1977 PNC meeting reaffirmed the option of a Palestinian ministate and approved contacts with progressive (anti-Zionist) Jewish groups inside and outside Israel.[75] The decisive new step in this direction was taken by the Palestine National Council meeting at Algiers. On November 15, 1988, the PNC declared the founding of an independent Palestinian state, side by side with Israel, and affirmed acceptance of UN resolutions 338 and 242, which implies recognition of Israel. The declaration called for the renunciation by both sides of terrorism, including state terrorism.

FROM THE LEBANESE CIVIL WAR TO THE 1987–88 UPRISING

A detailed description of the Lebanese civil war and the Israeli invasion goes beyond the limits of this brief account. All that will be attempted here is a basic outline of the effects of these events on the Palestinian presence in Lebanon. Other than Jordan, Lebanon was the major area into which Palestinians fled during the 1948 war. In 1975 about 400,000 Palestinian refugees lived around Beirut and in villages in the south. Many Palestinians had become integrated into Lebanese society. The Palestinian-dominated sections of Beirut had become the military, administrative, political, and cultural capital of the Palestinian national movement, with a network of social services, hospitals, research, information, and educational institutions under its control.

The Maronite Christians had become implacable foes of the PLO from 1967, seeing the PLO as upsetting the demographic balance of the national covenant that had given them dominant power. The Sunni and Shi'a Muslims and Druze were deeply dissatisfied with the system that belied their actual numbers in Lebanese society. (The Sunni and Shi'a are the two major divisions of Islam. The Druze are a Muslim-derived sect living in the mountainous border regions of Lebanon, Israel, and Syria.) Initially, the Muslim and Druze forces, pressing for national reform, welcomed the PLO as allies. But as the PLO increasingly transformed itself into a ministate with a regular army, they became antagonized.

The repeated Israeli shelling of southern Lebanon, and what was seen as the arrogance and affluence of Palestinian leaders and soldiers, led these former allies to become sympathetic to the Maronite view that the presence of the Palestinian refugees and the PLO guerrillas was the chief cause of the fragmentation of Lebanese society.[76] Thus, despite its efforts to cultivate Lebanese allies, the PLO had moved dangerously close to isolation in Lebanon on the eve of the 1982 Israeli invasion.

In 1975 civil war broke out between the Phalangists (Christian rightists) and the forces of the Lebanese national movement, under Kamal Jumblatt, with whom Palestinian commando groups were allied. The Phalangists sought to destroy the Palestinian refugees' neighborhoods in predominantly Christian West Beirut. On August 12, 1976, after a fifty-two-day siege of Tel al-Za'tar, some 1,500 unarmed civilians were massacred by Phalangists as they tried to evacuate the area.[77] At this point, *Fateh* openly allied with the Lebanese national forces, and together they seemed on the verge of defeating the Phalangists when Syria intervened on the side of the Christians. By shifting the balance of power, Syria hoped to become the arbitrator of Lebanese politics. Israel also intervened, with aid to the Maronite forces. After five months of heavy fighting, the Arab minisummit in October 1976 legitimated Syria's presence by consecrating it as an Arab peacekeeping army.

Israel had long seen the possibility of using the disintegration of the Lebanese system of political representation based on religious groupings as the opportunity to create a Christian puppet state dependent on Israel.[78] The civil war gave Israel not only an opportunity to fund the Phalangist leader, Bashir Gemayel, but also to set up a mercenary militia in southern Lebanon under former Lebanese army major Sa'ad Haddad and to create a buffer zone in Lebanon in a ten-mile area north of Israel's border. On the pretext of a bus hijacking in Tel Aviv, an Israeli army of 25,000 invaded southern Lebanon in March 1978, leaving some 700 Palestinians and Lebanese villagers dead and their homes destroyed.[79]

After 1978 the PLO began to upgrade their military power in expectation of a full-scale conflict with Israel. But they also sought to enhance their international political respectability, hoping to avoid an Israeli attack. They cooperated scrupulously with the United Nations Interim Force, Southern Lebanon (UNIFIL) troops stationed in southern Lebanon after the 1978 Israeli invasion. After six months of escalating cross-border hostilities with Israel in 1979, the PLO accepted and enforced a ceasefire for two years. In July 1981, Israel launched a series of unprovoked attacks against PLO positions, to which the PLO responded with strikes at over thirty Israeli military bases and towns in Israel. In the ceasefire, mediated by the United Nations, the PLO again became the enforcer of peace and seemed to be on its way to new international recognition.[80]

However, 1977–80 also saw shifts in the balance of power between Arab states. In November 1977, President Sadat of Egypt dramatically traveled to Jerusalem to announce his readiness for a bilateral peace agreement. This led to the Camp David accords in which Egypt received back the Sinai area occupied by Israel in 1967. Despite vague references, the Palestinian issue was actually marginalized. Egypt thus had effectively neutralized itself in the impending conflict between Israel and the Palestinians in Lebanon.

The PLO had received good marks, internationally, for its almost year-long enforcement of the July 24, 1981, ceasefire. But it had also isolated itself from its Lebanese allies. Israel, led by hard-line leaders Begin and Sharon, saw this as the opportune time to launch its long-planned invasion of Lebanon. The war was presented to the people of Israel as aiming only at a final pacification of the southern border of Lebanon, or "Peace for Galilee." But its planners had more ambitious goals. They sought the total destruction of the PLO military and political infrastructure, thus eliminating the PLO as a factor in international negotiation and opening the way for annexation of the West Bank and Gaza under the pretext of local "self-government." They also hoped to scatter the Palestinian refugee population, driving as many refugees as possible into Jordan, and to install a Phalangist government dependent of Israeli aid.[81]

After two days of continual bombardment of southern Lebanon, the coast, and Beirut (June 4–6), a massive invasion by Israeli armored columns was launched June 6, designed to link up with troops landing from the sea near Sidon and a combined drive up the coast to Beirut. However, from the beginning, PLO resistance was stronger than anticipated, and the Israeli timetable was delayed. The full-scale siege of Beirut began June 26 and continued until August 12 in a punishing onslaught that left tens of thousands, mostly civilians, dead or wounded.[82] In this siege of Beirut, the PLO forces not only were able to hold firm, to resist the takeover of their areas and the killing of their leadership, but also to provide basic civil defense for the civilian population, maintaining essential food, water, ambulance, and medical services.[83] The siege drew the Palestinians and the Beirut Muslims back into solidarity.[84]

During this period PLO negotiators were also active internationally. Already in late June it was evident that they would have to accept an evacuation of their forces from the city. But they hoped to do so in a way that would establish, on a new basis, their status in international diplomacy as political representatives of the Palestinian people. This position was also backed by the French government, but the Israeli government and the Reagan administration were determined to eliminate the PLO altogether. Finally, by late July, Arafat and the core *Fateh* leaders realized that they would have to completely evacuate their military forces from Lebanon. The important question was whether they could obtain firm guarantees from the United States government for an international peacekeeping force that would protect both the departing PLO fighters and also the unprotected Palestinian civilians who would remain behind.[85] Under U.S. assurances that both these goals would be accomplished, some 11,500 Palestinian fighters left Beirut for other Arab countries between August 21 and 30, triumphantly carrying their arms to show their undefeated status.

However, the vague promises of security for the Palestinian civilians left behind were soon forgotten by the Americans and ignored by the Israelis and Phalangists. On August 23, 1982, Israeli protégé Bashir Gemayel was elected president of Lebanon. On September 14 he died in a massive explosion of his headquarters. The next day the Israeli army, contrary to its pledges, moved to occupy the whole of West Beirut, as a U.S. peace-keeping force withdrew. Between September 16 and 18 there took place the infamous massacre of some 3,000 Palestinians (and poor Lebanese) in the Sabra and Shatila refugee neighborhoods. This massacre, while carried out by the Phalangists, was expected by Israeli leaders. Israeli troops surrounded the camps and prevented the residents from leaving. The intention of this massacre seems to have been both to eliminate these Palestinian enclaves and also to demonstrate to the Palestinian people everywhere the inability of the PLO to guarantee their security. Israel sought to facilitate the massacre in such a way as to shift the blame to the Phalangists, while pretending to be unknowing bystanders.[86]

These massacres crystallized opposition to the Lebanese invasion among progressive Israelis. Under the banner of "Peace Now," hundreds of thousands of Israelis took to the streets, calling for withdrawal of their army. Most of these Israelis did not object to an Israeli control of a border strip of southern Lebanon through a surrogate Lebanese army. But they objected to an ongoing direct occupation of Lebanon, one that was leading to an increasing death toll of Israeli soldiers. In the subsequent Israeli investigation of the massacres, Prime Minister Begin, Defense Minister Ariel Sharon, and Chief of Staff Rafael Eitan, among others, were blamed as indirect auxiliaries to the massacre for having failed to intervene to stop it. The Kahan Report did not deal with the issue that the massacre was jointly planned by Israelis, or with the larger atrocities of the entire invasion (in which some 20,000 people died and hundreds of thousands were wounded), or with the ongoing fragmentation of Lebanese society.[87]

The massacres precipitated a crisis in Arafat's leadership of the PLO. With the shattering of the PLO military and political infrastructure in Lebanon, and its relocation to areas no longer contiguous to Israel, Arafat had determined that the time had come to lay aside the option of "armed struggle" for a concentration on political negotiation. In early September 1982 the U.S. government announced the "Reagan plan," which called for a withdrawal of Israel from the Occupied Territories and the creation of a Palestinian "entity" in alliance with Jordan. Although this fell well short of Palestinian hopes for an autonomous state, Arafat was willing to consider this plan as a way to end what seemed like a process of continuous expropriation of land and eventual annexation of the Occupied Territories by Israel.

In October 1982 Arafat met with Hussein in Amman in an effort to end the long-standing animosity with Jordan and create a unified base for such a joint Palestinian-Jordanian entity. But it soon became apparent that the U.S. government had no real intentions of pushing Israel to withdraw, in the face of vehement assertions by President Begin that he would never give up "one inch" of those territories. Nor was Hussein really interested in a peer relationship with the PLO.

These diplomatic feelers of Arafat to Jordan, and also to Egypt and to Israel's peace groups, led to a mutiny in the spring of 1983 within the ranks of *Fateh*. Hussein's massacre of Palestinians in 1970–71 and Sadat's "treason" in the Camp David agreements were not forgotten. For many Palestinian *fedayeen*, negotiation with these "enemies" was unthinkable. This rebellion constituted an effort to create a new coalition of dissident *Fateh* and Rejectionist forces, in alliance with Syria, to oust Arafat from the leadership of the PLO. Syria sought thereby to achieve its long-sought goal of making the PLO an extension of its own policies.

The dissidents denounced the option of a ministate and reaffirmed the claims of the Palestinian National Charter of 1968, which looked toward the liberation of all of Palestine through armed struggle. This split, which briefly became an open war between *Fateh* forces, represented a deep division in the Palestinian movement between the growing moderation of Arafat's leadership and those who clung to the radical goals and methods of their foundations.[88] For them, Arafat's talks with Hussein even threatened to give up the basic claim that the PLO was the only legitimate representative of the Palestinian people. This tenet had been reaffirmed at the Arab summit meeting at Rabat in 1974 and was reluctantly accepted by Hussein himself.

However, as in the early Rejectionist revolt, the dissidents against Arafat's leadership were not able to show that they had realistic alternatives or to muster enough support to oust Arafat as chairperson of the PLO. As before, the dissidents also threatened to tie the PLO to the policies of another Arab state, in this case Syria. In the Palestinian National Council meeting in Algiers (1987), Arafat's leadership was reaffirmed and at least a show of unity restored.[89] The dissident leaders were reintegrated, and Arafat moved away from any suggestion of a Palestinian "entity" under Hussein of Jordan.

The destruction of the PLO military bases in Lebanon and the scattering of the PLO political infrastructure also meant that the primary focus of Palestinian resistance to Israeli rule must henceforth become the Palestinians living in the West Bank and the Gaza Strip. These Palestinians have generally supported the moderate direction of Arafat's leadership toward diplomacy and a political settlement that would allow a self-determining Palestinian state to be established in these Territories. Many would accept some relationship with Jordan, as long as self-government of the Palestinian "entity" is preserved, although few Palestinians in the 1967 Territories have any fondness for Hussein or accept him as their national leader. In a poll of political opinion of Palestinians in the Occupied Territories in the summer of 1986 by the newspaper *Al-Fajr*, it was shown that 93 percent of the population desired a Palestinian state under the PLO; 71 percent wanted that state headed by Arafat; and only 3 percent declared Hussein to be their preferred leader.[90]

On December 9, 1987, a major uprising of Palestinians in the Occupied Territories began, starting in the Gaza refugee camps in response to the crushing of four Palestinians by army transport. Between December 9, 1987, and September 27, 1988, 374 Palestinians had been killed, 248 by gunfire and 126 as a result of beatings, tear gas, and other causes. The Israeli military has been authorized to use extreme violence to repress the protest, including random roundups of people who were beaten with clubs in streets and alleys. It is impossible to estimate the numbers of severe injuries that have resulted from this policy. In February 1988, a group of

American physicians visiting the Territories estimated that the severe injuries were as high as 38,000. But most Palestinians are reluctant to visit hospitals because reporting to hospitals with injuries often results in arrests.

In addition to massive use of beatings, the Israelis have employed two different kinds of lethal tear gas, one a CS-type gas (with cyanide) and the other a yellow "mustard" gas. These gases lodge in the body cells and may do permanent damage. The gases have been lethal to elderly people, infants, and people with respiratory or heart conditions. In addition to 63 (as of September 27, 1988) people who have died from the gas, at least 80 uterine fetal deaths in Gaza alone are related to the effects of the gas, although the actual number may be much higher. This use of lethal gas raises the question of whether a kind of chemical warfare is being waged against the whole population.[91]

There have also been a large number of arrests of anyone regarded as exercising leadership, including journalists, human rights workers, attorneys, union activists, and Red Crescent (medical) workers. As of mid-July, 1988, about 10,000 Palestinian political prisoners were being held in Israeli prisons. Collective punishment, in the form of house demolitions, curfews (designed as much to keep journalists out as Palestinians in), and the cutting off of food, electricity, and phone lines have been among the methods used to repress protest. The magnitude of the repressive violence illustrates vividly the fundamental Israeli attitude toward Palestinians as a people who have no real right to exist. This violence raises the question of international responsibility for the basic safety and welfare of this entire population under Israeli control. International pressure needs to be brought to transfer control over these Territories to the United Nations and to force the Israelis to give up control. Negotiations could then begin for a more permanent political settlement of the relationship between Israel and Palestinian self-determination.

For several years there has been some discussion of how Palestinian resistance to Israeli rule might use techniques of nonviolent resistance. Mubarak Awad had been exploring these options in his Palestinian Center for Non-Violence in Jerusalem.[92] In June, 1988, the Israeli government deported Awad, despite efforts of Palestinians, Israeli peace groups, the U.S. government, and other international leaders to prevent this deportation.[93] However, any discussion of nonviolent resistance must be clear about the fact that, quite independently of Awad, most Palestinian protest against the Israeli occupation has been nonviolent. It has taken the form of massive strikes and boycotts, or what has classically been called "non-cooperation."

The Israelis treat any kind of resistance as though it were an assault on national security, making little distinction between a youth throwing a stone and a merchant closing a shop for a boycott, or even civil rights workers or journalists trying to gather information. Any kind of resistance to Israeli rule is seen as hostile action justifying extreme forms of violent repression. Because of the fundamental lack of identification of the Israeli government and people with the welfare of the Palestinians, the Palestinians in the Occupied Territories cannot be expected to carry the burden of their struggle for human and civil rights alone. The cost to their physical and social welfare is already overwhelming. The world community must intervene to protect Palestinian human rights.

PALESTINIAN NATIONALISM AND ZIONISM

As has been seen in this brief survey of the history of the Palestinian national movement, there has been a growing willingness to accept a compromise in which a Palestinian national authority would be established on the West Bank and the Gaza Strip. This seems to represent a significant change from the original ideology of the PLO, as stated in the National Charter of 1968. On January 14, 1988, in the midst of the uprisings in the Occupied Territories, Yasir Arafat took this development another step by declaring that he would recognize Israel's right to exist if it and the United States would agree to an international peace conference on the Middle East with PLO participation. In the context of such a peace conference, Arafat declared his willingness to accept UN Resolution #242.[94] This declaration removes the official reasons for U.S. refusal to negotiate directly with the PLO, as put forward in the secret agreement of the United States and Israel in 1975. The refusal of the United States or Israel to respond to these initiatives makes it increasingly clear that what these governments want is, not a moderate PLO, but no PLO at all.

American and Israeli citizens have been subjected to a disinformation campaign by their governments, designed to present the PLO as extremists who wish only to destroy the State of Israel and to drive the Jews "into the sea." This has been reflected in recent Israeli laws that make it a state security crime for Israeli citizens to enter into communication with PLO representatives any place in the world.[95] The successful effort of the Israel lobby in the United States (AIPAC) to persuade the U.S. State Department and Congress to close the Palestinian Information Office in Washington, D.C., on the grounds that it represents a "terrorist" organization, is a similar effort to deny American citizens access to corrective information about the PLO and Palestinians.[96]

To what extent does this evolution in PLO strategy represent an actual shift in ideology about Zionism or the acceptability of a Jewish state? In 1968 the revised Palestinian National Charter declared that "armed struggle is the only way to liberate Palestine." The goal of the Palestinian national movement was declared to be the liberation of all Palestine, as defined by the British Mandate borders. This area was said to be an indivisible unit. Palestinians were defined as all Arabs who lived in this area before the 1948 dispersal and their descendants (in the paternal line), including Jews who lived in Palestine before the Zionist settlements.

Zionism was completely rejected in the charter as an illegitimate movement with no historic rights in Palestine. Jews were said to be members of a religious, not a national, group, who are citizens of the various states to which they belong. Zionism was described as an ally of international imperialism, antagonistic to all progressive and liberation movements throughout the world. "It is racist and fanatic in its nature, aggressive, expansionist and colonial in its aims and fascist in its methods."[97] This judgment was echoed in the UN General Assembly resolution of November 10, 1975, which compared Israel to South Africa and declared Zionism to be a form of racism.[98]

Although the last twenty years have led the PLO leadership to change its strategy toward Israel and to give qualified acceptance to partition, nothing in these twenty years has served to change this fundamental judgment on the nature of Zionism. Indeed, if anything, it has become increasingly justified by the conduct of the government of Israel toward Palestinians, both inside and outside its borders. How then can Arafat declare that he will recognize the

State of Israel and accept a ministate within the present Occupied Territories? Is this, as Israelis frequently declare, a mere ploy to create a new base for armed struggle against Israel, aimed at ultimate destruction of Israel?

The fundamental vision of the PLO of a "secular democratic state for Jews, Christians, and Muslims in all Palestine" remains the optimum goal of the Palestinian national movement. However, a growing majority of Palestinians, including many PLO leaders, recognize that this goal cannot be achieved by force; it must be the end product of a cultural and political evolution within the Israeli Jewish and Palestinian Arab people.[99] This evolution must start with a mutual recognition by Israeli Jews and Palestinian Arabs of each community's rights to national existence and self-determination. Such recognition must be expressed by some kind of internationally guaranteed political recognition of Palestinian national self-determination, with the present 1967 Occupied Territories serving as the base for this "national authority." This could set in motion a political process of mutual accommodation, once the Palestinians are no longer the oppressed subjects of Israel's power.

But the future political shape of this development remains open. Two states, one binational state, a cantonal state—all are possible options, as well as economic federation with Jordan. The real issue is a recognition by Israelis that the Palestinian national community is not destructible and that the effort to create a single "Jewish state" that excludes Palestinians from civil and political rights has failed. It must be replaced by a political accommodation to the reality, already evident more than half a century ago, that two peoples, two national identities, have grown up in this area in the twentieth century. They must find a political and social structure that will allow them to share the land that one calls Israel and the other Palestine.

5. Contradictions of the Jewish State

> Woe to him who builds his house by unrighteousness, and his upper
> rooms by injustice; who makes his neighbor serve him for nothing, and
> does not give him his wages; who says, 'I will build myself a great house
> with spacious upper rooms' and cuts out windows for it, paneling it with
> cedar and painting it with vermilion. . . . You have eyes and heart only for
> your dishonest gain, for shedding innocent blood, and for practicing
> oppression and violence.
>
> JER. 22:13–14, 17

The definition of Israel as a Jewish state means a state of and for
Jews. As was noted in the chapter on Zionism, this ethnic exclusivism was in conflict with the universalist ideals of democracy and
socialism that were espoused by Zionists. Some humanist Zionists,
such as Judah Magnes, saw clearly this contradiction in the thirties
and tried to save the universalist values by political binationalism.[1]
Generally, however, this contradiction has not been admitted by
official Zionism but has been covered up by claims that "Israel is the
only democracy in the Middle East."[2] The concept of Israel as a Jewish state entailed a territory for this state cleared of Palestinians.
Any Palestinians who remain in such a state must be reduced to a
small minority and rendered politically impotent. What has to be
disallowed is any space where Palestinians might assert an autonomous national identity of their own, as Palestinians.

The logic of this connection between the formation of a Jewish
state and Palestinian removal began to become evident to leaders,
such as Ben-Gurion, in the late thirties,[3] when the Peel Commission
in 1936 recommended partition into two states, with "exchange of
population."[4] However, Zionist leaders concealed their intentions
to create an exclusivist state. In meetings before the Anglo-
American Committee of Inquiry in 1946, Ben-Gurion, Weizmann,
Moshe Sharett (then foreign affairs director of the Jewish Agency),
and other Zionist leaders offered effusive assurances that the Palestinians in the projected Jewish state would be treated as equal citizens. Ben-Gurion declared:

We will have to treat our Arabs and other non-Jewish neighbors on the basis of absolute equality as if they were Jews, but make every effort that they should preserve their Arab characteristics, their language, their Arab culture, their Arab religion, their Arab way of life, while making every effort to make all the citizens of the country equal civilly, socially, economically, politically, intellectually and gradually raise the standard of life of everyone, Jews and others.[5]

However, these assurances of equality remained vague and general. Other than Magnes and Buber, who were marginal to the Zionist establishment, Zionist leaders offered no political plan of how this equality would be shaped.

In the 1947 partition plan passed by the United Nations, the Zionists were offered a territory that encompassed 57 percent of the land. The remaining 43 percent, which included the western Galilee, the central hill areas, the West Bank of the Jordan and the Gaza, was to comprise the Palestinian state. In this plan, the two territories formed a crazy-quilt pattern in which each state was interwoven in the other. Of the 590,000 Jews and 1,320,000 Palestinians present in these lands, more than half of the Palestinians would have fallen into the projected Jewish state, while 10 percent of the Jews were resident in the area given to the Palestinians. The Zionist leadership worked for the passage of this plan and accepted it, while the Palestinians and the Arab world unanimously rejected it.

The Zionists accepted it as providing the basis in international law for a Jewish state. But they did not accept the territorial limits of this state, the residence of so many Palestinians in it, or a parallel Palestinian state. These aspects of the partition plan they expected to change by action.[6] From a Palestinian and Arab point of view, a Jewish state *qua* Jewish state was illegitimate. For them, this whole area was an integral part of the Arab world. Also a Jewish state would make the Palestinians a colonized group in their own land. They suspected a plan of gradual expropriation of the Arab land by the Jews, rendering the Arabs in the Jewish state both landless and stateless. They demanded a Palestinian Arab state. They declared that Jews could be members of such a state.

The European imperial world and the United States, which had mandated this partition, rejected the reasons for the Arab objections. For most Westerners, the division into two states seemed "fair." A common Western rationalization was that Arab objections represented an irrational hostility to Jews. This assessment has been promoted ever since by Zionists.

Although several leaders of the Arab League continued to hope for a change in the UN resolution in the early months of 1948, Ben-Gurion began to prepare for war. He saw the war as one that could be blamed on Arab intransigence and, at the same time, provide the cover to expand the territorial limits of the Jewish state and to remove as many as possible of the Palestinians resident in this area. The essential components of this plan had already been shaped from 1944 to 1947. They called for a terrorizing of the Arab towns and villages that would encourage most of the middle-class leadership to leave. Once the British departed and the Jewish forces were fully in command, then there could be a more forcible mass expulsion of Palestinian villagers, either razing their villages or transfering their property to Jewish immigrants.

Starting in early December, 1947, the *Irgun* and the Stern Gang, aided by the *Haganah*, began a campaign of terrorization with bombings and machine-gunnings of Arab crowds. A new stage in this campaign started on April 9, 1948, when *Irgun* soldiers entered the peaceful village of Deir Yassin near Jerusalem and massacred 250 residents. This massacre was intended to give the other Arabs a taste of what to expect. The campaign of terrorism was stepped up against the major Arab cities of Haifa and Jaffa. Radios and sound trucks broadcast horror noises and warnings to leave. Davidka mortars and barrel bombs were rained on the Arab areas. In Jaffa a truck of oranges, filled with dynamite, was planted in the center of town. Its explosion killed 100 people, including many children. By the end of April, both of these cities had been largely cleared of Arabs. Many were drowned as they tried to flee in boats by sea. Streams of refugees, carrying their possessions, were often fired upon by the Jews.

The struggle for control of Jerusalem took place in the early months of 1948. The Palestinian guerrillas retaliated on April 13 for the Deir Yassin massacre with a massacre of a hospital caravan on its way to Mount Scopus hospital, carrying *Irgun* soldiers and also doctors and nurses. The *Irgun* and *Haganah* were engaged in clearing neighborhoods around Jerusalem of their Arab residents. The dynamiting of the Semiramis Hotel, killing twenty-six people, was the signal for the Arab residents of the desirable Katamon district to flee. But the Arab Legion from Jordan was able to prevent the Jews from capturing the Old City and East Jerusalem. The soldiers of the Arab Legion also distinguished themselves by their restraint and humane treatment of captured Jews.

In April, the *Palmach*, the picked troops of the *Haganah*, began an organized clearing of Palestinians from the Galilee. Many of the villagers were taken by surprise, believing that the *Haganah*, who sometimes disguised themselves as Arabs, were soldiers from the Arab Liberation Army. The *Palmach* typically rounded up villagers, gave them orders to evacuate, and frequently shot groups of villagers to show what would happen to the rest, if they attempted to stay. Since the Arab Liberation Army had declined to help these villagers arm themselves, most were unarmed or had only a few rusty rifles and put up little resistance.

The clearing of the Arab towns of Ramle and Lydda fell to the 89th Commando Battalion, led by Major Moshe Dayan. These towns were subjected to a *blitzkrieg* shelling on the evening of July 11, 1948. In Lydda, the populace was told they would be safe if they went into a mosque, but once inside, more than eighty prisoners were machine-gunned to death. The populace of both towns was rounded up and marched in the blazing sun over the border (to Ramallah, which was in Jordanian hands). Many were shot as they fell by the wayside. About one thousand villagers of Lydda died in the massacres and death march and its aftermath. The clearing of the Palestinian population in areas in the Sinai and the Galilee occupied by Israeli troops continued into early 1949.[7]

The truce lines that were drawn in 1949 left the new State of Israel with some 20 percent more land than had been granted by the United Nations plan. The new land included the western Galilee and the Little Triangle that encompassed Beersheba and western Jerusalem, and a strip of the Negev that had been attached to the Gaza region (see map 2). Of the 900,000 Palestinians who had been resident in this region, some 780,000 had been driven out or had fled in fear. Most of them were located in the Gaza Strip (which had been occupied by the Egyptian army), in the West Bank (occupied by the Jordanian army), and in southern Lebanon and western Syria.

A tiny number of these were allowed to return, under pressure from the United Nations, which voted that the refugees should be allowed to return.[8] Many more attempted to infiltrate back, and most were ejected again by the Israeli defense forces. When this process sifted out, the State of Israel, in its 1949 truce borders, had 160,000 Palestinians. More than half were defined by the Israelis as internal refugees or "present absentees." The lands of those who had fled and also of the "present absentees" were put in the control of the Custodian of Absentees' Property. *De facto* this means that this land is lodged under the control of the Israel Lands Administration, which is jointly administered with what is, officially, a private, nongovernmental agency, the Jewish National Fund. Such lands are defined as state lands, to be held in perpetuity as the collective patrimony of the Jewish people. They are to be leased only to Jews.[9]

In 1947 the Jewish settlers, operating under the Jewish National Fund, had succeeded in buying about 7 percent of the land that fell into the 1947 UN partition borders (10 percent of the land in the 1949 truce orders). An additional 70 percent was added to this land through the confiscation of Palestinian land under the Absentee Property Law of 1950. With additional confiscations that have taken place since that time, it is estimated that about 92.5 percent of the land within the 1949 truce borders now falls into this category of Jewish national land.[10] This land included some four hundred villages, most of which were systematically razed by the Israeli army during the 1948–49 war and in the 1950s, although some of the housing stock in the larger towns was given to new Jewish settlers. It is estimated that this land included some 95 percent of all Israeli olive groves, ten thousand dunums (a dunum is one thousand square meters) of vineyards, 50 percent of all citrus groves, ten thousand shops, and some fifty-two stone quarries, producing one-third of Israeli stone production.[11]

The Law of Return, also passed in 1950, declared that every Jew in the world has a right to immigrate to Israel and claim automatic citizenship. Although Zionism was based on the assumption that Jewishness is a nationality or "race," the actual definition of who is a Jew under this law is religious; that is, it is based on Orthodox rabbinic law. For example, converts to Judaism, converted by Orthodox rabbis, are Jews. But illegitimate children of Jewish parents, children of Jewish fathers and non-Jewish mothers (including Jewish women who have become converts to another religion), Jews who are converts to other religions, and converts to Judaism in the Conservative or Reform movements are not defined as Jews.

This definition of who is a Jew by Orthodox rabbinic law, as well as the growing influence of rabbinic law on the laws of the State of Israel, gives the concept of Israel as a Jewish state a theocratic character. The definition of Israel as a Jewish state is a religiously defined nationalism.

In 1949 the remaining Palestinian population was put under military government, which lasted until 1966. This military government severely controlled their physical movements, political and cultural self-expression, access to employment and development. Most of these restrictions continue today, in different form. The general pattern of treatment of this population has been one of fragmentation, isolation from contact with Israelis and from one another, proletarianization (i.e., loss of land and reduction to a paid labor force in the lowest sectors of the Israeli economy), economic and educational underdevelopment, political neutralization and cooptation. In short, the Palestinians in Israel have been rendered politically invisible and economically exploited. Although those who could establish residence are defined as citizens of Israel, this citizenship is hedged around with such limitations that the Palestinian is constantly aware that he or she is a member of a state that is not their own, a state defined in almost all its aspects as being "for Jews only."

Under the Law of Return, some 666,400 Jewish immigrants entered Israel between 1948 and 1951, more than half being Holocaust survivors, mostly from Eastern Europe, and the rest being Jews from Arab countries, particularly from Iraq, Yemen, Egypt, and North Africa. The influx of Jews from Arab lands, and also Eastern European Jews, would continue in the 1950s, with Poland and Morocco being the largest senders. By the end of 1964 the Jewish population of Israel would have increased to almost 2.5 million, and to 3.28 million by the end of 1980, with 53 percent due to immigration and 47 percent due to natural increase.[12]

In the seventies and eighties the campaign to "free" the Soviet Jews would add several hundred thousand more immigrants to the Jewish population of Israel. However, migration to Israel was not the first priority for most Jews. By the late seventies and, even more, in the eighties, the trends of out-migration from Israel had begun to catch up with and even overtake immigration. The 1988 official statistics list the population of Israel as 4,208,000, with 83 percent being Jewish, or a Jewish population of 3,500,000, only a growth of 220,000 in six years. It is estimated that, in the years 1984 and 1985, the deficits between departing and returning Israelis was about 90,000 annually.[13] Since Israelis can hold dual citizenship, and some considerable number reside and work most of the year in other countries (especially in the United States) and are present in Israel for only a few months each year, the actual number of full-time resident citizens is difficult to know. At least half a million are permanent residents abroad.

The basic goals of the Jewish state thus can be defined as (a) building a commanding Jewish majority in control of most of the land, as well as of the economic, political, and cultural resources, and (b) reducing the Palestinians to an insignificant minority, deprived of most of the land and resources — in short, to turn a territory where two peoples, representing two national movements, were emerging (one primarily through settlement and the other through rising national consciousness) into an ethnic state reserved for only one of these national communities.

In 1967 this Zionist struggle to make Israel a Jewish state was exacerbated by the conquest (in Israeli terminology, "liberation") of East Jerusalem, the West Bank, the Golan Heights, and the Gaza Strip. The conquest or "liberation" of this territory added 1.1 million Palestinians to Israeli control. It is estimated that another 350,000 were displaced from these territories in the course of the war. By 1987 this Palestinian population had risen to more than 1.4 million, with 545,000 crowded into the Gaza Strip. An estimated 150,000 have been, in one way or another, expelled or denied the right to return after travel out of the area since 1967.[14]

If the remaining number were added to the present citizen population of the State of Israel through annexation, this would give Israel a total Palestinian population of more than 2,000,000 (the Palestinian remnant from the 1948 war having grown in the meantime to 715,000).[15] With the higher birth rate of Palestinians over Jews (especially Western Jews), this number threatens the definition of Israel as a Jewish state. With present rates of natural increase of the two populations, it is estimated that the Arab population will have risen to 43 percent by the year 2000, reducing the Jewish population to a bare majority of 57 percent. The only way to change this prognosis would be (a) for a new mass immigration of Jews, which does not seem to be forthcoming, or (b) a new mass expulsion of Palestinians.

Thus, Israel as a Jewish state is again faced with preventing some form of binationalism from emerging. The two populations could be accommodated either by acceding to the demands of a Palestinian state in the territories occupied in 1967, or by reshaping the entire state into a binational or a secular multicultural state. Since the majority of the Jewish population of Israel rejects any of these solutions and wishes to maintain the definition of Israel as a Jewish state, an impasse has been created. This entails an indefinite maintenance of the present situation in which the Palestinian population in the territories occupied in 1967 are kept under a regime of harsh military government.

In the rest of this chapter, the major aspects of this contradiction between a Jewish state and the reality of two national communities will be explored in fuller detail: (1) building a Jewish majority through immigration; (2) the ethnically exclusive character of Israeli state institutions; and (3) the expulsion and repression of Palestinians, in the 1949 truce borders and in the territories occupied in 1967.

BUILDING A JEWISH MAJORITY: IMMIGRATION AND SETTLEMENT

In 1882 there were 24,000 Jews in Palestine (a territory which included the West Bank and also the present state of Jordan). Most of these were religious Jews who rejected Zionism as a secular nationalist movement. By 1914 the number of Jews in Palestine had grown to 60,000, primarily through vigorous efforts by Zionist groups in Eastern Europe to attract the Jews being persecuted there. However, despite these Zionist efforts to attract immigrants to Palestine, less than 2 percent of the 2.4 million Jews who left Europe between 1882 and 1914 came to Palestine. Of those who left Europe, 85 percent came to the United States. Some of the Jews in Palestine left during the First World War. With new immigrants after the Balfour Declaration, the Jewish population climbed to 83,800, compared to 677,000 Palestinians, according to the British census of 1922.[16]

From the beginning of Zionist immigration and, even more, after the Balfour Declaration, the resident Palestinian population and its leaders offered strong resistance to Jewish immigration. This took the form of protest marches, riots, and strikes. Despite the vagueness of Zionist definitions of a Jewish state at this time, Palestinians recognized that this meant a state for Jews, a state from which they would be, in one way or another, excluded. This was evident even in the Balfour Declaration, which defined the Palestinian majority only as "non-Jews," thus implicitly denying them a parallel national identity.[17]

The persecutions of German Jews and then, during the Second World War, of all Eastern and Western European Jewry in areas under Nazi control, provided a major opportunity for a new influx of Jewish population to Palestine. However, in 1939, the British had responded to Palestinian objections to Jewish immigration by issuing a white paper that put a ceiling of 15,000 Jewish immigrants a year for five years, with the promise that in ten years the areas would be made a Palestinian state with a Jewish minority. "The independent State should be one in which Arabs and Jews share in government in such a way as to ensure that the essential interests of each community are safeguarded."[18]

In the United States, however, the traditional haven for persecuted Jews, the Congress had yielded to the anti-immigration agitation that had arisen in the late nineteenth and early twentieth centuries and had passed a law in 1924, to take effect in 1929, that limited immigration to 150,000 annually, with national quotas for each group limited to 2 percent of that group present in 1890. Through this immigration law, Jewish immigration to the United States was reduced to a trickle. The American Zionist leadership, anticipating perhaps as many as 4,000,000 Jews who might immigrate to Palestine because of Nazi pressure, refused to promote any significant easing of the barriers to U.S. immigration through the 1930s. In this period it was assumed by American Zionists that this persecution, like earlier ones, would have the primary effect of expelling this Jewish population. It did not occur to these American Jews that the Nazis would actually attempt to exterminate them *in toto*.[19]

As the news of the extermination camps filtered into the United States, American Jewish leaders found it difficult to believe the reports. As the magnitude of the situation became more and more apparent, American Zionist organizations continued to focus on the building of the *Yishuv* in Palestine, refusing to make major efforts to open up immigration to the United States or to pressure the United States to open up immigration elsewhere. The fault for this abandonment of European Jewry by the allied nations, especially by England and the United States, falls primarily on the shoulders of its leaders, Churchill and Roosevelt. But the lack of significant pressure from American Jews to open immigration to areas other than Palestine made it easy for those leaders to ignore the issue. Combined with British refusal to open immigration to Palestine beyond the 1939 limits, the major exits were closed to a trapped European Jewry.

This behavior of American Jewish organizations during the period from 1933 to 1945 is difficult to comprehend. The accounts of the official statements and minutes of American Zionist organizations during this period give one the sense that a certain Zionist dogma (i.e., that Jewish refugee populations must be directed primarily to building the Jewish state in Palestine) had become routinized. Unable to face the magnitude of the unthinkable reality, still clinging to the belief that a great influx of refugees would eventually be released and the doors to Palestine pried open, the Zionist leaders continued to insist that all concern for rescue of the remnants of European Jewry must be linked to building the Jewish state in Palestine. Thus, in the Zionist Hebrew magazine *Bizaron*, the editor wrote in October, 1943:

Many people complain that the American Jewish Conference did not deal seriously with rescue. This is not so. We, Zionists, have placed the creation of a Jewish State at the center, not because we are not concerned about the Jewish disaster, but precisely because of our concern. We are looking for a worldly solution, a constructive one, to this difficult question, because we believe that the creation of a Jewish state is the only ultimate solution to the troubles of the Jewish people.[20]

In a three-day meeting in Pittsburgh in September, 1943, in which almost all the major Jewish organizations were represented, the focus was primarily on how to build the Jewish state in Palestine after the war. The article on that conference in the Yiddish journal *Fakten und Meinungen* reported that attention to "the problem of the suffering of European Jewry was practically nil and only the American Jewish Labor Committee made a presentation on this subject."[21]

As the horror of the actual death toll of the Nazi "final solution" became undeniable, with the opening of the death camps in 1945, American Zionists were galvanized into action in three areas: (a) doing Zionist organizing in the displaced persons' camps to dispose the survivors to go to Palestine (this included an effort to transfer as many as possible to the American zone from the Russian zone); (b) organizing illegal immigration to Palestine (aimed, in part, at influencing Western opinion to open up immigration to Palestine by showing the tragic spectacle of death camp survivors packed into leaky boats and detained by heartless British officials); and (c) winning the UN partition vote.[22] Again, during this period, there was no effort by these Zionist Jewish leaders to open up expanded opportunities for immigration of Jews to the United States.[23]

During the period from May 1948 to May 1955, 342,895 emigrants from Europe arrived in Israel, compared to 200,000 who came to the United States and Canada between 1945 and 1956. Both the United States and Canada maintained nationality quotas that discriminated against Jews. However, 54,200 Jews emigrated from Israel between 1951 and 1954. One can only guess what the actual pattern of distribution might have been had all these emigrants been allowed to go to whatever country they wished. Only 1,815 Jews immigrated to Palestine from the United States during this same period.[24]

A second group of Jewish immigrants to Israel after 1948 came from the historic Jewish communities of the Muslim world. These Jews migrated because of rising anti-Semitism in the Arab nations. Their situation had gradually worsened. The nineteenth century had seen a marked deterioration of the status of Jews in the Ottoman empire, spurred by a sense of Muslim weakness vis-à-vis Western imperial power. Some of the worst of Western anti-Jewish tracts began to be circulated and accepted in Muslim countries. The Balfour Declaration heightened the perception of Arabs that Jews were agents of Western colonialism in the Middle East.

With the rise of Nazism and the exploration of Nazi-Arab alliances against the British, anti-Jewish propaganda accelerated in the 1930s and 1940s. Between 1941 and 1948, riots broke out against Jews in Iraq, Syria, Egypt, Saudi Arabia, and North Africa. Jews in Muslim lands, whose communities in those areas went back hundreds and even thousands of years, began to feel that life in these lands was becoming untenable for them. Most of the Jews in Muslim lands had been indifferent or hostile to Zionism, but the pressure of retaliatory violence directed against them increased their willingness to emigrate.[25]

Although Western Zionists were not originally interested in these "Sephardic" Jews as potential immigrants, as the paucity of European immigrants to colonize the open land in Israel became evident, the Israelis began to actively recruit these Arabic-speaking Jews. (The term *Sephardic* is used by Ashkenazi Jews—Jews from middle and northern Europe—to refer to all non-Ashkenazi Jews. But this term is a misnomer. It means Jews from Portugal and Spain. But most of these Arabic-speaking Jews are not descended from Jews that came from Spain or Portugal, but belong to ancient Jewries of the eastern Mediterranean. The blanket use of the term Sephardic seems to be a way of avoiding the term "Arab Jews" as a way of referring to Jews of Arabic language and culture.) The Israeli government facilitated their travel by sending airplanes to get them and arranged for their settlement in Israel, particularly in the border towns. Between 1948 and 1955 about 405,000 Arabic-speaking Jews immigrated to Israel. But not all the Jews who emigrated from Muslim states went to Israel. Many Jews of North Africa, particularly from Algeria, preferred to go to France.[26] The ancient Jewish communities in the Muslim world were almost entirely destroyed.

The Muslims themselves are largely responsible for this emigration, because they allowed the Jews of these areas to be scapegoated for Arab angers against Israel, even though most of these Jews were not Zionists. Several Arab governments did attempt to hold the line against this popular anti-Jewish violence, but their efforts were weak and ineffective against popular pogroms. However, some of the anti-Jewish violence was actually fomented by secret Israeli agents, anxious to spur Jewish exodus to Israel. Indications of this have come particularly from the case of Iraq, from which some 125,000 out of a population of 130,000 fled, mostly to Israel. Several of the bombs that were thrown at Jewish targets, precipitating this flight, were later shown to have been planted by Israeli secret agents.[27]

The 1948–49 war reduced the Palestinian population within Israel to a small minority. But this demographic relationship between

Jews and Palestinians has shifted during the last twenty years, putting two million Palestinians under Israeli rule. The fear that Jews may again become a bare majority in an expanded Jewish state has led to a new search for Jewish immigrants to Israel. But finding these new immigrants has been difficult. With the draining of the European and Arab Jewries, the only areas of the world with large Jewish populations are the United States and the Soviet Union. Six million Jews live in North America and more than 1.7 million in the Soviet Union.[28]

However, the prosperity and acceptance of Jews in the United States and Canada have meant that relatively few Jews from these areas choose to immigrate to Israel. Most Jews in the Soviet Union, and many who leave Israel, wish to immigrate to North America. Israeli and world Zionist leaders have looked to the Soviet Union as the prime source of new Jewish immigrants to Israel. Ironically, the success of nineteenth century Zionism in convincing the Russian revolutionary leaders that Jews were a national, and not a religious, group has meant that Jews in the Soviet Union, whether religious or not, are identified as Jews by nationality. This has been a primary way in which Jews have remained identifiable as a group within the Soviet Union and have been kept from assimilation, even though Soviet Jews are highly secularized.

Soviet Jews generally occupy better-paid sectors of Soviet life and are well educated. It is debatable whether they are more oppressed than other Soviet citizens. Certainly the denial of free emigration applies to all Soviet citizens and not simply to Jews. Much of the world Zionist crusade to "free Soviet Jewry" tends to conceal the fact that the primary purpose of the crusade is to provide a new population of Jews to counteract the Palestinian demographic "time bomb" in Israel. The fact that Soviet Jews are Ashkenazi or northern European Jews is also an important factor in this effort to enable them to emigrate to Israel. Since the numbers of Sephardic Jews are growing at a faster rate than Ashkenazi Jews, Russian Jews are seen as helping to keep northern European Jews dominant in Israel.

However, these Zionist efforts to bring Soviet Jews to Israel have been embarrassed by the tendency of many of the Soviet Jews, once freed from the USSR, to prefer to go to the United States, rather than to Israel. Since 1979, 80 percent of the Soviet Jewish emigres have preferred to come to the U.S.A. Pressure has been put on the

Soviet Union to force Soviet Jews to fly via Bucharest, Rumania, directly to Israel, rather than going to Vienna, where they can retain their refugee status and choose instead to come to America. Efforts have also been made by Israeli leaders to pressure the American government to deny Soviet Jews refugee status, on the grounds that they already have a country and that country is Israel.

In a February 1987 visit to the United States, Prime Minister Yitzhak Shamir of Israel asked U.S. Secretary of State George Shultz to stop offering special refugee status, outside of national immigration quotas, to Soviet Jews. However, most Jewish organizations in the United States have refused to support this Israeli effort to prevent Soviet Jews from coming to the United States.[29] Clearly American Jewish support for such restricted immigration of Soviet Jews to the United States would reveal the ulterior motive of the entire campaign to "free Soviet Jewry."

This brief review of Zionist sponsorship of immigration to Israel makes two things evident. First, Zionism has built immigration primarily on fostering nationalist identification with Israel as the true homeland of Jews. But it has not refrained, at various moments of crisis, from manipulating the Jewish population to force them to come to Israel, both by welcoming worsening conditions in their former homelands and by preventing opportunities of alternative immigration. Its concern with building a Jewish majority in Israel has sometimes been in conflict with the options of Jews to live in other lands.

Second, despite these efforts to attract and, sometimes, to force Jews to come to Israel, the Jewish majority in Israel is still not secure. If the 1967 Occupied Territories are annexed with their present population, Jews would soon become no more than a bare majority, not the 85 percent majority considered "normative" by Zionists. Moreover, a tipping of the demographic balance (particularly with the addition of the West Bank and the Gaza Strip), as well as further violent struggle, will increase the tendency for the present Israeli Jewish population to emigrate and discourage others from immigrating. Thus, despite one hundred years of zealous struggle to create a Jewish state, Zionism has not succeeded in creating the Jewish population base to sustain this project for the indefinite future.

MAKING PALESTINIANS INVISIBLE IN ISRAEL

The basic institutions of the State in Israel are built from organizations for immigration, land purchase and settlement, collectivization of labor and markets, and military defense developed by the Zionist movement before the state was founded. All these organizations were, by definition, for "Jews only." Several of these agencies, such as the Jewish National Fund and the Jewish Agency, continue to exist as a part of the World Zionist Organization, listed in the United States as tax-exempt philanthropies, as well as being an integral part of the state apparatus of Israel.

All these Israeli Zionist organizations form a coordinated network. Israeli Jewish elites typically move back and forth between leadership positions in the army, the government, the Jewish agency, and the *Histadrut* (Labor Federation), the holding company for the major corporations. Palestinians are excluded from this system of privilege, although for some time they have been allowed to belong to a subsidiary of the *Histadrut*.

From 1948 to 1966 the remnant of the Palestinian population in Israel was under military government. All travel outside their villages was restricted. Permits were granted primarily for employment, medical needs, and required contacts with the government, but not for Palestinian intercommunication such as family gatherings. The 1948 war shattered the infrastructures of the Palestinian economy that had begun to develop during the previous fifty years. Virtually all the Arab elites, including the small business class, left. The houses of these elites, their shops, and the best cultivated land were appropriated. Major cities such as Safed and Tiberias were cleared of all Palestinian population. Only Nazareth remained as a Palestinian urban area. Most of the population lived in small villages and were reduced to subsistence agriculture.

In his 1980 study, *Arabs in the Jewish State: Israel's Control of a National Minority*, Ian Lustick has analyzed the basic patterns of the system of repression of the Palestinians developed by the military government and continued thereafter in less overt forms. This system of repression has three components: isolation, dependence, and co-optation. Bedouin (nomadic shepherd people of the desert regions), Druze, Christian, and Muslim Palestinians are divided from each other by separate treatment. Villages find it difficult to communicate with other villages. Internal clan divisions within villages are used to divide the village against itself. By travel restrictions and denial of access to major Israeli institutions, Palestinians are isolated in their own local communities, kept apart both from the Jewish population and from one another.

Palestinians and Jews grow up separated from each other, never meeting in school, the army, work, or government, except in relations of strict subordination, such as a supervisor over Arab agriculture or construction workers, or a government or military officer over a detainee or petitioner.[30]

Studies of Israeli culture have shown that negative stereotyping of Arabs pervades Israeli publications, including children's literature. The Arab is typically viewed as a congenital liar and thief, lazy, aggressive, and incompetent. In a poll of Israeli Jewish opinion taken in 1971, 84 percent would be bothered if a relative or friend married an Arab and 74 percent would object if their children befriended an Arab. Further, 90 percent would prefer there to be fewer Arabs in Israel, and almost 90 percent agreed with the proposition that "Arabs understand only force." By contrast, polls of Palestinians show both a more realistic understanding of Israelis and also a greater willingness to develop personal friendships with Israeli Jews. For example, 90 percent said they would be willng to befriend Israeli Jews, and 42 percent thought that Israeli Jews were willing to befriend them.[31]

No countrywide Palestinian organization has been allowed to emerge, whether financial, commercial, cultural or, particularly, political.[32] Palestinian culture is repressed. Palestinian children study Hebrew classics in their village school, and they do not learn about Palestinian or Arab history. An occasional apolitical "nature poem" is the most that is allowed in the way of Arab culture in Palestinian village schools.

Dependency is the second aspect of control. This means the appropriation of most of the land, the denial of economic development, and the reduction of the Palestinians to a proletarian migrant labor force in the low-paid sectors of Israeli economy, such as services (i.e., restaurant workers), transportation, construction, manual and agricultural labor.[33] Even the bus system available to many Palestinians in more remote villages testifies to their isolation and economic exploitation. Buses typically run twice a day, out of the village in the morning to take workers to their jobs and back to the village at night to return workers to their homes.

The third part of the system of control is co-optation. All ordinary services, such as permits to travel, to build a house, and to obtain a job in the village school, are treated as favors dependent on a client-patron relationship to the Israeli government officials. Only the quiescent and compliant Palestinians are awarded these "favors," while anyone who shows "nationalist" tendencies is excluded.[34] The underlying ideology of this system is the denial that Palestinians are a national community. They are allowed to maintain a bare subsistence as individuals in isolated family support systems but not as a national community. All expressions of Palestinian national identity are regarded as subversive.

The official policy toward the Palestinian minority in Israel was summed up by the Ministry of the Interior's senior Arabist, Israel Koenig, in a memorandum entitled "Handling the Arabs of Israel," written in 1976. Koenig advocated "tough measures on all levels against various agitators among college and university students" and intensification of economic discrimination against Arabs in order to deprive them of the "social and economic security that relieves the individual and the family of day-to-day pressure [and] grants them, consciously or unconsciously, leisure for 'social-nationalist' thought."[35]

The basic Israeli institutions operate as a coordinated network to which Palestinians have access, if at all, only through separate and poorly funded Arab sectors. The most important expression of Israeli disempowerment of Palestinians is denial of Arab land ownership. In addition to taking over lands from refugees and "present absentees" in the period after the 1948 war, the government has devised a number of other ways in which land may be withdrawn from Palestinian control and use. Under the Ottoman and the British regimes, the open lands around each village were regarded as public property. This public property was understood to be collectively owned by the village and reserved for future expansion. However, under Israeli law, this public property has been defined as state property, under the control of the Jewish National Fund and thus to be reserved for exclusively Jewish use. Each village is denied room to expand, despite its growing population.

Property has also been taken from Palestinians in other ways. One of these is to declare land uncultivated (at times, after closing off access to it so that Palestinians are not able to cultivate it). Another way is to declare that land is needed for public purposes (which includes settlement of Jewish immigrants). Or it may be sold to be used as a security zone. Under these rubrics a large hill area around Nazareth was taken over and made into a Jewish settlement of "upper Nazareth." Also, a major fertile plain, that had been the prime agricultural land of Nazareth, was confiscated on the grounds that it was needed for a water conduit. The water conduit was placed above ground, even though it would normally have been put underground for an Israeli settlement, and the land on both sides of it was taken over to "protect" this conduit, to which Palestinian agriculture did not have access. All Palestinian claims of land ownership are challenged by the Israelis. Only the strictest proof of title going back twenty-five years is accepted, even though under Ottoman law, more informal methods of collective ownership and proof of title through tax receipts were understood as the normal proof of rights to residency and use of land.[36]

Palestinian villages do not fall under the land development services provided free to Israeli settlers by the Jewish Agency and the Jewish National Fund, which receives funds from international Jewry, including reparations from the German government. An Israeli settlement is typically completed in advance. The water and sewage systems, roads, houses, and electrical grids are installed, and then the settlers move in. By contrast, Palestinians must pay for any development from their own taxes, based on a much lower income base (although their taxes are generally higher since the Israelis count villages as "urban areas" because of their crowded conditions). Permits for any development, even a sports club, must be submitted to the central government (although Israeli settlements are allowed to be their own zoning authorities). These permits are endlessly delayed. Palestinians then often build illegally. These buildings are subject to threats of demolition. Strict compliance and quiescence to Israeli controls is the chief way of averting these threats of demolition.

At the time of Lustick's writing in the late 1970s, 44 percent of Palestinian villages still lacked electricity. Despite the fact that Palestinians still cultivate 20 percent of the agricultural land, they have access to only 2 percent of the water.[37] They are paid lower wages for their work and receive lower prices for their goods, than Jews. They are restricted to limited sectors of agriculture, particularly produce, such as olives, which cannot be picked mechanically and thus demand intensive manual labor. They cannot organize their own agricultural cooperatives for marketing but are dependent on Israeli marketing systems.

The *Histadrut* is the major Israeli organization for the collective organization of labor. It was developed as a Zionist organization in 1920 under the slogan "the conquest of labor." Thus its founding commitment was to the principle of exclusive development of Jewish labor and the exclusion of Arab labor. In 1959 it conceded to organize a separate "Arab" section to give Palestinians membership in it. As of 1979, 130,000 Palestinian workers belonged to it. Its chief benefit for Palestinians is access to its inexpensive health insurance system. But, otherwise, Palestinians are in no way equally represented, nor do they have equal access to its leadership. The *Histadrut* has not sponsored economic development in the Palestinian sector but has cemented the exploitation of Palestinians on the bottom rung of the Israeli economy. The *Histadrut* seems not to have sponsored any financial, commercial, or industrial enterprise in a Palestinian village.[38]

Cultural underdevelopment is another part of the system of repression and control. Palestinian villages have few cultural institutions that they are allowed to develop, other than churches and mosques. The village schools are crowded and undersupplied.[39] The job of village school teacher is one of the few forms of employment available to the educated Palestinian and is treated as a patronage award for quiescent and compliant persons. Palestinians have little access to the major media of Israel: television, radio, or newspapers. This contributes powerfully to their invisibility in Israeli society.

Religion is a key aspect of the Zionist establishment and its relation to minorities. The failure of the Israeli government to create the promised national constitution was partly a result of the conflict of secular and religious Zionist parties. The religious parties wish to make Israel a Jewish state in the religious sense of government by the Torah, as interpreted by Orthodox rabbinic law. In the first Knesset, Ben-Gurion took these religious parties into his ruling coalition by promising them control of key sectors of Israeli society, such as marriage, divorce, and burial. Restriction of travel on the Sabbath, kosher food laws in public institutions, and exemption from military service for Orthodox women are other areas in which the religious parties have won concessions from the government.[40]

The lack of secular marriage, divorce, and burial means that the other religious groups (Christians, Muslims, and Druze) also are allowed to have their religious courts and authorities that control these aspects of their lives.[41] These religious courts and authorities have quasi-governmental status. Thus, of the twenty-five Palestinians in the Israeli governmental bureaucracy in 1979, eleven were functionaries of religious courts (the rest being clerks in Arab departments). However, it is assumed that these non-Jewish religious functionaries will pay their expenses out of their own resources.

In 1946 the Muslim *Waqf* (organization for charity) owned 10 percent of Palestine. This included many businesses, social institutions, and farms. Most of this land was confiscated and added to the Jewish National Fund. Only land strictly related to religious functions, such as land with mosques on it, was allowed to remain. Muslim authorities are not allowed to use their funds for nonreligious developments, such as housing. The Israeli government has the right to appoint these religious officials and generally chooses the most conservative and compliant ones.[42]

The status of Israeli Palestinians is also evident in politics. The political parties of Israel derive primarily from combinations or splits in earlier Zionist parties. The Palestinians are not allowed to organize their own political party. They have relied for representation primarily on Communist parties, whose anti-Zionist views have made them advocates of a secular, pluralist society in which Palestinians would be equal citizens. However, these parties are small and ineffective and have no broad Palestinian support. Major Zionist parties, especially the Labor party, have organized separate Arab lists, which they use as rewards for compliant Palestinians. But this operates to co-opt, not to genuinely represent, the Palestinian community. So, effectively, the Palestinians have almost no political voice in Israel.[43]

One of the most important of the Zionist institutions is the Israel Defense Forces, which comes close to being idolized in Israeli society. A Zionist army became an integral part of Zionist settlement, at least since the second *Aliya* (1904–14). David Ben-Gurion organized a secret defense force about this time to defend the settlements against evicted Arab tenants who sought to return to their land. The British played a major role in shaping the *Haganah* from 1917 to 1945. Jews trained in the British army in the First World War went into defense units on *kibbutzim* afterward. During the Arab uprising of 1936–39, Jews were allowed to develop a settlement force that could operate "in hot pursuit" of Palestinian guerrillas. British officer Orde Wingate developed Special Night Squads to patrol Arab villages. Both Moshe Dayan and Yigal Allon were pupils of Wingate in this anti-Arab guerrilla warfare. Already in 1939 the *Yishuv* had begun to develop armament factories.[44]

The Second World War brought Jews of the *Yishuv* further service with the British, particularly in the North Africa campaign. After World War II, 25,000 trained troops were demobilized. In 1946 the Anglo-American Committee of Inquiry estimated the *Haganah's* strength at 40,000, to which were added 16,000 settlement police, 6,000 Palmach, and about 4,000 to 5,000 *Irgun* and Stern Gang commandos.[45] During this period the army began to develop a certain warrior cult that continues to characterize the Israel Defense Forces (IDF). The features of this cult are a conspiratorial mentality, a style of guerrilla warfare that prefers lightning blows (typically waged against the entire Arab population, not just against an opposing army), and a mystique of military violence as vitalizing. The warriors of Zionism saw armed violence as the way of transforming the weak, effeminate ghetto Jew into the new, masculine Jew.

During the 1948–49 war and for most of the next twenty years, Ben-Gurion held both posts of prime minister and head of the IDF. This allowed him to control both the political and the military systems but without integrating the IDF under civilian control. As a result, the military has remained largely autonomous and unaccountable to the civilian government. This has allowed it continually to plan raids and even major wars, while deceiving the Israeli public and even the government leaders about the actual necessity of such wars. With the exception of the war of 1973, which was an Arab surprise attack in retaliation for the 1967 conquest of territory and refusal to return it, all the subsequent wars of Israel, in 1956, 1967, and 1982, as well as endless major and minor border raids into Egyptian, Jordanian, Syrian, and Lebanese territory, have been planned by the military as wars of expansion. In each case incidents have been fomented or even invented in order to give the Israeli public and the world the impression that such wars were necessary for Israel's "defense."[46]

The IDF is a key institution that socializes young Israelis, male and female. The average Israeli male serves in the army for thirty-six years, first for three years as a conscript and then in the reserves for another thirty-three years, for between forty-five and seventy days a year. A man's status in society is determined by his service record, which must be produced when he applies for higher education, work or government financial assistance. Many benefits, such as housing and education, are linked to veteran status. Palestinians are neither conscripted nor allowed to volunteer for the army, so they are excluded from this entire system of benefits and social contacts. The Druze community is conscripted into a separate unit, and the Bedouin are allowed to volunteer as scouts, but these are small and marginal groups. Their separate treatment in this matter is intended to fragment the Arab groups in Israel.[47] The Palestinians do not accept this division. For them, all Arabic-speaking people of Palestine are Palestinians.

One of the few areas where Palestinians and Israelis might meet as peers is in university education. The poverty of Palestinian primary and secondary education, and the fact that Palestinians have to compete in a second language, Hebrew, in university exams, has limited the number of Palestinians who have been able to qualify for university. Palestinians also do not have the same access to scholarships as Jews. In 1977 about 4 percent of university students in Israel were Palestinians, although they were at least 17 percent of Israeli citizens.

Palestinian university students have been viewed with great apprehension and hostility by Israeli authorities as a potentially subversive group. Their student organizations were, for a long time, refused official status. They have been harassed and spied upon. Any Palestinian who is active politically as a student is almost certain to be kept from even that marginal employment open to the educated Palestinian. This repressive attitude toward the Palestinian student and emergent intelligentsia is intended to encourage them to emigrate, by denying to them any satisfactory use of their creative skills.[48]

Could the remnant of Palestinian people left in Israel after 1948 have been treated differently, given the Israeli view of them as an "enemy" community? It is instructive to compare them with the Jewish communities that immigrated to Israel from countries in the Middle East and North Africa and initially shared a common Arab language and culture. This population was treated as second-class citizens when they arrived in Israel. Despite significant elites and educational traditions among them, they have typically been viewed by European Jews in Israel as "primitive" people who need to be elevated to the Northern European Jewish level. This has meant particularly that they need to be stripped of their Arabic language and culture and assimilated into an Israeli Hebrew society, which had been defined by Northern European Jews.[49]

The Sephardic Jews also have found themselves excluded from the informal networks of power that have dominated the Israeli-Zionist organizations and state apparatus in the army, the *Histadrut*, the Jewish agencies, and the political parties. Even though some of them were Holocaust survivors from Greece and the Balkans, they did not receive the funds that came from German reparations. They were treated with cultural contempt and were located on the lower rungs of the Israeli economy. However, unlike the Palestinians, they are Jews. The definition of Israel as a Jewish state demands that they be assimilated, even if assimilation means a denial of their distinctive Sephardic Jewish cultures. Unlike Palestinians, they serve in the army and, in it, have risen to those positions that are the key to other career options. Thus, the Israeli system works toward closing the gap between Sephardic and Ashkenazi Jews and toward eventually creating a common Hebrew-speaking Israeli Jewish community.[50]

It is not farfetched to assume that a similar treatment of Palestinians might have had a similar effect. If they had been treated as equal citizens, given access to economic development and employment, they would have come to shape a distinctive way of thinking of themselves as Israeli Palestinians. Even with the harsh and negative treatment they have received, some Palestinian writers have sought such an Israeli national identity. Most Palestinians would have come to feel themselves loyal citizens of Israel, if there had been a genuine desire to include them.

But such inclusion contradicts the basic purpose of Israel as a Jewish state. Palestinians are excluded for ideological reasons, more

than for any security threat they have posed to Israeli Jews. Ironically, this means that they continue to think of themselves primarily
as members of a Palestinian national community. Israeli Jews have
worked to perpetuate, not to overcome, the enmity of Palestinians
toward Israel.

MAKING PALESTINIANS INVISIBLE IN THE 1967 OCCUPIED TERRITORIES

In 1967, in a lightning "six day" war, the Israelis occupied areas
that had been under Syrian, Jordanian, and Egyptian control since
the 1949 truce lines were drawn: East Jerusalem, the Golan Heights,
the West Bank, and the Gaza Strip. This caused new displacements
of Palestinians from their land. Many who fled were not allowed to
return. In the Gaza Strip, which had a population of 450,000 in
1967, about 100,000 fled or were absent at work in other countries.
These were not allowed to return. In the West Bank about 250,000
to 300,000 fled and were not allowed to return. East Jerusalem, with
a population of 65,000, was eventually annexed to Israel, as were the
Golan Heights, which was cleared of its Syrian population with the
exception of the Druze.

In the twenty years since 1967 the population of the Gaza Strip
and the West Bank has grown to about the same number as before
the conquest: 545,000 in the Gaza Strip (officially—the actual number may be as high as 650,000) and 900,000 in the West Bank. In
addition to those displaced in 1967, another 500,000 have been
expelled or denied reentry since 1967, including offspring of the
expelled. Thus, the total displaced population of the regions comes
to at least 850,000.[51]

Since the Old City of Jerusalem and the West Bank contain sites
going back to ancient Hebrew times, those Zionists who regard Jewish claims to the land as based on divine donation from biblical promises quickly expressed their beliefs that these areas should never be
given up. The official Israeli position was that these territories were
being held for purposes of future peace negotiations. But the appli-
cation of the Geneva conventions governing occupied territories was
rejected by Israel. These conventions forbid any land annexation, settlement, or expulsion of population. Instead, the government of
Israel invented a rubric called "administered territories" to avoid these

restrictions (although, from the point of view of international law, they are, in fact, occupied territories and thus such changes are illegal).[52]

Although Jewish settlements in these territories accelerated with the government of Menachem Begin beginning in 1979, already in 1967 two somewhat disparate plans were implemented for the settlement of the region. According to the plan put forth by Labor government leader Yigal Allon, a ring of settlements would be built around Jerusalem and this expanded area would be annexed. Another line of settlements would be placed down the Jordan valley. These were to secure Israel against future invasion. Eventually there would be a new partition and part of the land, together with the Palestinian population, would be returned to Jordan. Allon did not want to see Israel become a permanent ruler over this population or dilute the Zionist principle of Jewish labor further by using this Palestinian population as cheap labor. However, a second plan, put forth by Moshe Dayan, envisioned the eventual annexation of all the land, the encouragement of some Palestinians in it to emigrate and the control of the rest, to be administered in their day-to-day life through Jordanian civil services. This population would live in Israel but never become Israeli citizens.[53]

Beginning in 1967, appropriation of the land in the West Bank and the Gaza Strip has proceeded under a number of official rubrics. Military purposes, public purposes, and security purposes account for a considerable part of the land takeover. Such land is declared to be needed for firing ranges, military training grounds, and such projects as road buildings, but actually a considerable amount taken under these rubrics has been used for settlements. As in the 1949 truce lines, major categories of land that, under Ottoman law, were accounted public land but attached to villages for their collective use and future expansion, were appropriated by the Israelis as "state land," in the sense of "Jewish state land," and thus to be used only by Jews. Farmers who contest these appropriations have been required to prove title, something that few farmers possessed.[54]

The same methods of land confiscation used in Israel were applied to the territories. Land has been closed off (or water access denied to it) and then declared to be abandoned and, on these grounds, confiscated. Illegal land sales have also gone on. Since the land registration department keeps its records secret, it is difficult for Palestinians to contest a sale.[55] Under these rubrics, about 55 percent of the land in the West Bank and 30 percent of the land in the Gaza Strip has been taken over. Despite the small number of Jewish settlers (2,000) in the Gaza Strip, the most fertile farm land has been taken, as well as scenic areas along the seacoast for tourist developments. The more than 600,000 Palestinians in this area make the Gaza Strip one of the most crowded regions in the world.

In addition to the settlements that have taken place under the Allon plan, the Begin government approved many more settlements around historic regions in the West Bank, such as Hebron and Nablus. The government extended all the services of Israel to these settlements under especially generous terms. The settlers are governed by Israeli law, not the military law that controls the Palestinians of the regions. Males eighteen and over are in the military or reserves. Even when not on official duty, they are armed. So the settlements serve literally as armed camps, not only in defense of their settlements, but in aggressive harassment of the Palestinian population or mass armed retaliation against incidents such as stone-throwing. Thus the settlements are an extension of the military occupation.[56] About 52,000 settlers are present in the West Bank and 2,000 in the Gaza Strip.

The twenty-one years between 1957 and 1988 have also seen a steady integration of the infrastructures of these regions into Israel. This can be categorized under the headings of road systems, water supply, electricity, and labor and markets. The earlier road systems in the West Bank ran North to South, linking Palestinian settlements with each other. The new roads built by the Israelis typically run East and West, linking Jewish settlements with major cities such as Jerusalem and Tel Aviv in Israel, but skirting around Palestinian settlements, isolating and fragmenting them.[57]

Water appropriation is probably the most crucial factor in the denial of Palestinian existence on the land, since, without water, there can be no cultivation or, finally, even human residency. Israeli water development has diverted the water from the Sea of Galilee to Israeli agriculture in the Negev, while West Bank residents have been made dependent on water supplied from Israel. About 60 percent of the water supply of the West Bank is controlled from Israel, making it possible to cut off water needed by Palestinians. Palestinians are required to obtain permits to dig new wells or repair old ones, and these are often denied. Only five permits to dig new wells were granted to Palestinians between 1967 and 1983. Wells dug by Israeli settlers have caused nearby springs, traditionally used by Palestinian villages, to dry up.[58]

The electrical grid of the West Bank has been almost entirely integrated into that of Israel. This has involved the dismantling of autonomous electrical generation plants. For example, the city of Hebron had its own power station before 1967. In 1973 the city was refused permission to replace the generator with a new one, and so had to connect its electrical system with sources supplied from Israel.[59]

The integration of labor and markets means that Palestinians from the West Bank and the Gaza Strip provide a cheap labor supply for Israel. Agricultural seasonal labor, restaurant workers, maintenance and construction work—jobs seen as unbefitting Jews—are now largely done by Arab labor. Palestinians, in turn, are prevented from developing their own industry and so become dependent on finished goods from Israel. The West Bank and Gaza have, in fact, become the largest market for Israel-produced goods. The agricultural produce of the Palestinian farms has been marketed through Israel, although at times there have been successful efforts to market some Palestinian agricultural produce autonomously.[60]

The control of the Palestinian population in these regions falls under the military commander, who holds combined dictatorial powers as chief legislator, executive, and judge. Although a local system of Jordanian courts exists, these have become practically defunct through denial of funds, of jurisdiction, and of cooperation from the Israeli police and military. Not only in matters of security violations, but for all matters essential to daily life, such as licenses to build, open a business, or travel, the Palestinian is dependent on the granting of permits from the military government—permits that are typically delayed and denied.[61]

Every Palestinian of the Occupied Territories must carry an identification card. They are also identified by the license plates of their car. These identifications are regarded as the property of the State of Israel and can be confiscated at will. For persons whose cards are confiscated, any movement is illegal, since the Palestinians can be charged with a security violation if they do not have their ID on their person. Palestinians are also not allowed to spend the night in Israel and so must travel back to their homes each night.

The military orders that have been passed by the military commanders allow any means deemed necessary to control protest or resistance from Palestinians. This regularly involves house demolition, both to check unlicensed houses and also as a means of collective punishment for a family or neighborhood suspected of harboring someone who has taken a violent act against the occupation. These charges do not have to be proved for such collective punishment to be carried out. Other kinds of administrative punishment, without trial or conviction, are house arrest or town arrest, which may be indefinitely renewable. The person under such arrest is typically required to report to the military commander one or more times a day.[62] Since the basis of charges of security violations is kept secret, it is almost impossible to challenge such charges in a court of law.[63]

Military orders also prevent Palestinians from assembling and expressing themselves politically. Under these orders, books and newspapers freely available in Jerusalem, such as the Palestinian paper *Al-Fajr*, are forbidden (even in individual copies) in the West Bank and Gaza. It is forbidden to state publicly that one supports the PLO. A poll taken by *Al-Fajr* in the summer of 1986 revealed that about 93 percent of the residents of the West Bank support the PLO and would favor a Palestinian state set up under its control.[64] The pollster, Dr. Mohammed Shaddid of An Najah University in Nablus, was arrested and denied a work permit for taking the poll. Even to unfurl the Palestinian flag or to display any sign with the four colors of that flag together is forbidden. The Gazan artist Fathy Chapin was imprisoned for three months for painting a picture of a horse whose mane was depicted in the colors of the Palestinian flag.[65]

In 1975 the Israeli government attempted to provide a facade of local self-government and allowed major cities to elect mayors. However, since the mayors who were elected were overwhelmingly supporters of the PLO, the Israeli government withdrew support from them. In incidents that have been officially blamed on settler extremists (but are generally believed to have been coordinated by the Israeli military and secret police), assassination attempts were made on several of these mayors. The mayor of Ramallah, Karim Khalaf, suffered a foot blown off, and the mayor of Nablus, Basaam Shaka'a, lost both his legs, while the mayor of El Bireh, Ibrahim Tawil, escaped unharmed. All the elected mayors were deposed by the Israelis, and Rahad Kawasme, the mayor of Hebron, was deported and later assassinated in Jordan. His successor, Mustafa Natsche of Hebron, was also deposed.[66] There has been an effort to claim that the appointment of village leagues constitutes a new form of Palestinian self-determination; but, in fact, the village leagues are primarily mercenary militia recruited from criminal elements in Palestinian society to supplement the occupation military forces.[67]

Students at universities, and even in secondary and elementary schools, are particularly harassed by the military government. The universities on the West Bank (which are founded and funded independently of Israel) have been repeatedly closed down by the Israelis on the grounds that the students either have been engaged in protests or are suspected of planning a protest.[68] High school students have experienced mass arrests during the days they were to take their matriculation exams, thus delaying their opportunity to take those exams for another year. Students on the way to school or returning from school are frequently the object of harassment and arbitrary arrest. It was estimated that 90 percent of the school children between twelve and twenty in the Occupied Territories have been arrested at least once.[69] (This was before the 1987–88 uprising.)

Anyone who is arrested in the Occupied Territories can be held without trial or consultation with a lawyer for eighteen days. During this period (and also during extensions of this period) those arrested are typically subject to brutal treatment, ranging from kicking and beatings to elaborate forms of torture, such as being forced to stand with arms extended and head covered by a wet sack into which tear gas is injected, or continuous deprivation of sleep, or being confined to tiny cells deep in sewage water from latrines. The Al Fara'a prison in the West Bank — a prison used particularly for arrested young people — is particularly notorious for its unsanitary conditions and brutal treatment.[70]

Palestinians in the Occupied Territories live under a constant regime of restrictions and harassments, culminating in threats of torture, physical injury, and death or expulsion without right to return. Although the official justification of this regime is that it is needed to protect against "terrorists," in fact the need for it for security purposes is minimal. It must be seen as an integral part of a total scheme of occupation, the ultimate purpose of which is to induce a large percentage of the Palestinian population to leave, so that the land can be annexed to Israel without this population. There is a growing danger that Israel will attempt a new mass expulsion of Palestinians. In a poll reported in the *Jerusalem Post* (August 12, 1988) 49% of Israelis endorsed this option.

As seen in the previous chapter, in December 1987 the Palestinians in the Occupied Territories began a sustained resistance and protest against the occupation. Before the *intifada*, the uprisings begun at that time, protest had been sporadic. There were occasional knifings and bombings and frequent rock-throwing. There were many nonviolent demonstrations of protest. All these expressions of resistance were met with extreme violence by the occupation army. Few Israelis have died from such Palestinian resistance, while Palestinians have died and been injured in large numbers.[71]

The main form of resistance to the occupation is what Palestinians call "steadfastness," the quiet determination to refuse to leave the territory. Steadfastness means a constant day-to-day struggle to survive under these conditions of repression; it includes the struggle to raise children and hold families together, to create means of keeping up morale and maintaining Palestinian culture and identity. Steadfastness takes the form of simply trying to get the word out about violations of human rights, about university closings, house and town arrests, house demolitions, killings and injuries and mistreatment of prisoners. Such publication of conditions in the territories may range from personal letters to the development of information services designed to provide material for journalists.[72]

Steadfastness also means the development of Palestinian cultural centers where folklore and artisan work can be collected. Artistic expressions of Palestinian national identity are developed and distributed in posters and tape recordings. Resistance also takes the form of careful documentation of the actual history of occupation, such as the development of historical maps showing the more than five hundred villages that have been destroyed by the Israelis, with their locations under what are now national forests or monuments, settlements, and universities.[73] Palestinians continually try to counter the Israeli story with the story of their own experience. Survival takes the form of subversive memory that keeps alive the history of a national identity that refuses to be destroyed.

Women play a key role in this work of survival, since it is they who bear the large families considered, not only traditional, but now an act of commitment to the nation. It is women who hold the family together when their fathers, husbands, and sons are in prison, are deported or dead, or are demoralized by unemployment and repression. Networks of women's groups have sprung up and have created sewing and embroidery cooperatives as ways both of earning income for the family and of keeping alive a cultural identity. Women's organizations have also founded kindergartens, orphanages, literacy projects, and improvements of medical services and sanitation in villages.

All these self-help projects have a double aim: both to improve conditions of life and also to create spheres of Palestinian autonomy that encourage the will to resist. Such projects are vital to grassroots leadership training for women. During 1988 many of these cultural and self-help institutions have been closed by the Israelis, and their leaders arrested, in an effort to quell rising Palestinian resistance to the occupation.[74]

The struggle over the West Bank and the Gaza Strip is a struggle between two national identities. One people, the Israelis, backed by the funding of the wealthiest nation in the world, the United States, and with massive military power, seeks to deny the Palestinians' right, and shatter their will, to exist as a national community. It seeks a gradual erosion of Palestinian presence in the Territories to the point where these can be fully annexed. A second people, the Palestinians, unarmed and without rights, tenaciously hangs onto the remnants of its historic homeland but with much more limited access to funds and communications media on the outside. Palestinians worry about losing more of their land, the destruction of their culture and physical health, and being expelled en masse, while more sensitive Israelis worry about losing their souls.

PART 3.

CHRISTIAN RELATIONS TO
JUDAISM AND TO ZIONISM

6. Contemporary Christian Responses to Judaism and to Zionism

> And they asked him, "Teacher, when will this be, and what will be the sign when this is about to take place?" And he said, "Take heed that you are not led astray, for many will come in my name, saying 'I am He!' and 'The time is at hand!' Do not go after them. And when you hear of wars and tumults, do not be terrified, for these things must happen, but the end has not yet come."
>
> LUKE 21:7–9 (RSV adapted)

With the defeat of Nazism in 1945 and the founding of the State of Israel in 1948, the Christian churches have been faced with the need to respond to both of those realities. Western churches particularly have had to face the question of whether their long history of anti-Judaism was not a key factor in the passive and perhaps the active acceptance of Hitler and his "final solution" to the Jewish question. Christians have also had to ask themselves how they should respond to the existence of the State of Israel. In this chapter we will survey responses of Christian groups to Judaism and to Israel since 1948 and mostly since 1967.

To simplify a very complex picture, the chapter will concentrate on representative statements from four main sectors of world Christianity. For Roman Catholicism, we will discuss the position taken by the Vatican in its statements on relationship to the Jews and on relationship to Israel; for mainline Protestantism, the statements on Judaism and on Israel by the World Council of Churches. For American fundamentalist Protestantism we will discuss particularly the position taken by Jerry Falwell. Finally, for the Arab Christian world, we will discuss a statement issued by a group of Middle Eastern theologians and also the writings of Canon Na'em Ateek, leading Palestinian Christian theologian.

THE VATICAN: RELATIONS TO JUDAISM AND TO THE STATE OF ISRAEL

The attitude of the Vatican to the State of Israel cannot be understood by referring to the ancient patristic ideas that the Jews are to be in a state of exile until the end of history. However much such ideas may have still lingered and conditioned the mind of Pius X in his negative response to his first encounter with Zionism in his meeting with Theodor Herzl in 1904,[1] this old tradition does not explain the present reluctance of the Vatican to grant full recognition to the State of Israel. The global Catholic church has been in a state of dramatic transformation in the twenty years between the mid-1960s and the 1980s. The Vatican has both led this transformation, through the convening of the Second Vatican Council in October, 1962, and, in recent years, tried to restrain the changes unleashed by the Council. Among the important develop- ments of the Council was a new ecumenism, not only toward the other Christian bodies, but toward Judaism, Islam, and other world religions.

The Vatican II statement on relationship to non-Christian reli- gions starts out with a general affirmation that authentic relation to God has been present among many peoples and their religions.[2] This affirmation is based on the Catholic tradition of general reve- lation, which sees all human beings, on the basis of their natural or created relation to God, as having some authentic access to knowl- edge of God.[3] Such a view is in contrast to both fundamentalist and neoorthodox Protestantism, which have believed that human total depravity removes all access to God based on "original nature" and that relation to God is established through Jesus Christ alone.

After mentioning Hinduism and Buddhism as having some true insights, the decree then speaks of even greater affinity with Islam as a faith that affirms "one God, living and enduring, merciful and all powerful, Maker of heaven and earth and Speaker to men." Islam is seen as claiming a relation to Abraham, as honoring Jesus as a prophet and also his virgin mother, Mary, and as believing in a strict moral life, prayer, and hope for a final resurrection and judgment.

The closest affinity of all is affirmed in relation to the Jewish peo- ple. The church acknowledges that Jesus himself, and all the early disciples and apostles, were Jews and that God's election of the Jews is the root into which the gentile church has been ingrafted. God's covenant with the Jews has not been rescinded, and the church looks forward to a future time when the reconciliation of Jew and Gentile in Christ will be accomplished. In the most important state-ment of a decree, any notion of collective guilt of the Jews for the death of Christ is repudiated. Although some individuals were involved, this could not be construed as blame either upon all Jews at the time or upon Jews today. "The Jews should not be presented as repudiated or cursed by God." All persecutions or displays of anti-Semitism are repudiated, and the decree specifically mandates that efforts be made to eliminate such attitudes from preaching and catechetical instructions.[4]

This decree set relationship between the Roman Catholic church and Judaism on a new footing. Catholic-Jewish dialogue was institu-tionalized with the creation in 1970 of the Catholic-Jewish Liaison Committee, which brought together five Vatican representatives with delegates from five leading Jewish organizations (the Jewish Council in Israel for Interreligious Consultation, the World Jewish Congress, the Anti-Defamation League of B'nai B'rith, the Ameri-can Jewish Committee, and the Synagogue Council of America). In 1974 the Pontifical Commission for Religious Relations with Juda-ism was created, linked to the Secretariat for Christian Unity. These agencies, and their counterparts under national episcopacies, have worked to eliminate anti-Semitic references in liturgy and catechet-ical materials.

The statement on Judaism brought an outcry from Eastern Chris-tian delegates to the Council, who feared it would be understood as an endorsement of the State of Israel. The supporters of the decree answered these objections by asserting that it had to do with reli-gious relations with Judaism, not with political relations with Israel. As a result, most of the prelates from Arab countries voted for the decree in the final session of the Council.[5] This confusion also indi-cates the chief problem that the Vatican has in dealing with the State of Israel. The Vatican wishes to strictly separate religious rela-tions with Judaism from relations with the State of Israel as a politi-cal entity. Zionists, on the other hand, insist that the two cannot be separated, that the Jews as a covenanted people are a nation and that the State of Israel is the political expression of this biblically based identity. Not to recognize the State of Israel, in their view, is to repudiate an intrinsic aspect of Jewish identity. This, to them, is anti-Semitism.

The attitude of the Vatican to the State of Israel has been in a state of transition since 1948. At the beginning of this period, the Vatican was motivated primarily by a traditional view that wished to see the Holy Places under Roman Catholic jurisdiction. The Vatican supported the UN resolution that favored the preservation of Jerusalem as an international zone.

Since 1967 this view has shifted in adjustment to changing political realities and growing ecumenical sensitivities. By receiving Israeli ministers, and in statements affirming Israel's right to security as a sovereign nation, the Vatican has granted *de facto* recognition to the State of Israel.[6] It has also accepted Israeli administration of Jerusalem, asking only for international guarantees of access to the Holy Places for all three faiths, no longer just for Roman Catholics or even just for Christians.[7] The 1984 Vatican statement *Redemptionis Anno* stressed the need to make Jerusalem a city of peace for all three monotheistic faiths.[8] This also implies a continuing protest against the Judaization of the city, i.e., the confiscation of Muslim or Christian property for exclusively Jewish use, thus diminishing the interreligious character of the city.[9]

The reasons why the Vatican has stopped short of full formal recognition of the State of Israel have to do primarily with a desire to preserve an outreach to the Muslim Arab nations, the cultivation of Christian-Muslim dialogue and coexistence (particularly in Lebanon), and a growing support for Palestinian self-determination. The Vatican maintains two institutions that help support Palestinian human rights: the Pontifical Mission for Palestine, founded in 1949, that oversees relief for the refugees; and Bethlehem University, founded in 1973, which seeks to maintain educated Palestinian Christians in the West Bank[10] (although today about 70 percent of its student body is Muslim).

In 1975, Paul VI made a statement supporting Palestinian rights to national self-determination, a statement that was reiterated in stronger terms by John Paul II in 1980.[11] John Paul II also met with Yasir Arafat in 1982[12] after the Israeli invasion of Lebanon, which had sought to destroy the PLO. This meeting, which gave official Vatican recognition to the PLO as the representative of the Palestinian people at precisely the moment when the Israeli government hoped to destroy the PLO, particularly angered supporters of Israel.

In effect, the Vatican has assumed a position that gives *de facto* recognition to both the PLO and the State of Israel. But it withholds final recognition of Israel until a parallel right of the Palestinians can be established. An added consideration is the Vatican policy of not giving formal recognition to states with undefined borders. Thus, as long as Israel occupies the territory that might be a Palestinian state, formal recognition is withheld.

THE WORLD COUNCIL OF CHURCHES: RELATIONS TO JUDAISM AND TO THE STATE OF ISRAEL

Since 1948 (and particularly since 1964), a number of statements on the relationship of Christianity to Judaism have been issued by world and national Protestant ecumenical and denominational bodies. The Vatican Declaration, which was being debated in the Council in 1963–65, had a major effect on Protestant decisions to issue like statements. Protestant statements — particularly those coming from the Reformed tradition, such as the statement of the 1970 synod of the Reformed Church in Holland, "Israel: People, Land, and State"— have been willing to make a positive theological connection between relationship to the Jews and recognition of the State of Israel as an ongoing expression of a covenant with God that includes the gift of the land.[13] World Council of Churches' statements have not been willing to make this connection, since they must balance the positions of many Protestant traditions as well as those of the Orthodox traditions.

The 1948 statement on Christian approach to the Jews, issued at the first assembly in Amsterdam, while deploring anti-Semitism and declaring that it should be repudiated among Christians, nevertheless unequivocably renewed the call for Christian mission to the Jews. Indeed, rejection of anti-Semitism was seen as aiding in the conversion of the Jews to Christianity (as though anti-Semitism were simply a question of social hostility and not also a part of theological teachings of Jewish incompleteness).[14] However, between 1964 and 1967, the Faith and Order Commission and the Committee on the Church and the Jewish People studied this question of mission to the Jews in depth. Its report was accepted and also recommended for further study in 1968.[15]

The report specifically puts aside any consideration of the State of Israel as a theological issue, although this also is recommended for further study. The word *Israel* is used only for the Jews in the biblical context, not in reference to a present state. The report is inconclusive about the question of mission to the Jews. It is still assumed that there will be an eschatological reconciliation of Jews and Christians when Jews will accept Christ in the Second Advent as their Messiah. But whether Christians should do anything about converting Jews now, and in what sense the covenant with Israel continues as a parallel covenant with that of the Church or has been superseded by the covenant with the Church, remain unresolved questions.

The general tone of the report suggests that Christians should not actively proselytize Jews but hope that, by their good works, the Jews will see the light. This means that Christians should get busy and do some good works, particularly purgation of anti-Semitism from their churches. In a number of areas the report also suggests that Christians can understand Hebrew Scriptures and their own faith better by dialogue with the Jewish tradition, a tradition that is not to be identified with the "Old Testament" but includes the ongoing rabbinic tradition.

Since 1948 the World Council of Churches has also made a number of statements on the question of justice and the Middle East conflict. The World Council was involved in this area from the beginning through refugee work, but conflicting views of the solution to the refugee problem soon developed. Western Protestants, who saw the issue from a distance, favored an effort to integrate the refugees into host Arab countries, while missionaries, who were attentive to the views of Palestinians themselves, opted for the advocacy of a political solution — either a binational state or a parallel Palestinian state.[16] Since the expression of such political views brought down the wrath of the Israeli government, making Christian work in the camps difficult, expediency also suggested a focus on humanitarian aid, without reference to a political analysis of the causes and possible solutions of the refugee situation.

After 1967 this situation began to shift. The emergence of the Middle East Council of Churches as a vehicle for indigenous Arab

Christianity made it no longer possible for Western churches to speak for the Palestinian or other Arab Christians. The emphasis shifted to work with rather than work for the refugees. Also, the emergence of the PLO meant that Palestinians needed to be recognized as agents of their own national self-determination, not simply as victims and objects of charity. In 1969, Gabriel Habib, then Mideast secretary for the World Student Christian Federation (WSCF), sponsored a WSCF consultation on "Peace and Justice in the Middle East" that brought together Arab and Western European and American delegates. This resulted in the decision of the WSCF to recognize the PLO, thus being the first international Christian body to do so.[17]

These shifts in relationship between Western and Arab Christians, as well as increasing evidence of injustice in the Israeli treatment of Palestinians in the Occupied Territories, are reflected in the World Council of Churches' statements after 1967. The statement of the Consultation of the Middle East Council of Churches and the Council's Division of Interchurch Aid, Refugee, and World Service, in Nicosia, 1969, declares that

in supporting the establishment of a Jewish state in Palestine, without recognizing the rights of the Palestinians to self-determination, injustice has been done to the Palestinian Arabs by the great powers and this injustice should be redressed.[18]

In the February 1974 statement of the World Council of Churches (WCC) Executive Committee, from Bad Saarow (East Germany), the "even handed" approach has become evident. This means an effort to balance statements of the rights of Palestinians to self-determination with statements of guarantees of the existence and secure borders of the State of Israel: "What we desire is equal justice for both Palestinian people and Jewish people in the Middle East." Support for a Geneva international peace conference is also indicated; this should include representation of the "Palestinian people." Protection of Jerusalem as a city, not only of shrines, but of living representatives of the three monotheistic faiths, also comes in for special emphasis in the Berlin WCC Central Committee statement of August 1974.[19]

In 1975, Philip Potter, general secretary of the WCC, issued a statement repudiating the UN declaration that Zionism is racism, on the grounds that Zionism doesn't fall within the UNESCO definition of racism, i.e., of the biological inferiority of certain races. But the statement also urges that ways be found "to enable the Palestinian people to achieve their legitimate rights to nationhood and state-hood, while recognizing the right of the state of Israel to exist peace-fully within internationally agreed boundaries."[20]

The fifth WCC assembly in Nairobi in 1975 issued a comprehen-sive statement that called for withdrawal of Israel from the territo-ries occupied in 1967, the rights of Palestinians to self-determination, the convening of the Geneva peace conference with all parties con-cerned (including the Palestinians), and the cessation of all military activity "both regular and irregular" (thus putting Israeli military activity on the same footing as that of the Palestinians). A separate statement on Jerusalem reiterates the belief that it should be a city of all three faiths and that its status must be part of a general peace settlement.[21] In 1980 the annexation of Jerusalem by the State of Israel was opposed as a threat to regional and global peace. The 1975 Nairobi statement also mentions that the PLO is ready to accept a two-state solution to the conflict; it thus implies that the PLO should be the representative of the Palestinian people in any peace negotiations.

These WCC statements are not put in the context of any biblical or theological references to themes such as covenant, election, or Promised Land. One gathers that the WCC, as well as the Vatican, maintains a separation between the religious or theological issues of relationship of the churches to Judaism, on the one hand, and their relationship to the State of Israel as a political entity, on the other. However, for the WCC this separation seems to be more of an expression of the indecision about how to connect these two frame-works, rather than an explicit assumption that the two are not connected.

The Canterbury Statement on the Middle East, adopted by the WCC Central Committee in 1969, included a call to study biblical interpretation "to avoid the misuse of the Bible in support of parti-san political views and to clarify the bearing of faith upon critical political questions."[22] The fact that this has not happened indicates that the WCC (which includes Eastern Orthodox as well as Protes-tants) would be divided and unable to reach an agreement on any effort to create a comprehensive theological perspective within which to discuss the relationship with Jews as a religious community and the relationship of Israel as a Jewish state. Consequently the two are discussed separately. Reltionship to Judaism is discussed in biblical and theological terms. Relation to the State of Israel is discussed in terms of the criteria of international peace and justice that would be applied to any other international conflict.

AMERICAN FUNDAMENTALIST CHRISTIANS, JEWS, AND ISRAEL

During the 1940s it was liberal Protestant Christians, such as Reinhold Niebuhr, in the Christian Council on Palestine, who were the main allies of the emerging State of Israel in the Christian churches. But the growing criticism of Israel in mainline Protestant bodies, especially after 1967, caused increasing dissatisfaction with liberal Protestants among Zionists. On the other hand, Christian fundamentalists, who maintained a totally supportive view of the State of Israel, were growing in political power in the United States. This fundamentalist view of Israel is derived both from their dispensationalist biblical theology and also from their views on international politics as a contest between God and Satan, with the United States and Israel on one side and the Russians and Arabs on the other.

As we have seen in the earlier chapter on Christian Zionism, premillenialist evangelicals had long incorporated the return of the Jews to Palestine into their eschatological scenarios and were quick to hail the State of Israel, when it was founded in 1948, as the fulfillment of prophecy. One of the most widely read books among American Christians in the 1970s was the premillenialist apocalypse by Hal Lindsey, *The Late Great Planet Earth*, which adapts the dispensationalist timetable to current global politics.[23] In Lindsey's book, the State of Israel is the centerpiece of the world historical events that will lead to the Second Advent of Christ. All Christians are urged to support Israel unequivocably. They should also urge Jews to rebuild the Temple and restore the sacrificial cult as well (an act that would necessitate destroying the present al-Aqsa Mosque, revered as the third holiest shrine, after Mecca and Medina, in the Muslim world). Lindsey identifies four evil kingdoms that will clash in the final destruction: a northern power (the Soviet Union), a southern power (the Arabs and Africans), an eastern power (which he called the yellow peril and identified with China), and a western power, identified with the European Common Market. It is from this western power that the Antichrist will emerge.

By the mid-1970s, evangelicals were playing an expanding role in American national politics. They were important in the election of Jimmy Carter in 1976 and even more so in the election of Ronald Reagan in 1980. In Israel as well, after 1978, a more religiously fundamentalist and aggressively expansionist government held power under the leadership of Menachem Begin, a former leader of the *Irgun*. Thus the time seemed ripe to many Zionist leaders, both in Israel and in the United States, for an alliance of Zionism and Christian fundamentalism.

Such an alliance was, however, embarrassing to many American Jews whose cultural and political perspectives were secular and liberal. Most Jews had little understanding of Christian fundamentalists. The one group belonged to secular urban America, the other to rural and small-town America. Fundamentalists stood for principles that were anathema to Jews, among them, a belief that everyone, including Jews, must convert to Christianity to be saved and that "Christian" values should predominate in American society. The enthusiastic patriotism of fundamentalists for the State of Israel was viewed by some Jews as a hypocritical cover for a scheme of evangelization.[24]

Still, fundamentalists as a group were gaining wealth and political power, and they were unswervingly dedicated to the State of Israel. These facts could hardly be ignored. In 1982 Merrill Simon, a Zionist Jew who supported this alliance, conducted a series of interviews with Jerry Falwell, leader of the "Moral Majority," a center of both the religious and political power of fundamentalists, in order to present Falwell's views on Judaism, Israel, and American society to American Jews.[25] The account of Falwell's views will be taken primarily from these interviews.

Falwell is unabashedly conversionist in his belief that Jews, like everyone else, must be converted to Christ to be saved. By conversion, he does not mean simply a cultural identity as a Christian, but a personal "born again" experience that applies Christ's atonement for sin to the individual and makes a person dead to sin and alive to God, a vessel of the Holy Spirit. By this reckoning, most Christians

are not really Christians at all, because they have not been converted in that sense. According to Falwell, no one who has not been
personally converted in this "born again" relation to Christ will be
saved. Christians have a mandate to witness to Christ for all people,
including Jews; but only God can convert a person. Christians can
only witness to Christ; they can't convert another person unless God
has elected that person and provides the transforming grace.[26]

In this view, God has elected the Jews in the Abrahamic covenant.
This covenant is permanent and unbreakable, so Jews are still God's
elect people. Jesus is the Jewish Messiah who completes and fulfills
the promises of the Jews. Christianity is the completion of this
promise to the Jews, but it does not replace God's covenant with the
Jews. According to Falwell's dispensationalist theology, the covenant
of God with the Jews continues and plays a key role in the final
eschatological events of redemption in the future.

The promises of God to the Jews — return to the land and rebuilding of the Temple — must be fulfilled first. Then Christ will return,
and the 144,000 Jews (12,000 from each of the twelve tribes) will
acknowledge Christ as their Messiah. They, together with believing
gentile Christians, will be "raptured" to heaven with Christ during
the "time of tribulation," while Christ prepares the earth for the
millennium by purging it of all evil. Then the saints (Jewish and
gentile Christians) will reappear with Christ and reign over the
earth with Christ for a thousand years.[27]

Thus Falwell's scenario for Jewish conversion is eschatological.
He is not concerned about conversion of Jews now, although he
believes that Christians must witness to Christ for all people, including Jews, on an individual basis. But the corporate conversion of the
Jews, to make up the reconciled community of the messianic people
of God, is assured by a future divine plan. Meanwhile, fundamentalist Christians (such as himself) and non-Christian Jews can work
together on their present agenda of common interests, which
includes defending Jews in all lands from anti-Semitism and, particularly, total commitment to the survival of the State of Israel.

Falwell presents his loyalty to the State of Israel as resting on three
bases. First, there is a humanitarian concern. Every people has a right
to a national homeland, and so Jews have a right to Israel as a part
of this general human right to a national homeland. Second, there
is a political commonality between America as a "Judaeo-Christian,"

freedom-loving, democratic" state and Israel as a Jewish, "freedom-loving, democratic" state. Both nations rest on the same religious and cultural values. Indeed, in Falwell's mind the two nations are like Siamese twins, linked together not only by common self-interest of a pragmatic kind but because they are identical in values. Together they represent these values over against an evil world dominated by "Communists" and "totalitarian governments." Communist states and Arab states represent evil, as totalitarian systems that are the antithesis of the values of America and Israel.[28] Falwell holds a dualistic, Manichaean view of global politics: America and Israel stand together against an evil world.

However, the third and most crucial basis of Falwell's commitment to Israel is theological—or, rather, is based on his interpretation of biblical prophecy. God's covenant with Abraham, which is permanent and irrevocable, includes the land. Falwell, using Genesis 15:18–19, interprets God's permanent gift of the land to the Jews as stretching from the river of Egypt to the Euphrates. Thus, according to Falwell, the Jews have a permanent right, not only to the land within the pre-1967 borders of Israel, but also to the Golan Heights and the West Bank (which Falwell calls "Judaea" and "Samaria") and, of course, to East Jerusalem, and they also have the right to southern Lebanon, the Gaza Strip, part of the Sinai, Jordan, and Syria. He thinks that they shouldn't give up any of this land. Particularly, they should not give up any of the land that was occupied in the 1967 war.[29]

The capture of this biblical homeland (East Jerusalem, Judaea, and Samaria) in 1967, according to Falwell, is the fulfillment of prophecy. This means that ancient Israel is now "ingathered" in its historic homeland. This is the signal for the end of the "time of the Gentiles" (Luke 21:24, understood as the end of the period of mission to the Gentiles).[30] The apocalyptic scenario of the "last things" is thus ready to roll, although exactly when it will roll is entirely up to God. God is completely in charge of history, in Falwell's view. So there is no "delay" of the messianic events; nor can they be hastened by human action. They unfold on a divinely determined schedule.[31] So the Jews did not return to Palestine, found a state, and capture these additional territories in 1967 simply as human agents, but as agents of God, according to a divinely determined plan.

Falwell sees the conflict of American and Israeli "democracy" against "totalitarian" states, the conflict between Christian fundamentalists and their critics, and that between Jews and their persecutors, all as aspects of one ultimate conflict between God and Satan. The enemies of Israel and America are enemies of God and agents of Satan. All who persecute Christian fundamentalists and Jews are also agents of Satan.[32] The New Testament itself, rightly understood, is in no way responsible for anti-Semitism; nor has any true Christian ever been anti-Semitic. All anti-Semitism has come from pagans pretending to be Christians. Jews and true Christians are one people of God whose final unity is in the process of unfolding against their perennial enemies, the agents of Satan.

In God's good time the final events of world redemption will unfold. In the final crisis of world history, the Antichrist will lead an attack against Israel — the ultimate battle of Satan against God. Israel will be saved only by the appearance of Christ, the acknowledgement by the 144,000 Jews of Christ as their Messiah, and their ingathering into the community of saints that will reign with Christ over the whole world during the millennium. Thus the conversion of the Jews, and also the full security of Israel within its biblical borders, is for Falwell a millennial event, beyond purely human history. Israel will never be secure within premillennial history.

Meanwhile, all true Christians must be against anti-Semitism and also unshakably loyal to the State of Israel. This includes three billion dollars in military aid for Israel — or even more — whatever is necessary for its military security.[33] Israel has only one true friend in the world, the United States. It can never hope to trust in any promises from the Arab states, for they will always be unreliable.[34] Israel is in no way responsible for the Palestinian refugee "problem"; this has been created entirely by the Arab states who made these people refugees and who have kept them refugees by preventing them from assimilating into the Arab countries. This problem should be solved by assimilating them into these Arab countries. There is no need for a Palestinian state. No such state can be allowed, for Arafat and the PLO are the epitome of the bloodthirsty terrorists of the world and prime agents of Satan.[35]

Unlike the pope and the World Council of Churches, Jerry Falwell has no concern about the Christian or Muslim Holy Places in

Jerusalem. Jerusalem belongs to the Jews and only to the Jews as their historic national capital. The Catholic and Orthodox Christians who predominate in these Christian shrines are, for Falwell and other fundamentalists, apostates and even representatives of the Antichrist, while Islam has, in his view, nothing in common with the biblical tradition. It is an evil, satanic religion, and its claims to Abrahamic roots are a sham.[36]

To understand Falwell's perspective, one must see that his apocalyptic perspective annihilates all human history between biblical times and the coming return of Christ. Catholic Christian or Muslim claims to Jerusalem have no relevance, because they are not "in the Bible." For him, too, the Jews are people solely of the "Old Testament." They have no relevant history between the first century C.E. and the founding of the State of Israel in 1948. Oddly enough, this makes his view quite compatible with a certain type of Jewish Zionist that wishes to "negate" the Diaspora.[37]

For Falwell, an unshakable bond ties Jews and Christians together in the promises of God. Moreover, the Jews have a special protection from God. This includes the Jewish state as well. Whoever blesses the Jew (and the Jewish state) will be blessed by God. Whoever curses the Jew (and the Jewish state) will be cursed by God (Gen. 12:1–3). Thus Americans and Christians assure their own prosperity by protecting the Jews and supporting the State of Israel. Any individual person who is hostile to Jews, or any nation hostile to Israel, has their downfall assured; they are cursed by God and will be destroyed.[38] This, then, is Falwell's vision of the world—a vision that makes him unhesitatingly call himself a "Zionist." It is a vision and a commitment that one has every reason to believe is totally sincere.

The Christian messianic Zionism of Falwell—and of even more militant spokesmen of this position, such as Mike Evans, author of *Israel—America's Key to Survival*; Hal Lindsey, *The Late Great Planet Earth* and *The 1980s, Countdown to Armageddon;* and David Allen Lewis, *Magog 1982 Cancelled* (which sees Israel's invasion of Lebanon as the prevention of a takeover of the Middle East by the Soviet Union, interpreted to be the biblical Magog)[39]—has great affinity with the militant political messianism that has arisen in Israel in the *Gush Emunim* settler movement. This group has taken to an extreme the organic messianism of Rabbi Abraham Isaac Kook (which was discussed in chapter 2) but without his humanitarian universalism.

They are supported by a number of prominent rabbis in Israel, such as Rabbi Zvi Yehudah Kook, the son of Abraham Isaac Kook; Rabbi Abraham Kahana Shapira, a member of the rabbinic court in Jerusalem; Rabbi Haim David Ha-Levi, chief rabbi of Tel Aviv and Jaffa and of *Yeshivot* (rabbinic schools), such as Merkaz Harav and Kfar Haroeh.

The basic perspective that emerges from this militant political messianism is that Israel's wars of conquest are a religious obligation and herald the dawning of the messianic age. The messianic age is not to be seen as a time of supernatural miracles or cosmic changes but rather primarily as a time of Israel's military victory over its enemies and of its conquest and settlement of the land. Several of these rabbis interpret the ancient commandments to annihilate the Canaanites and the people of Amalek as applicable to the Arabs today. Israel's wars against these peoples are holy wars, and the Israel Defense Forces are sanctified holy warriors. Thus, Rabbi Zvi Yehudah Kook had declared that

this is already the middle of redemption ... the return to Zion, its settlement and conquest is the Kingdom of Heaven built anew. ... The Israel Defense Force is total sanctity; it represents the rule of the people of the Lord on His land. ... We must know that the Kingdom of Heaven is being revealed in this Kingdom, even in the kingdom of Ben-Gurion.[40]

Basic to the *Gush Emunim* (which is engaged in quasi-illegal settlements of the Occupied Territories) and its supporters is the belief that it is forbidden to return "one inch" of the historic Promised Land to the enemies of Israel. Israel's wars against its enemies are wars against Satan. Those who fight against Israel fight against God and attack God by attacking Israel. The late Rabbi O. Hadya provided some of the *halachic* (religious-legal) interpretation that underlies this position. Rabbi Hadya taught that the events of the 1967 war had changed the metaphysical status of Israel. The victory was a miracle that signaled that

the end of days has already come ... behold, now through conquest *Eretz Yisrael* has been redeemed from oppression, from the *sitra achra* [Satan's camp]. It has entered the realm of sanctity. Thereby we have raised the *Shekhinah* [presence of God] from the dust, for it has been in Exile amongst foreigners. If, God forbid, we should return only a tiny strip of land we would thereby give control to the evil forces, to the *sitra achra*.[41]

The presence of Muslim property in the old city of Jerusalem (the *Waqf*: property used to support Muslim religious work), and especially the Dome of the Rock and al-Aqsa mosque, which grace the site of the ancient Jewish Temple, particularly infuriates these Zionist militants. Since 1967 there has been a continuous takeover of property in the old city from Muslims for exclusively Jewish use.[42] In recent years this has also involved radical *Yeshiva* students who have been engaging in a house-by-house takeover of Muslim property, particularly in the Muslim quarter that adjoins the Temple Mount. On a number of occasions these militant nationalists, including armed rabbis and *Yeshiva* students, have tried to storm the Temple Mount and blow up the Muslim buildings there.[43]

In the dark streets of the old city adjoining the Temple Mount, *Yeshivot*, particularly the *Ataret Kohanim* (Crown of the Priests) are preparing for the day when the Dome of the Rock and the al-Aqsa mosque will be destroyed, either by force or by a "divine miracle," and the rebuilding of the Jewish Temple can begin. Their students are studying the ancient laws for the temple sacrifices and weaving the priests' garments that will be used in the restored Temple.[44]

Christian Zionist groups, who have long believed that the rebuilding of the Jewish Temple is one of the events of prophecy that must be fulfilled, have become actively involved in helping these Jewish nationalists to fulfill their "dream." Terry J. Reisenhoover, a wealthy California oil and real estate magnate, is the founder and president of the Jerusalem Temple Mount Foundation, which raises money for *Gush Emunim* militants in Jerusalem and for their settlements in the Occupied Territories.[45] Stanley Goldfoot, a former Stern Gang member and reputedly the one who actually set the bomb that blew up the King David Hotel in 1946, has been tapped by Reisenhoover as the international secretary for the Temple Mount Foundation.[46]

Other Christian Zionist organizations allied with Jewish militants are the Christian Embassy and the Institute for Holy Land Studies, both in Jerusalem. The Christian Embassy was founded in 1980, when the Israeli annexation of East Jerusalem caused most Western nations to move their embassies to Tel Aviv in protest. The Christian Embassy was established with Christian fundamentalist money from America, South Africa, and Holland and was built to express Christian solidarity with the Jewish annexation of Jerusalem as the capital of the Jewish state.[47] Jan Willem van der Hoeven, the spokesman for the Christian Embassy, has denied funneling money to the Temple Mount Foundation; but a cassette distributed by the embassy, on which van der Hoeven speaks, describes plans to build the restored Temple on the site of the Dome of the Rock.[48]

The Institute of Holy Land Studies conducts archaeological research and Christian tours. Its interpretation of archaeological finds of ancient settlements is designed to establish direct connections between ancient Hebrews and the rights of modern Israelis to occupy east Jerusalem and the West Bank. Organizations such as Christians United for Israel and the National Christian Leadership Conference for Israel network Christian Zionist support for Israel in the United States.[49] In short, Christian fundamentalist support for Israel is not simply a matter of apocalyptic theories; it is a matter of garnering major economic and political support behind an expansionist vision of the State of Israel.

ARAB CHRISTIANS, JUDAISM, AND ZIONISM

The Arab Christian voice is almost entirely unknown in the United States. When it is mentioned at all, as in its opposition to the Vatican statement on the Jews at the Second Vatican Council, it is presumed to be viscerally anti-Jewish. Their objections to the State of Israel are assumed to reflect their anti-Jewism. Although such anti-Jewism may exist among some Arab Christian leaders, in fact, several Arab Christian spokespersons have attempted to put forth carefully reasoned statements on relations of Christians to Judaism and of the Arab Christian world to the State of Israel. These statements are notable for their recognition that the claims of Zionism must be dealt with as a problem of biblical hermeneutics for Christians, a topic avoided by the Vatican and the WCC, as we have seen.

Before discussing these theological statements of Arab Christians, a word about the situation of Middle Eastern Christian churches is in order. Middle Eastern churches represent the remnants of the ancient Christian churches of the region, which arose in the first centuries of Christianity. These churches have suffered repeated fragmentation and colonization by political and religious powers beyond their control. In the fourth to seventh centuries these churches were split between Chalcedonism and Monophysite branches in the conflict over Christology. The christological conflict was intertwined with the conflict over allegiance to the Byzantine state, whose capital city was Constantinople.

In the seventh century these churches were inundated by the rise of Islam. Many Eastern Christians converted to Islam, both because it had become the dominant political power and also because they wanted to distance themselves from a Christianity identified with the Greco-Roman empire of Byzantium. Those who remained Christian became members of the Christian *dhimma*, defined by Muslims as a protected, but distinctly inferiorized, people.

Western colonialism in recent centuries has further split the Eastern churches, with Roman Catholicism drawing Eastern Christians into "Uniate" churches (united with Rome), while Protestants founded local branches of various Protestant denominations.[50] This dividing and subdividing of an already weakened Eastern Christianity has made it very difficult for Arab Christians to find their own voice, much less to be heard by Western Christians, who tend to ignore their very existence in their dealings with the Middle East. The World Council of Churches, which now numbers these ancient Oriental churches among its members, has become aware of the need to facilitate their own self-representation, rather than dominating them through Protestant church representatives based in the Middle East.

The Middle East Council of Churches, organized in 1974, has become such a voice for Arab Christians. It was preceded by the Orthodox Youth Movement, which was an important force in the revitalization of the indigenous Middle Eastern churches. Metropolitan George Khodr, presently bishop of Mount-Lebanon in the Greek Orthodox Church of Antioch and one of the founders of the Orthodox Youth Movement and its general secretary for many years, has emerged as one of the major spokespersons of an indigenous Arab Christianity. He is one of the authors of the 1967 statement by Middle Eastern theologians, entitled "What Is Required of the Christian Faith Concerning the Palestine Problem."[51]

The major emphasis of the statement is on the spiritual and universal meaning of Christian faith. Christianity is called to be a witness to God's salvific love for all human beings. Therefore it must reject any kind of nationalism based on religious, ethnic, or cultural exclusivism. Today this Christian commitment to a spiritual univer-salism is represented by the secularization of the state. Separation of religion and state resolves the confusion of religious faith with political citizenship that has plagued the monotheistic religions for so many centuries. Political communities must be committed to pluralism, religious and ethnic, giving full and equal citizenship to all those resident within their boundaries, without setting up hier-archies of majority and minority groups. For the Middle East, and for Israel in particular, this means that the optimum goal must be a secular, pluralist state where Christians, Jews, and Muslims can live together as equal citizens.

In their stress on the separation of civil and religious identities and on the creation of states with civil equality for all, regardless of religion or ethnicity, the Middle Eastern theologians are question-ing both Zionist and Muslim types of religious nationalism. The Zionist concept of a Jewish state has resulted in a quasi-theocratic type of ethnic exclusivity, where only Jews enjoy full citizenship. The resurgence of Muslim fundamentalism in the Islamic world pro-motes Islamic nationalism where non-Muslims or heterodox Mus-lims are reduced to inferior status.

The Middle Eastern theologians criticize the tendency of some Arab Christians to reject the Old Testament altogether because of its use by Zionists and their Christian supporters to sacralize the State of Israel. For them, this reflects a new form of the ancient Marcionite heresy that splits the Bible into a wrathful "Jewish" God of this world and a loving, Christian God of heaven. They insist that there is only one God revealed throughout the two Testaments. This one God is the Creator of all peoples, not the founder of ethnic separation.

The Jews were elected by God, and continue to be elected by God, as a paradigmatic people with a universal vocation to witness to this one God. Their vocation is summed up in, but not superseded by, Jesus Christ. The destruction of the ancient Temple and, with it, the ancient seat of Jewish national identity scattered the Jewish people among all nations to be witnesses to God among all people. They should be accepted among all people as civil and religious equals. This implies a dissolution of all tendencies to set up political enti-ties that are religously exclusive.

The theologians see Western Christianity (which, for them, includes Greek Orthodoxy) as having distorted its universal spiritual vocation by its merger with imperial and national states. Such mergers resulted in various forms of Christendom where Jews were persecuted. Such politicization of Christianity as Christendom is the root of anti-Semitism. By separation of church and state, Jews and Christians can live together as equals. They can witness in different ways to the universal God of the Bible, without confusing this witness with their political identities.

Zionism and Muslim nationalism represent parallel distortions of monotheistic religion into religious nationalism. The new resurgences of such religious nationalism in the Middle East are regressions from the authentic spiritual vocations of these religions. Discriminatory political systems arise where minorities—Arab Christians and Muslims in Israel, Christians and Jews in Muslim states—are inferiorized.

Western Christianity confused religion with politics and committed the crimes of anti-Semitism. It now wishes the Middle East to pay for these crimes by supporting an exclusively Jewish state. This has resulted in more than a million Arab refugees. The Jews, made refugees in Europe, should have been reintegrated into their former homes; instead, they were sent to Palestine to create a second injustice, this time against the Arabs.

But these states refused to carry out this act of justice. Because the Christians of Europe and of America denied their responsibility for a million Jews who were their brothers, they threw one million Arabs out of their homeland of Palestine. "What have you done to your brother?" In rejecting one million Jews and in dispelling one million Arabs, the Christians of the West have committed a double crime which cries to heaven for redress.[52]

The Arab Christian theologians deny the Zionist claim that Jewish peoplehood makes Jews a nation. They do not suggest that Jews are religiously inferior or that they should accept Jesus as their Messiah. Rather, Jews are seen has having transcended their earlier national form of existence and become a universal people with a distinct vocation to witness to the universal God, paralleling the Christian witness to Jesus Christ. The Promised Land, to which both Judaism and Christianity point in their messianic hope, is not a national territory but the Kingdom of Heaven, a transhistorical human destiny in the world to come.

The Jewish people is prophetic, not a nation, but "a witness of God among the nations...." The Jewish race was chosen to serve the Salvation of Humanity and not to establish itself in any particular religious or racial way. In the same fashion the Church is "called to serve the World and not to enfold itself in any particular cultural or religious shroud...." The vocation of the Jewish people is universalist, not particularist.

From the Christian point of view it is clear from this that the creation of an exclusively Jewish state of Israel goes directly against God's plan for the Jewish people and the World. Just as the creation of exclusively Christian states, in former times and today, was directly contrary to the calling of God and the Salvation of the world.[53]

The statement by the Middle Eastern theologians ends with some suggestions on the solution of the Palestinian problem. Christians should reject all anti-Semitism. This means every nation should integrate its Jewish citizens in the "full freedom of the children of God." For Christians to purge all anti-Semitism will eliminate the goad that gave rise to the parallel aberration among Jews of setting up a counterpart exclusive Jewish state. Zionism is, in effect, the mirror image of a previous anti-Semitic Christian exclusivity: "This people is the mirror of humanity. Their temptations are ours; our victory against all discrimination will be therefore their own."[54] Israel must then, in turn, work to eliminate its own Jewish exclusivity, which has been born and perpetuated in violence. This is not a question of toleration of minorities, but a modern pluralistic state—ethnic, religious, and social—for all the inhabitants of Palestine—Christians, Muslims, and Jews.

This will mean a true conversion for the modern state of Israel from racism to the universal vocation of the Jews that will make it:
· integrate all refugees who have been thrown out of their homes.
· make reparation toward them....
· accept that all the inhabitants of Palestine be considered citizens with full rights in their own homeland.
· promote active participation in the political life of Palestine without any discrimination for all of the inhabitants.
· use all the available resources for the development of all the citizens and those of the neighboring countries.
· submit to all international decisions.[55]

Palestinian Christians themselves have been the most invisible party in this whole Christian discussion. Several factors have made it difficult for Palestinian Christians to articulate a response to the situation that most immediately affects their lives. First, Palestinian Christians have been a minority community of about 10 percent, nonetheless they have been prominent in the leadership of the Palestinian community because of their greater opportunities for Western education than their Muslim counterparts have had. But they have also been more likely to emigrate under pressure, and so their numbers have dwindled to about 5 percent of the Palestinians in Israel and in the Occupied Territories. Also, their churches are divided among all the historic splits of Christendom: Old Catholics, Roman Catholic, Uniate, Eastern Orthodox, and Protestants. Many of their clergy has been foreigners from outside Palestine.

One Palestinian theologian who has attempted to articulate the dilemmas of biblical interpretation faced by the Palestinian Christians in Israel is Father Na'em Ateek, rector of the Arab-speaking congregation at St. George's Episcopal Cathedral in East Jerusalem. Many Palestinian and Arab Christians have found it almost impossible to use the Hebrew Scripture as part of their worship. The term *Israel* which occurs so frequently there, and which was historically understood by Christians to be the religious people of God's promise that was continued in the Christian church, now becomes painfully negative. The word *Israel* has now come to mean the State of Israel. This name now thunders with the military and territorial claims of the modern state that has established itself at the expense of Palestinian residents in the land.

Religious imagery drawn from Exodus also resounds with negative connotations for Eastern Christians. For an Arab Christian in Jerusalem, Bethlehem, or Nazareth, the message that God has elected Israel, led them from bondage in Egypt, conducted them through the Sinai and mandated their conquest of the land of Canaan now becomes a concrete religious justification of the conquest of the land by modern Israelis and the dispossession of Palestinians. Moreover, Jewish religious Zionists march around in the West Bank using these biblical texts in exactly that way.

The creation of the State of Israel, its history of appropriation of Palestinian land, and expulsion or repression of the Palestinian people have caused a crisis of belief for Palestinian and Arab Christians. Many have responded to this contradiction by refusing to use the Hebrew Scripture in their worship or sermons. Yet, since the language of Hebrew Scripture (Old Testament) is so interwoven with Christian theology and worship and is the background of the New Testament, this does not solve the problem. Father Na'em Ateek is engaged in developing the biblical hermeneutic for a Palestinian liberation theology that would address this dilemma.[56] In this theology, Ateek wishes to address three audiences: Palestinian Christians themselves, the global Christian community and, finally, the Jewish community.

For Palestinian Christians, the question raised by Zionist use of Scripture is not God's existence, but God's nature. Palestinian Christians assume that God exists; the troubling question is, "What kind of God exists?" Is God a God of war and vengeance, a tribal god who chooses one people, the Jews, at the expense of another people, the Palestinians? Ateek is clear that the true God is a God of justice, truth, and peace for all peoples, a God who calls all peoples into relations of justice and peace with one another. His biblical hermeneutic seeks to vindicate this view as the authentic biblical God. This means providing criteria for distinguishing between passages of the Bible that portray God as a tribal god (who sides with the Jews against other people) and those passages of Hebrew Scripture that point to a universal God of justice and peace for all people.

Ateek would distinguish three traditions in Hebrew Scripture. One is a tribalistic tradition that sees God as electing the Jews in an ethnically exclusive way, thus allowing for violent rejection of the other peoples in the land. Then, there is a prophetic tradition that criticizes the tribal tradition and moves toward a vision of God as a God of justice for all people. Finally, there is also the development of a legal tradition that enshrined patterns of Jewish particularity but that also relates Jews to other people in an ethical, justice-seeking way. The rabbinic tradition has developed this third line of Jewish tradition. Modern ethical Judaism was shaped by a Jewish appropriation of the Enlightenment and by the search for a more adequate ethical universalism.

Ateek sees Christianity as rooted in the prophetic, universalist tradition. He wishes as a Christian to dialogue with the second and third traditions of Judaism. Both communities need to renew the prophetic, universalist tradition against tendencies to regress toward nationalist and militarist patterns of religion. Ateek thus believes that there is progress and development of insight in biblical revelation. There are narrow, chauvinist, sinful views of people toward each other that shape their understandings of God into their own images. There are also better insights that call us to a fuller vision of God as Creator and Redeemer of all people. The two traditions, both found in Hebrew Scripture, are not equally authoritative: the tribal tradition must be rejected as bad theology and bad ethics.

This supercession of an ethical, universal understanding of biblical monotheism over a tribal, ethnocentric view of God does not, for Ateek, set Christianity against or above Judaism. More adequate insights into God's nature are not a matter of simple chronological progress. The sinful, tribalistic attitudes of the God of Joshua are still with us. Both Jews and Christians need to renew their better ethical traditions and overcome self-interested religious attitudes. The Book of Joshua remains in the Bible, not as adequate or normative tradition, but as a bad example of religious attitudes that need to be continually overcome.

But Ateek is concerned that Palestinian Christians not identify the tribalistic concept of God of the Book of Joshua with Hebrew Scripture as a whole. Palestinian Christians need to reclaim for themselves the universal God of truth and justice of the prophetic tradition. The God of the poor and the oppressed, whose voice cries out in the prophetic texts against the powerful who appropriate the land of the poor and steal the sustenance of the widow and orphan, is of the greatest relevance to the Palestinian. Here they find a God who is for them, who shares their agony, who demands justice for those who have been robbed and truth for those who have been victimized by lies and deceptions. This God is active in history to create a new era of justice and peace for all people.

Both Na'em Ateek and the authors of the statement of Middle Eastern theologians understand that the issues of relationship to Judaism and to the State of Israel cannot be split into a religious/secular, or theological/political dualism. There must be a unifying framework within which Christians distinguish the separate issues of relation to Judaism and relation to Zionism. That unifying framework is an understanding of God as a universal God of justice for all people. That universal God, on the one hand, demands that Christians relate to Jews and Judaism as a people and as a religious community of equal value with themselves. That same universal God also calls both Christians and Jews to question their tendencies to regress toward religious nationalism or ethnocentrism or to construe God as a God who elects one community exclusively. Jews and Christians are peer people of one God, called to live justly with each other.

This survey of Christian attitudes toward Judaism and toward Zionism suggests that, for much of Christianity, pro-Judaism and pro-Zionism are incompatible. Those Christian traditions most willing to accept the equality of Judaism as an autonomous, salvific path are also the ones most critical of Zionism, while Christian groups that are the most enthusiastic about Zionism maintain the traditional Christian view that a Jew cannot be saved unless converted to Christ. Willingness to accept the equality of Judaism goes with a universalism that is willing to see both Judaism and Christanity as instances of a universal faith, while pro-Zionism is related to an endorsement of an ethnocentric Jewish particularism as provisional and ultimately to be liquidated into a Christian particularism. The Arab Christians fall at the universalist end of this spectrum, while American fundamentalist Christians fall at the other end of the spectrum—for they believe in a god who elects one nation and one limited body of the saved to the exclusion of the rest of humanity.

7. Jewish and Christian Responses to the Holocaust: The Link to Zionism

Come, let us return to the Lord; for he has torn, that he may heal us: he
has stricken, and he will bind us up. After two days he will revive us; on
the third day he will raise us up, that we may live before him. . . . He will
come to us as the showers, as the spring rains that water the earth. . . . For
I desire steadfast love and not sacrifice, the knowledge of God, rather
than burnt offerings.

HOSEA 6:1–3, 6

In the midst of the Second World War, Adolf Hilter, leader of the
German people, conducted a systematic campaign to exterminate
European Jewry. This genocidal campaign was directed at all Jews,
on the basis of what was presumed to be a shared racial nature. It
did not matter if the Jew was male or female, infant or elderly, culturally assimilated into German or other Western European societies, or set apart by a traditional Jewish dress, speech, or way of life,
whether the Jew was secular or religious or even a convert to a Christian church. For Hitler, a Jew was a Jew. All belonged to one racial
nature, which he regarded as inimical to the presumed racial virtue
of the Germanic or Aryan race.

In Hitler's paranoid worldview these two races, Aryan and Jew,
were set apart, not simply as superior and inferior types of humans,
but as opposite ontological species of good and evil. The Aryan was
raised above the merely human to the heroic; the Jew was sunk
below the creaturely to the pestilent and the demonic. To exterminate the Jew was, in Hitler's mad fantasy world, to redeem the
Aryan from all danger of "contamination" by the forces of weakness,
whether mental, moral, or physical, and to inaugurate the Third
Reich, the Germanic millennial age of undiluted virility.

This crusade of redemption through genocide almost succeeded.
Six million Jews were annihilated. This meant not only more than

one-third of the Jews of the world, at that time. It also meant ninety percent of the rabbis and religious scholars of Eastern and Western Europe. The Holocaust pulled up the worlds of European Jewish culture by the roots. Although individuals may survive from these communities, these communities themselves can never be reconstituted. The more traditional Jews of the Eastern stetls were the least likely to escape. Although remnants of this traditional culture may have been transplanted to America or Israel, the Holocaust has left a void at the heart of the human community of peoples that can never be filled.

This enormity happened in the "heartland" of Western Europe, the land of Goethe, Beethoven, and Mozart, of Kant, Hegel, and Schelling, of Schleiermacher, Ritschl, and Troeltsch. It happened in the center of the Christian Enlightenment, from which has flowed the classics of modern literature and music, philosophy, theology, and biblical studies. It happened with the passive acquiesence or active participation of most Christians in Europe, and with no decisive protest from church leadership, Catholic or Protestant. Many individual Christians sought to save their Jewish neighbors, but official church bodies did not mobilize in protest. Even the Confessing Church in Germany limited its protest against Hitler to the heresy of a Nazi "cultural Christianity" and failed to mention anti-Semitism.[1]

For both Jews and Christians of the post-Holocaust period these events throw the viability of their traditions into question, but in quite different ways. Reflection on the meaning of the Holocaust was slow in coming. For almost two decades there was virtual silence from theologians, Christian or Jewish. Even the stories of survivors came slowly and hesitatingly. Elie Weisel's first book, *Night*, was published in Yiddish in 1956 and became available in French in 1958 and in English in 1960.

JEWISH HOLOCAUST THEOLOGY

RICHARD RUBENSTEIN

The first theologian to recognize the Holocaust as a major crisis for traditional theology was Richard Rubenstein in the mid-1960s. Rubenstein, a nonestablishment Jewish religious scholar, published

After Auschwitz: Radical Theology and Contemporary Judaism in 1966, questioning the possibility of faith in God after the Holocaust. Emil Fackenheim, a German Jew transplanted to Canada, courtesy of British detention camps, who has been writing primarily on Hegel and religious philosophy, took up Rubenstein's challenge and began to write about the possibility of religious faith after the Holocaust. Fackenheim himself admits, in an article published in May, 1970, in the *Christian Century*, that before 1967 he was "at work on a theology that sought to show that nothing unprecedented could call into question the Jewish faith — that it is essentially immune to all secular events between Sinai and the Messianic days."[2]

Rubenstein, in a reply to Fackenheim, published July 29, 1970, in the *Christian Century*, said that Fackenheim was the first establishment Jewish theologian to "agree with me concerning the unique and decisive character of Auschwitz for Jewish religious life." He went on to say that "at the time I wrote *After Auschwitz*, one could search through almost everything written by contemporary establishment theologians without finding the slightest hint that they were living in the same century as Auschwitz or the rebirth of Israel."[3]

This slowness of the Jewish theological world and, even more, the Christian theological world to respond to the Holocaust can have many explanations. There is the general aversion of theologians to respond to contemporary events. Perhaps there was the added impetus to restore, rather than further destablize, a world already deeply shaken by the events of the Second World War, with its revelations of Nazi death camps and also the first atom bombs dropped on two cities. There was the collective guilt of Christians, and even of U.S. and Israeli Jews, who preferred not to look too closely at their own complicity. There was a stunned horror before the face of vast evil and suffering that made most responses seem inappropriate. Silence, as Elie Wiesel has said, is the most appropriate response to the Holocaust.

But there are many kinds of silence and also various reasons for speech. It is not insignificant that the Holocaust, as a central theme for religious observance, "caught on" for American Jews after 1967, after the third Israeli-Arab war captured the West Bank, the Gaza Strip, the Golan Heights, and East Jerusalem for the State of Israel. This chapter on Jewish and Christian theological responses to the

Holocaust (responses given mainly by Americans or emigres to America) will focus primarily on the connection established by these theologians between the Holocaust and support for the State of Israel. There are others, perhaps more important, points that many of these theologians wish to make about the shape of religious faith after the Holocaust. These points will be mentioned briefly. But, for the purpose of this particular study of Zionism and the Palestinians, the central question will be to what extent the theologian sees support for the State of Israel as an integral part of a new worldview necessary after the Holocaust. How is the link between the two established, theologically or ethically?

For Rubenstein, Auschwitz brings to an end the possibility of belief in the God of traditional Judaism. This God was the Lord of history, providentially in charge of historical events and directing them to an ultimate redemptive end. Belief in the God of history demands a theodicy to justify the ways of God to humans. The central problem of theodicy, or the defense of the doctrine of a providential God of history, is why God allows unjust evil to happen. If God allows it, God is not wholly good. If God cannot prevent it, God is not omnipotent and hence not Lord of history. Theodicy attempts to break this conundrum by asserting that there are hidden reasons for God's allowance of evil. Out of such evil God is bringing good, although its full design is hidden from our eyes.

The classical strategy of the Jewish tradition for explaining evils that befall human beings, or, specifically, evils that befall the Jewish people, is to assert that these evils are punishment for sin. God is chastening God's people. When they learn from this punishment and become wholly obedient, then rewards and blessings will follow. For Rubenstein, no such theodicy can rationalize the enormity of the unjust suffering of the Holocaust or vindicate divine justice in the light of innocent Jewish victims. No possible sins could justify such vast destruction of innocent victims, victims chosen without regard to any actual particularities of moral or immoral activity but simply because of a shared identity as Jews.

The God who could will the destruction of the very people whom he had elected as his own would be a cosmic sadist. One could not honor or respect such a God but recoil from him in horror. This God of traditional Judaism is dead after Auschwitz. Henceforth, Jews must cease to look beyond history for rationality and justice that can make sense out of senseless evil. There is no divine plan that will make it all work out for the best in the end. Such hopes should be renounced, rather than justify the existence of a sadistic God who could use the Holocaust to further his ends.

Rubenstein also believes that Jews should abandon the idea of special election or chosenness by God. They must cease to see themselves as paradigmatic of humanity as a whole and of human relation to God. Such notions of Jewish specialness have created cycles of self-inflation, gentile hostility to or over-identification with these Jewish claims of chosenness, with their denouement of competitive violence against the Jews who taught Gentiles such an idea. Rubenstein particularly sees Christians as the Gentiles who sought to claim for themselves this Jewish idea of being God's chosen and, in the process, to deny this claim to Jews. Christian anti-Semitism is thus the underside of a Christian competitive relationship to Jewish claims of divine chosenness.[4] Rubenstein would have Jews accept their particularity, but as one particularity among others. Jews are special in the same way that each people claim their own uniqueness. Rubenstein seeks to "normalize" Jewish identity, as one cultural community among others.

In keeping with his Freudian interpretation of collective psychology, Rubenstein views civilization pessimistically. In a subsequent book, *The Cunning of History*, he denies the uniqueness of the Holocaust. Rather, the Holocaust is an outstanding expression of a general trend of modern bureaucratic technological societies and sovereign states.[5] While modernity has brought the human capacity to express arts and skills to a higher level of prowess, it is at the same time perfecting the arts of mass death. Nazi extermination of the Jews is not an expression of the outbreak of irrational passions but rather the perfection of bureaucratically achieved extermination. The danger of the human metropolis is that it will move, more and more, toward this finale as necropolis, the kingdom of objectification and annihilation. To avoid this, Rubenstein speaks of becoming a political conservative who seeks to avoid redundant people in contemporary society whom the state will wish to annihilate.[6]

But, underneath Rubenstein's pessimistic account of history and technological civilization, there lurks the romantic striving to break free and return from historical alienation to nature. It is in this context that he introduced his interpretation of Zionism and the reclaiming of a Jewish state after the Holocaust. The Jew of rabbinic Judaism, with his belief in a transcendent God of commandments and punishments, is the alienated Jew, the Jew in a state of exile or estrangement from embodiment. This self-alienated Jew was the Jew of Diaspora, the Jew in exile among the nations.

But lurking under the ethical Jew, with his self-estranging ethics and punishing God, is the natural Jew, integrated into the rhythms of nature, the seasons, and the life cycle. Much of this natural or "pagan" Jewishness Rubenstein would see as derivative from the Canaanite background of ancient Hebrew religion, which Jewish tradition repressed but preserved in its festivals. The Zionist is the Jew who has returned from exile, not only in the political sense of statelessness, but also from exile from "his" own natural embodiment. (Rubenstein's thought is androcentric, so we have followed his male generic language here.)

The Zionist is restored both to his relationship to his sexuality and to his community, rooted in his historical homeland. He (she?) has returned to the bosom of his particular part of mother earth from which all come and all shall return at death. Rubenstein's views seem to have been influenced by the "Canaanite" movement among Israelis. The Canaanites claimed to be, not Jews, but Israelis as a national ethnic identity.[7] Israeli dance and folk music represent this reintegration of the Jew with his nonrational collective embodiment in Israel.

Rubenstein goes on to suggest that the real deity that exists is not the Lord of history but rather the cosmic matrix, the void of nothingness from which all things spring and to which they return at death, the nonethical God (dess?) of natural fertility. This idea coincides with Rubenstein's description of himself as a "Catholic" Jew rather than a "Protestant" Jew. For Rubenstein, what binds him to Judaism is not its ethical commandments but rather its priestly or cultic side. These are the collective rituals that bind the community in collective solidarity, not to solve the human dilemma of ultimate meaninglessness, but rather to share it together, and thus to comfort one another in a common affliction.[8]

This celebration of the Zionist as the natural Jew rings a little hollow twenty-two years later. Israel as a spartan society of ever-redoubled militarism and repressive concern for "national security" looks more like Rubenstein's fears of the death machine of the modern sovereign state, rather than the happy Hebrew peasant, dancing at the harvest festivals. One wonders if Rubenstein fails to realize how closely his own romantic vision of the release of the natural Jew corresponds to the Nazi dream of the release of the natural German, once the alienating urban Jew was cleared out of the picture. In 1930s Germany, the dream of return to spontaneous, nonethical folk-culture masked the very different reality of the death machine. Rubenstein's dream of folk-Zionism seems to be an integral part of a similar contradiction.

EMIL FACKENHEIM

Although Emil Fackenheim agrees with Rubenstein that the Holocaust has created a crisis for traditional Jewish theology, he vehemently disagrees with Rubenstein's Freudian methodology and his demythologizing of Jewish chosenness. For Fackenheim it is a blasphemy to say the Holocaust is simply one expression among others of "tendencies of Western civilization in the twentieth century."[9] Fackenheim rejects comparisons between the Holocaust and other modern evils, such as Hiroshima, Vietnam, or black enslavement. Auschwitz was an evil of a different order from any other human evil. It is evil without remainder or purpose, evil for evil's sake. It stands out beyond all other relative human evils as unique, absolute.

This means for Fackenheim that the Holocaust also calls the Jew back to Jewish uniqueness and particularity, from all attempts to be assimilated into generic universals. Jewish faith must be rebuilt by reclaiming a primary commitment to this Jewish unique status of chosenness and its ongoing continuation. It is by committing oneself to raising Jewish children after the Holocaust that one reaffirms one's Jewish faith in the ongoing life of the people Israel. By raising Jewish children one refuses to give new victories to Hitler.[10] This commitment carries over to the collective life of the Jewish people. It is by committing oneself to the defense of the State of Israel that one commits oneself to Jewish survival as a nation.

Through these commitments to ongoing Jewish life, familial and political, one can also reaffirm faith in the eclipsed face of God. One can redeem God from the abyss of Auschwitz by affirming faith in Jewish survival. Auschwitz overcame all distinctions between the religious and the secular Jew. All Jews who commit themselves to ongoing Jewish life witness against Satan. They witness against the triumph of evil and death over life and hope and hence implicitly prove that the bond between God and the Jewish people is stronger than Satan. Fackenheim does not dispute Rubenstein's assertation that one cannot construct a theodicy of the Holocaust itself. But he believes that Jews can rebuild faith in God and hope for the victory of life over death through human redemptive acts.

In an essay entitled "The Holocaust and the State of Israel: Their Relation," Fackenheim constructs a theological relationship between these two events that he would see as total and unbreakable. This is not a causal nexus between the two events. Fackenheim does not suggest that the State of Israel happened "because of the Holocaust," either in the sense that God allowed the State of Israel to redeem Israel from the Holocaust or that the world community did so out of remorse or pity. Rather, the bond between the two events is established by the overwhelming and continuous response of Jews themselves, whose commitment to the State of Israel is their negation of the threat to their existence poised by the Holocaust. Fackenheim makes this relation total and exclusive. He says "The heart of every *authentic* response to the Holocaust—religious and secularist, Jewish and non-Jewish—is a commitment to the autonomy and security of the State of Israel."[11] Presumably this means that any Jewish and Christian response to the Holocaust that is not focused on the autonomy and security of the State of Israel is inauthentic.

Fackenheim sees the founding of the State of Israel as "the beginning of the dawn of our redemption."[12] In traditional rabbinic thought the Jewish people would only be restored in their homeland by an act of divine intervention in history, by the coming of the Messiah. Fackenheim concurs with those modern Jewish thinkers who reject this distinction between human effort and divine action. Human effort can, in effect, overcome divine inaction and make a beginning of redemption within history. The heroic efforts that have gone into founding the state cannot be explained simply by human causation within ordinary historical developments. There is a miraculous element of these events that could do such deeds as reunite a people scattered all over the world and rent apart by cultural gaps of centuries, revive an ancient language as a national language, and create self-government and self-defense in the face of overwhelming odds. These heroic acts are, for Fackenheim, an indication that Zionism represents a human will "in touch with the Absolute."[13]

Fackenheim creates a direct and dangerous symbolic relationship between Jewish resistance to the revelation of the demonic in the Holocaust and their present resistance to the Arabs, who would deny them their security and their state. In Fackenheim's language the Arabs are turned into Nazi surrogates. By fighting the Arab "enemies" of Israel, one fights the Nazis. He paints two pictures of the Jew in the face of the absolute evil of the Holocaust. One is the calm, dignified rabbi who insists on praying Kiddush Hashem for his flock before the Nazi began to shoot them in their mass grave. The second picture is that of a butcher who leapt out of the grave and sunk his teeth in the throat of the Nazi officer and hung on until the Nazi died. These two pictures represent redemptive acts that are complementary to each other, the one of a transcendent goodness in the face of absolute evil, the other of absolute will to refuse to let evil triumph.[14]

For Fackenheim, the Israelis represent the collective will of the butcher who has leapt out of the grave, while the Arabs have become the surrogates for the Nazi officer into whose throat they sink their teeth. In them, Jewish powerlessness is overcome, and Jewish redemption begins. In 1943, Mordecai Anielewicz, a leader of the Warsaw ghetto uprising, perished in the flames with the satisfaction that Jewish passivity has been breached and Jewish self-defense had begun. A kibbutz in Israel was named for him that same year. Five years later a small group of members of Kibbutz Yad Mordecai held off an invading Egyptian army in a battle critical for the survival of the Jewish state. Thus does Fackenheim make the direct connection between the Warsaw uprising and the battle against the Arabs in 1948. The spirit of the leaders of the Warsaw ghetto has risen and is present in the members of the kibbutz defending their state against the Egyptians.[15]

This transference of the unsuccessful resistance against the Nazis to the contemporary conflict with the Arabs represents a dangerous mystification of the issues involved in the State of Israel and its conflicts with the Arabs. By making the Arabs the surrogates of the Nazis, defined as revelations of Satan, it becomes impossible to see the Arabs as fellow human beings. One can not discuss the differences between Israelis, Arab states, and Palestinians in terms of relative and negotiable differences. One is transported to the mythical plane of the battle between pure goodness and absolute evil. The Arabs are not perceived as having specific objections to the political arrangements of the Jewish state but rather a Satanic desire to continue the Holocaust and to destroy the "Jewish people," an idea completely foreign to Arab and Islamic tradition.[16]

Contemporary Jewish rhetoric speaks constantly of the possibility of the failure of the Jewish state as "another Holocaust," as though the issue were absolute life and death of all Jews rather than relative and historical reforms in a political organization of an existing state or states. This mythical linking of the Holocaust and Israel as absolute death and absolute life, a contest between God and Satan, is a great disservice to both events. While the Holocaust may come close to being a revelation of the demonic, Hiroshima surely also was such a revelation of the demonic as well. Fackenheim's refusal to link the Holocaust with other such events of mass murder prevents the linking of Jews and Gentiles in solidarity in a shared struggle for human survival.

Moreover, the State of Israel is looking more and more unredemptive for Jews. It was a sign of negation of the existence of the Palestinians from its beginning. To turn Palestinian villagers — men, women, and children, being driven out of their country in 1948, so their land could be expropriated for a Jewish state "clean" of Arabs — into surrogates for Satan is to add the ultimate insult to injury. Palestinian exile is the sign of contradiction against all efforts to make the State of Israel a messianic sign. The test of a messianic sign is that it signals overcoming of evil, not the release of new evils. The founding of the State of Israel does not pass this crucial test. Neither does the founding of other modern states, especially colonial states founded by Westerners in lands already inhabited by native people.

The State of Israel needs to be brought down from its theological heights of absolutized redemption from absolutized evil and seen as a human state with all its defects. Its critics may wish that it had never existed, but this is not to be equated with a wish that Jews not exist. Today these critics are calling, not for its annihilation, but for its adjustment in relative political terms, so that other people can exist within and alongside it. The claim of messianic status is thus the barrier, not the basis, for those relative reforms that might make it less of a sign of evil for Palestinians. When Jews also are able to see such reforms, that allow both people to coexist, as a positive sign for themselves also, then perhaps we can speak authentically of a "sign" of redemption.

IRVING GREENBERG

Irving Greenberg is director of the National Jewish Center for Learning and Leadership in New York City. Greenberg wishes to synthesize radical insights about the crisis of God-language and human responsibility for redemption, found in Rubenstein and Fackenheim, with more traditional Jewish religious language and with the ethics of American Jewish liberalism. Greenberg speaks in the calm, judicious tones of one who wants to bring the best of everything together in balance. He speaks for an American Jewish establishment that has increasingly moved from a progressive to neoconservative stance in domestic and foreign politics.

In a major address given at the International Symposium on the Holocaust held at St. John the Divine Cathedral in New York City, June 3–6, 1974, Greenberg discussed the challenges to both traditional Jewish and Christian theology from the Holocaust.[17] Both Judaism and Christianity, he said, were religions of redemption. Both hope that the evils of human history will be finally overcome by divine salvific action. Both base their hopes that goodness and life will win over evil and death on foundational paradigms of redemption in the past that shape subsequent ways of life and self-understanding.

For the Jews, the foundational paradigmatic event is the Exodus from slavery in Egypt and the giving of the covenant on Sinai. For Christians, it is Easter, the revelation of the Resurrection of the Crucified One. In the light of Easter, the Crucifixion becomes not simply a meaningless evil but a divine act of atonement for sin. Both religions insulate themselves from further revelations or crises in history by living between this foundational paradigm and their expected fulfillment in the messianic deliverance at the end of history. The Holocaust challenges these Jewish and Christian strategies of insulation from history. For Jews, the Holocaust threatens the basic faith in a God who has entered into a permanent covenant with the Jewish people. There can be no covenant if there is no covenant people. There can be no God of the covenant if that God would will or allow the covenant people to be exterminated.

An even more devastating challenge is given to Christianity by the Holocaust. For Christians have not been innocent victims but collaborators with the Holocaust. Christianity was the major root of that "teaching of contempt" for Jews and Judaism that was translated by Nazism into secular terms as anti-Semitism. Christianity not only claimed to hope for a deliverance from evils in the future messianic advent but to already have experienced its foundations in Jesus. To say that Jesus is the Christ is to say that we already have received the down payment on messianic times. But a Christianity that, not only produced individual Christian sinners, but that, collectively, could be a prime source of genocide for the Jewish people has perhaps lost the last shreds of credibility in its claims to be a beginning of messianic fulfillment. It has been revealed as a font of new evils, rather than of human hope.

Greenberg also perceives in the Holocaust a challenge to modern secular messianisms of the Enlightenment, scientific rationality and liberal universalism. All these secular gods of modern civilization failed in the death camps. The claims of progress through scientific rationality turned out to be a mere mask for racist destruction of a despised people. Science provided the tools of mass murder. Nor did world Jewry rise to the occasion, but everywhere Jews outside of Europe proved more concerned about their own well-being in their own countries than with the fate of their brothers and sisters in Europe.

The failure of human projects of redemption, whether religious or secular, points also to an absence of the divine presence in our experience. We live in a time of the silence of God. For Greenberg this does not mean a denial of God's existence. Here Greenberg speaks more in the mystical Jewish language of Elie Weisel, rather than the demythologizing language of Rubenstein.[18] We have entered into a profound religious silence that no longer knows how to speak adequately about God. In the light of the Holocaust, all our past assertions about God and how God is acting in history have become questionable.

For Greenberg, new tentative ways of speaking about God must grow experimentally from human redemptive acts. Greenberg speaks of this cautiously and not with the absolute tones of commands issued from Sinai assumed by Fackenheim. Humans must show by real actions on behalf of life that faith in human goodness is possible. Through building up the signs of commitment to life, one may begin to believe that there is a divine life and goodness that is stronger than human evil and violence.

Greenberg sees commitment to the State of Israel as one such sign that hope is possible. It shows not only that the Jews arose from the Holocaust to affirm their collective survival, it also brings a closure to those efforts to snuff out Jewish collective life that began almost nineteen hundred years ago, with the Roman defeat of the Jewish national uprisings and the destruction of Jerusalem. Unlike Fackenheim, Greenberg wishes to balance Jewish particularity and Jewish universalism, the concerns of the State of Israel and the concerns of the Jews of the Diaspora. Jews today, together with all human religious cultures, must seek to overcome those denegrating stereotypes that deny full and equal human dignity to others. "This is the overriding command and essential criterion for religious existence today." Whoever joins in the work of the creation and rehabilitation of the image of God in one another, by implication, also rehabilitates the presence of God in the world and in history.[19]

In subsequent writings, Greenberg has developed what he calls the "third age" of Jewish history that begins with the Holocaust and the State of Israel. The first age of biblical Jewish history was one of the direct presence of the voice of God in the midst of his people. The second rabbinic age was one of a mediated presence through the Law and the teachers. The third age must be one of holy secularity. Jews, having overcome their powerlessness, claim the power to assure their own survival. At this point Greenberg begins to start to sound like a Niebuhrian political pragmatist. He says that the possession of political power can never provide perfect moral virtue. Jews need to adapt themselves from utopian expectations to pragmatism and ethical ambiguity in pursuit of their justifiable goals. Sometimes it is necessary to use immoral means for moral ends. (One wonders what he means by this: the bombing of civilians in refugee camps?)

Greenberg speaks of secular monuments to Jewish life replacing religious ones; the new temples are Yad Vashem (memorial of the victims of the Holocaust) and the Diaspora museum in Israel. In America, Jewish agencies supplement the synagogue as expressions of the Jewish community assembled together. Greenberg accepts the close alliance of the foreign and domestic policies of these Jewish agencies with neo-conservative American policies. He says that Jews should approach all policy questions by asking, Is it good for the Jews? — and should assert their group self-interest without apologies and without illusions.[20] Greenberg declares that Palestinians can be allowed national sovereignty over their own state, only in the distant future, if they manifest their intention to live in peace with the Israelis over an extended period of time.

As Marc Ellis, a progressive Jewish theologian, has put it, Greenberg seems to have adopted an obfuscating religious language for American and Israeli *Realpolitik*.[21] To assume that such policies are signs of global redemption is to assume a Western colonialist posture toward Palestinians and Third World peoples' desires for self-determination. White Westerners apparently are able to use power responsibly, while Palestinians, Africans, and Latin Americans need to be kept under the guardianship of their superiors and only allowed internal self-government in their "homelands," while their external political and economic affairs are controlled by those who have assumed the "white man's burden."

For Greenberg, Palestinians are not Satan. But they are reduced to undisciplined children who can be allowed some rights to the extent that they learn to control their irrational outbursts of temper. One would never guess from such paternalistic language that there were issues of justice involved.

CHRISTIAN HOLOCAUST THEOLOGY

Christian responses to the Holocaust were even slower to develop than Jewish ones. Moreover, in contrast with the Jewish community, those Christians who have made this a central theme of their thought remain isolated individuals. It is true that church bodies, both Catholic and Protestant, have felt the need to respond collectively to the Holocaust. As was seen in the previous chapter, at the Second Vatican Council, a document on the relationship of the Roman Catholic church and the Jews focused on rejecting the concept of deicide. The death of Jesus was said to be the responsibility of some Jewish persons (as well as Gentiles) in the first century. This does not connote any collective guilt of the Jewish people, either at the time or in ongoing history.[22]

Protestant responses have focused on the question of mission to the Jews. This was central to the statement of the German Evangelical Church that appeared in 1975.[23] This statement confessed the historical complicity of Christianity with anti-Semitism. It pledged to oppose anti-Semitism, including that anti-Semitism that assumes the form of anti-Zionism. Support for the independence and security of the State of Israel was declared to be, not simply the recognition of a human need and achievement, but an event in the salvation history of the people of God. But the statement stopped short of full rejection of a superior salvific status for Christianity. By implication, Jews remain religiously inferior as long as they have not responded to the revelation of Jesus as the Christ.

A number of denominations have developed statements on Jewish-Christian relations and also have developed programs to purge their denominational, liturgical, and catechetical material of anti-Judaism.[24] Yet, despite these gestures, the issue cannot be said to have become a deep concern for Christians, as it is for Jews. Those theologians who have taken up this issue as central for their theology are exceptional, rather than representative of their church communities. Three such figures will be discussed: A. Roy Eckardt (together with his wife, Alice), Franklin Littell, and Paul Van Buren. These figures have been selected because they have made a revised relation of Christianity to Judaism in the light of the Holocaust determinative for their whole theological enterprise (Van Buren more recently so — in the last ten years — while Littell and the Eckardts have been working on this concern since the 1960s).

For Jews, the central theological question posed by the Holocaust is theodicy — the question of divine justice, or whether it is possible to speak of a just God working in history after the Holocaust. The question for Christianity arises from Christian culpability for almost two millennia of anti-Semitism, which fed the hatred and indifference that made the Holocaust in "Christian" Europe possible. If Jews, or some Jews, ask about the silence of God, the failure of God to act to save his people, Christians must ask about the silence of "man," specifically Christians, who not only failed to act to save their Jewish neighbors but, in many cases, aided and abetted the violence.

Some more Orthodox Jewish theologians, such as Eliezer Berkovits, would say that the question raised by the Holocaust is not "where was God?" but "where was man?"[25] Berkovits would explain the possibility of radical evil in history by a voluntary withdrawal of divine omnipotence in God's act of creation, which makes possible human freedom and choice. Thus the Holocaust is an extreme example of humanity using its freedom to make the evil rather than the good choice, but it does not disturb the fundamental framework of Jewish understanding of God.

However, for Christians, this question of human culpability is more radical since it is also a specifically Christian culpability. Most Nazis were not Christians, but neopagans. But their neopaganism was rooted in and fed upon a European Christian background of scapegoating the Jews as the "cause of our misfortune." It is this Christian background of a religious anti-Judaism, translated by modern racists into anti-Semitism, for which Christianity must take responsibility. Christians must ask whether there is not a deeply buried, false theology, going back even to the New Testament itself, that has constructed Christian relationship to the Jews and Judaism in a hostile and antagonistic way.

Is it possible to excise the roots of this Christian anti-Judaism without pulling up foundations of Christian faith itself? As *Faith and Fratricide* puts the question, is it possible to affirm that Jesus is the Christ without, at the same time, proclaiming a negative and supercessionary relationship to Judaism as the "old" faith that has failed to accept its own transcendence?[26] If, as was argued in that volume, Christology and anti-Judaism are interwoven, not only recently, but within the New Testament itself, then anti-Semitism cannot be dismissed simply as a product of an ancient or modern "paganism." Whether or not some forms of ancient or modern paganism were or are also anti-Jewish is not the central issue here. But rather, Christians have to take responsibility for a particular kind of anti-Judaism, rooted in a Christian rivalry with Judaism and a desire, simultaneously, to inherit and supercede God's election of the Jews.

This anti-Judaism cannot be regarded as unrelated to political and racial anti-Semitism because it was originally religious, rather than racial. This religious rivalry was translated in Christendom into a series of ecclesiastical and imperial laws that segregated Jews into a despised status in Christian societies.[27] It is this fifteen centuries of hostility to Jews, incarnated into political and social systems in Christian societies, that is the background of modern political anti-Semitism. Thus Christian anti-Judaism is not simply a matter of theological "ideas" but of ideas that have borne hostile social fruit for more than a millennia and a half.

Christian affirmation of ideas, such as Jesus' status as the fulfillment of Jewish messianic hope and the Church as the "New Israel" that supercedes God's covenant with the Jews, is integrally intertwined with a Christian teaching of contempt for Jews and Judaism. This theological revision is not simply a matter of abstract "ideas" but rather of ideas that have consequences. For example, if Christianity takes seriously that God's covenant with the Jews has not been superceded by Christ, and that the Torah continues to be the expression of Jewish faithfulness to God, then it cannot continue to organize programs of evangelization of Jews. Christianity must relate institutionally, not just as individual Christians, to institutional Judaism as a religion having its own salvific efficacy. It is not in need of Christian evangelization in order to come into a fullness of relationship to God.

Although there are many critical aspects of this rethinking of Christian identity that are implied by such a shift in relationship to Judaism—aspects that were delineated in the last chapter of *Faith and Fratricide*[28]—in these pages we will focus on one particular question that was only slightly touched upon in that book.[29] To what extent does a Christian rethinking of its identity necessitate, theologically, a partisan support for the State of Israel as a Jewish state? This question was not addressed in the earlier book because, at that time, it was not apparent that anyone would draw such a connection between Christian rejection of anti-Judaism and partisan support for the State of Israel. It was assumed that the implications of a Christian critique of anti-Judaism pointed primarily toward a reevaluation of Christian-Jewish relations as religious systems; Christians needed to move from a supercessionary to a peer relation between Christianity and Judaism, as religions of salvation of equivalent value.

Such a conceptual shift in relationship between Christianity and Judaism as religions would have political implications. It would imply equal rights of Jewish organizations with Christian ones, as well as of Jewish persons with Christians within pluralistic secular societies. However, it was not evident that this implied that Jews should also be seen as a nation that had a unique right to have a

Jewish nation-state (Jewish in both the ethnic and the theocratic sense). This was and is a kind of nationalism that we reject for Christianity or indeed for any religious-ethnic group.

However, it has become apparent to us that many Jews now assume that Jewish identity resides, not primarily, or even at all, in a religious communal identity, but rather in a national-ethnic one. For them this national-ethnic identity is to be expressed normatively in a Jewish state. Not to accept the Zionist Jewish state is, therefore, to reject the core of Jewishness. For anyone, including Jews, to be anti-Zionist is to be anti-Semitic. Thus, it is becoming less and less possible to differentiate between a religious and civil libertarian rejection of anti-Semitism and the endorsement of a Jewish state. It is said that anyone who wishes to purge themselves of anti-Semitism must be pro-Zionist.

The three Christian theologians whom we have selected to discuss in this chapter have concurred with this fusion of Jews as a religious community and as an ethnic-national one. They have accepted the thesis that anti-Zionism is anti-Semitism.

A. ROY ECKARDT AND ALICE L. ECKHARDT

Roy and Alice Eckardt have expressed their views of a necessary Christian Zionism, in response to the Holocaust, in several volumes, such as *Long Night's Journey into Day: Life and Faith After the Holocaust* (1982) and *Jews and Christians: The Contemporary Meeting* (1986).[30] For the Eckardts, a full and adequate Christian response to the Holocaust necessitates a revolutionary revision in Christian theology. All notions that Judaism has an inferior moral or salvific content vis-à-vis Christianity must be rejected. This means rethinking the basic interpretation of the Resurrection and Jesus' status as the Messiah. Jesus cannot be said to have risen from the dead in a physical sense (and there is no other way to interpret this original Christian assertion) or to be in an already achieved messianic status, because the world is unredeemed.[31] The Eckardts take seriously the Jewish tradition that the coming of the Messiah does not refer to simply a changed spiritual relation to God but the total salvation of the earth from evil. Since this obviously has not happened, it is not possible to say that the Messiah has come. Jewish rejection of Jesus as the Christ is, not unfaithfulness, but faithfulness to God. It means that Jews remain faithful to the one covenant that God has made with them. They continue to hope and work for a future redemption that has not yet come.

For the Eckardts, this unification of the religious and the political, which they see as a central Jewish insight that Christians need to learn from their Jewish "elder brothers," also has implications for a Christian support of Israel as a Jewish state. The Eckardts do not wish to make absolutist claims for a relationship of Jewish peoplehood to a divinely given land in Palestine. They would assert that no people has an absolute claim to anything. All human claims to states or land are partial and relative. They would particularly reject the fundamentalist type of Christian Zionism that assimilates a Jewish return to the land with a Christian dispensationalist eschatology. They characterize such as theology as ultimately anti-Semitic, since the Jewish state is celebrated only as a step to final Jewish conversion or annihilation.[32]

While seeking to avoid a "territorial fundamentalism," the Eckardts nevertheless characterize any criticism of Israel, from either the Arabs or Christian peace activists, such as the Quakers, as anti-Semitic. It is motivated by a fundamental hostility to Jewish self-determination.[33] They assert that "the worst fate that can befall any people is to be bereft of political sovereignty."[34] Jews have a right to a state because every people has a right to political self-determination. To reject a Jewish state thus is rooted in a anti-Semitic ideology that believes that Jews, of all the peoples of the world, are to be homeless and powerless wanderers among other people and are not to have a home (state) of their own. Thus, for the Eckardts, the Jews don't have a special God-given right to a state above other people. They have the same right as every people to a state. This is the fundamental base for defending one's existence against hostile enemies.

However, the Eckardts fail to examine carefully whether such a universalistic identification of every ethnic group with an autonomous nation-state is really realizable or desirable in a world where forced or voluntary migration patterns have diffused ethnic groups and mingled them in the same territories. They compare the Jewish right to self-determination with the Black Power movement in the United States,[35] failing to notice that black Americans are not asking for a separate black nation in some autonomous territory within North America. Nor are they asking to return to found an Afro-American state in Africa (this was already done in Liberia with consequences somewhat analogous to Zionism).[36] Rather, they are asking for equal civil rights within an ethnically pluralistic state, where being an American is not construed to mean membership in a particular religious or ethnic-racial group.

If all peoples should have political sovereignty, then one should imagine that the Eckardts would also support a Palestinian state. However, they refuse to draw this conclusion from their universal principle of the right of every people to national self-determination. They do so by using selective and biased information about Palestinians. Palestinians are said to already have a state, which is the state of Jordan, so they don't need a state. Palestinians in the Occupied Territories, the West Bank, Gaza, and the Golan Heights, are ignored completely, and Palestinians within Israel are said to already have full and equal rights with Israelis (which, of course, is not the case). So the only "Palestinian question" is that of Palestinian refugees in other Arab areas, such as Lebanon and Syria. Their prolonged refugee status is caused entirely by Arabs who have "manipulated" the "Palestinian problem" to forment hostility to Israel.[37] Presumably the solution to the problem of these Palestinians is to be allowed to move to Jordan.

FRANKLIN LITTELL

Franklin Littell has developed his views of anti-Zionism as anti-Semitism in a number of writings. His *Crucifixion of the Jews* is representative of his perspective. Littell's earlier book, *The Anabaptist View of the Church* (1952), established him as a major advocate of the free church tradition of ecclesiology. Any unity of church and state is an apostasy to the authentic understanding of the Christian Church as a counterculture that must stand as a prophetic critique of all worldly power systems. The Church is a community set apart from the state as witness to an alternative redemptive lifestyle of the Kingdom of God, characterized by pacifism, egalitarianism, and communal sharing.[38]

Littell brings this free church critique of Christendom to his battle against anti-Semitism in the Christian tradition. Christian failure to reject Hitler is a radical instance of a "culture Christianity" that sells out the gospel to a pagan nationalism and idolatrous sacral state.[39]

However, these free church principles come out oddly when confronted by what Littell sees as a necessity to support the Jewish state in order to be fully affirmative of Jewish identity. Jews in medieval and Reformation Europe were a people set apart, without power in Christian theocratic states. He can readily identify this type of Jewish life with his free church principles. Such Jewish communities are an analogous type of "counterculture," witnessing to redemption apart from existing political systems. Indeed, Christianity should have seen this Jewish counterculture within Christian states as a faithful witness to what the Church was supposed to be.[40]

However, Jews in a Jewish state are obviously not a counterculture within that state but rather a fusion of religious and ethnic identity with a state. Israel is a quasi-sacral or quasi-theocratic state, exactly everything Littell supposedly opposes for Christians. Littell covers up this contradiction in three ways. First, he scores any criticism of Israel, whether from Arabs or from Quakers, as anti-Semitism. Like the Eckardts, he identifies any opposition to a Jewish state as a lingering expression of an ideology that decrees misery and powerlessness for Jews as normative. Jewish power or self-determination is seen as a threat to this Christian prescription of Jewish misery.[41]

Second, he identifies Jewishness with a social, historical community, not just a "spiritual identity," scoring what he sees as a false Christian spiritualization of peoplehood. He then identifies this idea that Jews are a community with having a state of their own. Unlike the Eckardts, Littell is willing to give a special or unique status to this Jewish right to a state. It is not simply that every people should have a state but rather that the Jewish people uniquely have a right to a state on a particular, God-given piece of land. This expresses a special promise of God to the Jews. God chose the Jewish people as an ethnic community and promised them a land. Thus an identification of peoplehood and land are unique to the Jews. While a sacral ethnic state would be wrong for everyone else, it has been mandated by God for the Jews. The Jews are set apart from all other people as the only people whose ethnic identity is mandated by God and who have been given a land in which to express this ethnic identity.[42]

Littell simply ignores the Palestinians. All objections to the State of Israel from the Arab side is presumed to be motivated by baseless hatred. It is even suggested that the presence of the Jewish state challenges Islam, since Islam represents an extreme example of a sacral political order that fuses religion, culture, and the state.[43] It is hard to understand how the Jewish state could challenge this idea in Islam, if it is doing essentially the same thing. But Littell does not ask how Israel can be, simultaneously, a de-politicized "countercul-ture" within the Middle East, over against the Islamic idea of a Mus-lim state, and, at the same time, be the only divinely mandated instance of an ethnic theocratic state.

PAUL VAN BUREN

A Christian Zionism, which is present only in sketchy form in the Eckardts and Littell, has been fully developed in the recent writings of Paul Van Buren. Van Buren is engaged in a thoroughgoing revi-sion of Christian theological identity in which Christian Zionism assumes a central role. Van Buren is developing his theology of Jewish-Christian relations in a four-part *magnum opus*. The second volume, *A Christian Theology of the People Israel*, presents his basic view of the Jewish people and the relationship of the Christian covenant to the Jewish covenant.[44]

Van Buren's theology was deeply shaped by the theology of Karl Barth. Barth shaped his theological system around a christological monism. Barth's neoorthodox theology rejected the liberal univer-salism of nineteenth-century Protestant theologians, such as Schleiermacher. The doctrine of original sin was again taken with radical seriousness. All human beings are fallen and alienated from God and so lack any natural connection with God. Only through Christ has connection with God been restored. This view makes it impossible to give a positive evaluation of any non-Christian reli-gion. Judaism, at best, could have only a preparatory role in the economy of salvation. But, without faith in Christ, Jews remain in darkness.[45]

Van Buren seems to have transferred this monistic concept of his-torical revelation to the covenant of God with the Jewish people. God (or at least the only God that Jews and Christian know) has made himself known only in one way, as the God who chose the peo-ple Israel as his people.[46] The covenant of God with Israel at Sinai is God's foundational and normative work in Creation and the redemption of Creation. All other work of God in history (it is not apparent that God is at work in nature at all, according to Van

Buren's rejection of all "natural" theology) flows exclusively from this one elect center.

Van Buren typically uses the metaphor of light and darkness for the relationship of this one revelatory center to gentile peoples who lack this elect relation to God. He draws this metaphor, not only from its Christian usage, but also from its use in Jewish messianic Kabbalism.[47] The covenant of God with Israel is not only the one place where God is revealed but also the one place where Creation itself is being healed from its brokenness. The gentile world lacks any natural relation to God and is sunk in darkness, spiritually and morally. Gentiles exhibit the godless nature of humanity, which is to be idolatrous and morally perverse. The Gentile, or natural human being, is a "pagan," in the negative sense of the term.[48]

However, God is not only the God of Israel but the creator and redeemer of all nations. He has chosen to reach out to the Gentiles through his covenant with Israel. Israel is called, not only to be God's people, walking in the Way of Life that God has given them in the Torah. But it is also called to be a light to the Gentiles, to communicate its revelation of God and its healing of Creation to the Gentiles. Christianity, or the Christian Church, has its identity solely in this extension of God's covenant with Israel to the Gentiles. Christianity does not have a new covenant, in the sense of a covenant that supercedes the covenant of God with Israel. This covenant is eternal and unchangeable. The Church is not a new Israel. The announcement of salvation to the Gentiles is, in one sense, a new work of God in history, but in a strictly auxiliary and dependent relation to the one covenant of God with Israel.[49]

Jesus is not the Messiah of Israel.[50] Christianity completely misunderstood its own foundations by giving Jesus the title of Messiah (Christ). This misunderstanding comes from the fact that Christianity became a gentile movement, and Gentiles, being by nature "in darkness," make bad biblical theologians. They need to be constantly taught by Jews to understand biblical revelation. Thus the greater disaster of Christianity was that it cut itself off from its Jewish roots, where it could be taught to properly understand itself by the Jewish tradition. Falling back into the pagan darkness from which it came, gentile Christianity set itself up in a supercessionary relation to Israel. It developed a teaching of contempt for Jews and Judaism based on the failure of Jews to recognize Jesus as their

Messiah. It demanded that Jews abandon their faithfulness to Torah in favor of the new way of salvation in Christ. Such a gospel Jews could only reject with a resounding no. This rejection of the Christian gospel by Judaism, thus, does not represent Jewish unfaithfulness but rather Jewish faithfulness to God. Christians should come to recognize this Jewish no to the Christian gospel as a witness to the truth, recalling Christianity to its true identity.[51]

The culmination of this Christian self-deception, expressed in hostility to Jews, was the Holocaust. But this was simply the extreme expression of a root error, going back to a foundational misunderstanding that appeared as Christianity became a gentile movement in the second century C.E. Van Buren does not allow that this error appears in the New Testament itself. He contends that, rightly interpreted, the New Testament, including Paul, supports his reading of the auxiliary relationship of the Christian mission to the Gentiles to the one covenant of God with Israel.[52]

Jesus is central for Christianity, but not as the Messiah of Israel or as the basis of a new covenant superceding that of God with Israel. Rather, Jesus is the paradigmatic expression of the covenant of God with Israel for Gentiles. It is where Israel is summed up and given to Gentiles. Gentiles plug into the covenant of God with Israel through Jesus. Therefore, he is central for our salvation, but he is not necessary for the salvation of Jews, who are this covenant themselves.[53]

Once Christians return to their true, auxiliary relationship to the covenant with Israel, then Israel will be able to claim and use the Christian Church as its own vehicle for its mission to the Gentiles. This it has not been able to do heretofore because of Christian hostility and misinterpretation of its role. But this depends on the willingness of the Christian Church and its teachers to humble themselves and become disciples of the Jewish tradition.[54] Only by being continually instructed by Jews can Christians keep clear about who they are and what their role in history is. Because of their background as Gentiles, who came into the light from pagan darkness, they can never understand this by themselves.

Central to the faithfulness of Jews to their covenant with God is observance of the Torah. Thus the heart of the Christian false gospel was the effort to invalidate the Torah for Jews. Christians do not need to observe the Torah, for Jesus is their Torah. But the Torah is central to the ongoing response of Israel to its election. Jewish apostasy consists in nonobservance of Torah. God's covenant with Israel also implied a Promised Land. The land has been given by God to Israel in perpetuity, whether they are actually present in it or not. No other people, whether they may have dwelt there for cen-turies or millennia, have any right to this land.

Jewish presence in the land normatively takes the form of a Jew-ish state. This means a state where Jews alone are full citizens, although the "stranger or sojourner in the land" (non-Jews) should observe the same laws as the Jews (Exod. 12:49; Num. 15:15ff). This Jewish state cannot be like other states. It is called to a higher des-tiny, not only to be an exemplar to all other nations, but the place where Creation itself is being healed. The Jewish state is the begin-ning of the redemption of Creation. This state is mandated by God to be a theocratic state, a state that is governed, not by a secular con-stitution, but by the Torah. The Torah is and must be the Law of a Jewish state in order to fulfill its redemptive task, both for itself and for the rest of Creation.[55]

The role of the Christian Church is to extend the revelation of the God of Israel — and the healing work of God in and through Israel — to the nations. Christianity should do this, not only by preaching this gospel to the nations, but also by rendering service to the people of Israel. This service takes an external and an inter-nal form. Externally, the Christian Church must become the exten-sion of the Anti-Defamation League, combating all anti-Semitism among Gentiles.[56] It also takes the form of defense of the State of Israel, both raising money for Israel's defense and also defending the State of Israel against all anti-Zionist calumny.

All criticism of the State of Israel, whether based on alleged injustice to the Palestinians or claims that Israel is unjust to Third World peoples, such as black South Africans or Central Ameri-cans, are simply lies, according to Van Buren. The so-called Pales-tinian problem was caused solely by the Arab states, who made the Palestinians refugees and have kept them refugees.[57] The claims against Israel made by black South Africans and Central Ameri-cans are expressions of base ingratitude for Israel's generosity.[58] It is the job of the Christian Church to combat all these lies against Israel, being taught the truth by Jews; i.e., the government of the State of Israel.

Christians should also render an interior or spiritual service to the people of Israel by encouraging all Jews to return to faithful observance of the Torah.[59] By implication, this also means encouraging the State of Israel to become a fully theocratic state, where the commandments of Torah are publicly enforced as state laws. The fact that most Israelis are secular, and are vehemently antipathetic to any further extension of the power of the Orthodox rabbinate over their daily lives, matters not to Van Buren. He has definite ideas about who is a "true Jew"; a true Jew is a Torah-observant Jew. A nonobservant Jew is not only apostate from God's commands but threatens the work of redemption of Creation that comes from Jewish Torah observance. Thus it is vital, not only for Jews, but for all Creation, to see to it that Jews are Torah observant.

Van Buren's *Christian Theology of the People Israel* undoubtedly springs from a sincere desire to overcome Christian anti-Semitism and to promote reconciliation of Jews as a people and Christians. But he seems to have checked his critical faculties at the port of entry to the State of Israel. He has uncritically accepted a version of religious Zionism of the Kabbalistic tradition of Abraham Kook. He has also swallowed entirely the Israeli government party line on the history of Israel's relations to the Palestinians and to the Arab world.

Theologically, he operates out of a monism of revelation that can allow for only one revelation of the one God of history. If this becomes the revelation through the people of Israel, rather than Christ, then Christian revelation and Christian existence must be totally subordinated and auxiliary to the projects of the Jewish people, religious or secular, as defined by themselves. Christians are denied any right to question these Jewish self-definitions, even though Jews themselves are vehemently disputing these definitions between each other. Thus Van Buren's theology seems to exhibit a peculiar flip side of Christian relationship to Judaism, in the form of a self-abnegating philo-Semitism. This is expressed in an overcompensatory identification with Jews that, finally, is unable to allow Jews to be ordinary human beings.

CONCLUSIONS

To accept Jews as equally human means appreciating their traditions but also recognizing that they are as capable of organizational, as well as personal, errors as any other people. One of the most dangerous errors of any political system is to set itself up in such a way as to mandate the expropriation of land from an indigenous people and their expulsion and/or reduction to politically second-class and economically exploited status. This is exactly the error committed by the State of Israel, an error that does not make them worse, but much the same as many other nation-states. To criticize this error, to point out its effects on the victims, and to call for change is not anti-Semitism but simply justice. This does not call Jews or Israel to a higher morality than other nation-states. This is the same political morality that needs to be expected of any state in the twentieth century community of nations that seeks to overcome the heritage of colonialism and to establish a minimally just global social order.

Israel may be more visible as a nation than some other countries with similarly unjust patterns. This is because it is the meeting ground of the three monotheistic faiths and the major geopolitical systems of the world. Yet, despite its visibility, the actual situation of the Palestinians in Israel, in the Occupied Territories and in surrounding Arab nations, has been kept remarkably invisible until recently, or, rather, covered up by disinformation. The highly biased statements about Arabs and Palestinians, found in those few passages in Eckardts, Littell, and Van Buren that notice this question at all, reflect this disinformation. This must be regarded as culpable ignorance on their part. Corrective information can be easily found by talking to Palestinians themselves, critical Jews in Israel or in the Diaspora, and even from Israeli government sources. The ideological bias of these thinkers has blocked them from making the most minimal efforts to verify their views with alternative information.

Frank criticism of political injustices in Israel is not anti-Semitism. One must be clear what anti-Semitism, or any prejudice, is and not confuse it with justified criticism. Prejudicial views against a particular people have several aspects. One element is that crimes are claimed against a group that did not, in fact, happen, such as the medieval ritual murder charge. Or, even if some members of the group, or organized expressions of the group, did commit some evil at some particular time, this is not treated as an instance of a general human capacity but rather of a stereotypic characteristic of the group. Finally, and most importantly, the criticism is made to justify hatred and injustice against the group.

Thus, for example, to say that the papacy is an autocratic form of church government is not anti-Catholicism but to state historical fact. However, to say that all Catholics are autocrats by nature, that they desire to establish autocratic governments that deny other peoples' liberties, and therefore one should prevent Catholics in Protestant societies from being elected to governmental office is anti-Catholicism.

No one's anti-Semitism is justified because some Jews, too, may be oppressors. The proper response to any revelation of injustice is compassion for the victims but also sorrow for the victimizers, for theirs is the moral tragedy. The point of authentic criticism of evil is not to justify more hatred and violence but to end the cycle of hatred and violence. This is what Jewish and Christian Holocaust theologians have failed to do, precisely by accepting the Zionist view that response to the Holocaust means uncritical support for the State of Israel.

This critique of the Holocaust theologians, Jewish and Christian, reveals two fundamentally different ethical stances toward anti-Semitism and the Holocaust as expressions of evil. One stance elevates Jewish suffering to unique status. It becomes incomparable with any other human suffering. To mention any other great massacres, such as the destruction of millions of American Indians, or millions of Africans during the middle passage, in the same breath with the Holocaust is seen as trivialization. To even mention Palestinian suffering, the two million refugees, the tens of thousands killed and wounded in assaults on refugee camps and villages, most not commandos but unarmed civilians, is an abomination and a blasphemy. Jewish suffering is innocent and sacred. Palestinian suffering is despicable and deserved.

This effort to elevate Jewish suffering to unique status, incomparable with any other suffering, is self-defeating. It signals to other people a lack of generosity and solidarity with their suffering. It evokes a response of like ungenerosity. Some human rights activists, concerned about all other forms of human suffering, refuse to be concerned about anti-Semitism. They become convinced that this concern is manipulative, a cover for special privileges for the Jews and for the State of Israel in particular. They equate all Jews with their criticisms of Israel, mirroring the Zionist effort to equate Zionism and world Jewry. They refuse, not only to mention the Holocaust in their "list" of great human evils, but to be concerned about swastikas on synagogues or bombs thrown into cafes in Europe, simply because the people sitting there are primarily Jewish.

This ungenerosity of some persons of the Left toward Jewish suffering drives those convinced that anti-Semitism is unique and incomparable into further isolation. Leftist human rights activists are labeled the new anti-Semites.[60] The anti-anti-Semites become even more convinced that anti-Semitism is a unique cosmic mystery that must ever spring up in new forms from "nowhere." Anti-Semitism becomes the negative side of Jewish election. This adds to their belief that only the State of Israel, as a militarist state, surrounded by ever higher iron walls against the rest of the world, can keep the Jews safe from anti-Semitism.

A fundamentally different ethical stance toward anti-Semitism is one that grounds concern about Jewish suffering with concern for all human suffering. This does not deny that anti-Semitism has unique aspects in its intertwining of religious and ethnic hostility or that the Holocaust was one of the great infamies of human history. But each of the great human systems of evil has its unique and special peculiarities. Each people experiences its suffering as unique and special to them. But this particularity of each community's suffering is interconnected in human solidarity. To be concerned about Jewish suffering obliges one to be concerned about black South African suffering, women's suffering, the suffering of homeless refugee people in many parts of the world, and Palestinian suffering.

This interconnecting of the Jewish suffering and universal human suffering is found in theologians and peace activists, such as Arthur Waskow and Marc Ellis. For Waskow, the Holocaust as the genocidal assault on one people becomes the signal to warn us all against that final holocaust that would annihilate all people and the planet. To remember the Holocaust is to bind all humans together in solidarity to avert that ultimate fire that would destroy us all.[61] Marc Ellis has been developing a Jewish theology of liberation beyond the dialectic of Jewish victimization and empowerment. He seeks to restore a Jewish prophetic voice toward Jewish power and bring Jews into solidarity with other victimized people.[62]

For Ellis, Holocaust theology, as the consensus theology of Jewish-Christian dialogue, which has been forged since 1967, has proved inadequate. Its dialectic of absolute suffering and absolute empowerment has been unable to encompass the realities of the abuse of power. This theology has made both Jewish and Christian Holocaust theologians morally blind to the failure of the Jewish state and the oppression of the Palestinian people. A new theology needs to arise that would encompass the Holocaust and Jewish empowerment but that would transform this dialectic into a theology of solidarity between peoples. Such a theology of solidarity would struggle against human oppression but also realistically recognize that former victims can become new oppressors.

Mutual criticism does not mean a competitive put-down but a concern of communities to help each other be truthful about their failures and to regain their prophetic voice. Thus Christian-Jewish solidarity today must include both a critique of Christian anti-Semitism and a concern to liberate the Jewish community to regain its prophetic voice toward its own system of power. This is not an illegitimating of Jewish power but a quest for a mutual empowerment of all peoples that can create a more just use of power. The concluding chapter of this book will explore some of the issues that block such a theology of solidarity and mutuality between peoples in the Israel-Palestinian conflict.

8. Zionism and Inter-national Justice: A Theological and Ethical Evaluation

> In that day Israel will be the third with Egypt and Assyria, a blessing in the midst of the earth, whom the Lord of multitudes has blessed, saying, "Blessed be Egypt my people and Assyria the work of my hands and Israel my heritage."
>
> ISA. 19:24–25 (RSV ADAPTED)

The history of the Israel-Palestinian conflict is a story of two tragedies. The Palestinian people have suffered the tragedy of uprooting from their homes and lands, creating forty years of suffering as refugees for the majority of its people. The remnant of Palestinians left in the 1949 truce borders of the State of Israel have been ghettoized and marginalized from real exercise of their reputed legal citizenship in Israel. Since 1967 another large segment of the Palestinian community has lived under harshly repressive military rule. Tens of thousands of Palestinians have been killed or wounded in the conflicts with Israel that have ensued,[1] due to the refusal of the Palestinians to "fade away" into other Arab nations and their insistence on maintaining their national identity and claims to political rights.

The punitive violence meted out to the Palestinians by the Israeli military far exceeds any actual military threat that Palestinian commandos have ever offered to Israel's national security. This excessive fury must be seen as a response to the challenge to Israel's legitimacy posed by Palestinian nationalism. Israel's absolute claims are asserted by seeking to silence all expressions of Palestinian nationalism, even of the most symbolic and non-violent nature, as well as by the repression of political dissent among Jews who question the justice of the treatment of Palestinians.

The second tragedy of this story is the moral debacle of the Jewish state itself, which was bred in the sick world of Western anti-Semitism, racial nationalism, and imperialist colonialism in the Middle East. Despite its idealistic hopes and pioneering foundations, Zionist settlement was tainted from the beginning by a need to assert an exclusive claim over the land that it saw as its ancestral homeland, by excluding the claims of the Palestinian Arabs. The decisive turning point in this moral decline of Zionism was the 1948 war. It was in this war that Ben-Gurion and the dominant Zionist leaders determined to remove as many as possible of the Palestinians from within the State of Israel's expanded borders. This decision was rooted in the determination to create a Jewish state; i.e., a state where Jews would be the overwhelming majority and only effective citizens, rather than a binational state that would have accepted the reality of two national communities in Palestine.

From this decision to expel the Palestinians, and to create a Jewish rather than a binational state, has flowed endlessly worsening results. Starting with a denial of the fact that the Palestinians were expelled or terrorized into leaving, Israeli ideology has constructed a tissue of falsifications that have become almost automatic in the public utterances of its spokespersons. The excesses of Israeli violence against the Palestinians are routinely denied or, when too egregious to be totally denied, minimized. Efforts by either Gentiles or Jews to bring out the truth are attributed to a priori anti-Semitism or Jewish "self-hatred" and, thus, dismissed.

The myth of Israeli "purity of arms" (i.e., that the Israeli army only fights when attacked, does the minimum of damage, and avoids violence against unarmed civilians)[2] began to be unmasked in the war in Lebanon. That "purity of arms" is a subterfuge and a self-delusion became more and more evident in the 1987–88 uprising in the Occupied Territories. A gaping world witnessed Israel Defense Forces soldiers and also settlers *repeatedly* using live ammunition, three-foot clubs, and cyanide gas against any Palestinian, young or old, male or female. Such violence suggests, not the requirements of law and order, but a need to act out a collective hatred and frustration against the Palestinians.

Courageous human rights activists, Jewish and non-Jewish, have striven to make visible the massive human rights violations of the State of Israel against the Palestinians in the Occupied Territories. This system of repression has increasingly made Israel into a police state not only for Palestinians but for dissenting Jews as well.

Revisionist historians of Zionism and Israel have brought to light the repressed history of the state, in contradiction to its official ideology. Some revisionist history has come particularly from those older Zionists who adhered in their youth to the binationalist perspective of the Zionist Left, i.e., *Hashomer Hatzair*. Simha Flapan, founding editor of *New Outlook Magazine*, presented in *The Birth of Israel: Myths and Realities*, published in 1987 shortly before his death, a landmark expression of this revisionist history of the State of Israel.[3]

The seriousness of the moral debacle of the Zionist experiment is denied by Zionist ideologues in two ways. Jews, in Israel or in the Diaspora, who worry about the loss of Israel's "soul," are mocked by being labeled "the beautiful souls," implying that they are weaklings who lack the virility needed for the tasks of power. Such language reflects the ambivalence of Zionism toward the moral culture of the Jewish Diaspora. Traditional *sabras* (native-born Israelis) saw themselves as the reborn "masculine" Jews, against the weak "feminine" religious Jews of the Diaspora. Gentile criticism of Israel is rebuffed by claiming that Gentiles are demanding a higher level of morality from Israel than that expected of any other "normal" state faced with comparable security risks. This moral "double standard" is attributed to gentile anti-Semitism.[4]

The claim that the gentile world judges Israel by a moral "double standard" is misleading. Judgments of Israel vary considerably, depending, for example, on whether the critic is also a critic of Western imperialism and colonialism. The most vehement ideological criticism of Israel has come from the Arab world, which rejects Israel as a "colonial settler state" and hence a product of Western colonialism, with no legitimate rights as an expression of indigenous nationalism in the Arab world. Parallel language has been used by Third World allies of the Arabs and also by Western leftists who identify with the Third World and Arab perspectives. The rhetoric of such criticism of Israel has little influence in Western circles, especially in the United States where Israel secures the preponderance of its support.

U.S. administrations and mainline media have not been biased against Israel. Any double standard has been overwhelmingly in the other direction, reflecting a Western hostility to Arabs and a perception of Israel as part of the Western world, racially and ideologically, and as a crucial ally in the Middle East.[5] The excesses of

Israeli military violence, the oppressiveness of its occupation, remained largely invisible in the mainline press until the 1982 war in Lebanon opened the eyes of some journalists. This questioning has accelerated with the revelations of dubious Israeli espionage, with or against the United States, such as the Pollard and the Iran-gate scandals,[6] and also with the violence of the repression of the 1987–88 uprising in the Occupied Territories. But critical coverage of Israel continues to be apologetic and anxious about "balance"; for example, stories of Israeli soldiers agonizing over their unpleasant duty of beating unarmed Palestinians.[7]

The claim that outside critics harbor a negative bias against Israel that causes them to judge it by an unreasonably high moral standard, conceals the real locus of this issue. The call to a higher moral standard for Israel than for other nations is internal to Zionist identity. It is not a bias that originates in the gentile world. It was Zionism itself that justified its project by claiming that its state would be a "light to the nations," a model of democratic equality and socialist justice. It is Zionism that has sought to cement the loyalty of the Jewish people to its project by presenting itself as the solution to anti-Semitism, the redemption from the Holocaust, and the first fruits of the messianic age.

As Israel is revealed to be an "ordinary" state, not on the benign model of a noncolonialist social democracy like Sweden, but on the militarist and repressive model of a racist, colonial state such as South Africa, the moral basis of Jewish loyalty to Israel threatens to erode. Morally sensitive Jews leave Israel to emigrate elsewhere. Some Jews in the Diaspora, discouraged by official Jewish organizations from making a positive critique, turn away from it in silence and sickness of soul. Many Diaspora Jews experience a deep sadness over Israel, but a sadness allowed limited public expression. Many others are filled with rage at what they interpret to be a conspiracy of hatred of the whole world against the Jewish people. As Zionist triumphalistic rhetoric rolls on, asserting its righteousness, the rage, confusion, and sadness grow and turn into intra-Jewish conflict. Some Diaspora Jews begin to mount expressions of public protest.[8] But most Diaspora Jews are kept silent by the fear that Jewish self-critique in public will feed gentile anti-Semitism.

Zionist ideologues constantly stoke Jewish fears and insecurities by claiming that Israel is in danger of "disappearing" and that, if this happens, there will be "another Holocaust." Such fears belong more to the realm of Jewish subjective feelings than to objective realities. The Israeli military was never stronger. It enjoys the lion's share of American military aid. It is the fourth strongest army in the world and the only nuclear power in the Middle East. This nuclear capacity was developed secretly, even from the Israeli public, but now is a known fact.[9] So there is no danger of Israel as a state "disappearing," except perhaps in a world war sparked by the Middle East conflict, that might well take the rest of the planet with it.

Jews in the Diaspora, especially in North America, enjoy unparalleled power, prosperity, and acceptance. The Christian world, by and large, has come to identify with their rights, not only to exist, but to prosper as a religious and ethnic group. This is the positive and appropriate expression of Christian repentance for its sins of anti-Semitism. Never in the last seventeen centuries, since Christianity became the ruling religion in Europe and the northern Mediterranean, has there been less danger of a major organized outbreak of discrimination against Jews. This does not mean that there is no anti-Semitism in the West and that Christians do not need to remain vigilant in support of Jewish rights in these Christian-influenced nations.

A primary cause of hostility to Jews today springs from anger against the policies of the State of Israel. The scapegoating of all Jews for the mistakes of the State of Israel interacts with the Zionist efforts to link all Jews everywhere in uncritical support of Israel. And so Jews sitting in cafes in France, for example, become victims of random acts of violence done in retribution for actions of the State of Israel. These acts of violence, in turn, reinforce the Zionist claim that all Jews need Israel to "save" them from anti-Semitism. Thus, once again, world Jewry is caught in the double bind of a Zionist ideology that both feeds and exploits anti-Semitism.

This cycle of fear and insecurity is one that Christians need to understand. But in our view, such understanding is not correctly expressed by collaboration with Zionist-bred ideologies that only continue this cycle of fear and insecurity. Rather we believe that those who care about the Jewish people should support their liberation from a Zionist bondage to Israel as the supposed solution to anti-Semitism. The actual injustices of Israel, and the ideological cover-up of these mistakes, need to be clearly exposed to critical

examination. At the same time, the negative energy of disappointment might be transformed into a positive energy of reform, both
of Israeli and world Jewish institutions.

The break with Zionist ideology might create the new freedom
and energy for a broad religious and social renewal of Judaism. It
would provide the opportunity for restatements of what it means to
be a religiously based and morally concerned global community.
This does not mean a rejection but rather a new relationship of
world Jewry to the State of Israel, as a political project of Jewish people. Instead of trying to make Israel into a messianic state, it will be
recognized as an "ordinary" state that needs to become a more credible expression of normal political justice than is presently the case.

Any transformation from repression of criticism to positive
prophetic critique can only spring from the creative capacities of
the Jewish people themselves. It would have to be seen both as possible and as necessary for themselves. This rests on finding other
sources of confidence and security than the State of Israel. Zionism
has fed on a "macho" concept of power as invulnerable might. This,
in turn, rests on a fear of both physical and emotional vulnerability
as the sign of weakness. It is assumed that any sign of weakness will
be despised by the *goyim*, who will use it as the invitation to attack.

This psychology of power and fear of vulnerability is directed
particularly at the Arab world, which is presumed to "only understand force." But it includes assumptions about the Western Christian world as well. Thus, one has the sense that, while the State of
Israel poses political problems, freedom for appropriate analysis of
these problems demands some kind of intergroup psychotherapy.
It is hazardous to imagine how that can be done or who can
appropriately do it. But part of what is involved in this conflict is
the facilitating of an inner growth and empowerment of traumatized people that can free them to take up a more generous stance
toward the outside world.

It is typical of Israelis to suggest that Palestinians are primarily
responsible for this task of removing Jewish fear.[10] But we believe
that such "therapy" cannot be expected to come solely or primarily
from a wounded and traumatized Palestinian people. It needs to
come from the larger world community, as well as members of the
Jewish community, who need to communicate to traumatized Jews
a message of firm acceptance of their rights to prosper as a religious

and political community that will not "disappear" with the revelation that Jews are not superheroes but normal human beings subject to frailties and mistakes. This must go hand in hand with equally firm insistence that Palestinian rights to self-determination must be recognized and that the horrors of the occupation must cease.

This shift of consciousness demands a critique and revision of foundational assumptions of Zionist ideology. This does not mean that these assumptions are totally wrong and to be rejected out of hand but rather that these assumptions have been falsely construed and need to be reinterpreted in order to become life-giving, rather than destructive.

In the following sections of this chapter we will discuss three assumptions that are basic to Zionism: (1) that Jews are not a global religious community but, first and foremost, a nation and even a "race" and that the Jewish community as a nation can only be authentically expressed in a Jewish nation-state, that is, a state by and for Jews and Jews alone; (2) that the ancestral homeland and necessary land base of this Jewish state is Palestine (Ideally this means the "whole" of Palestine, not just the 1949 truce borders but also Judea and Samaria [the West Bank] and perhaps the east bank of the Jordan and southern Lebanon. This was the ancestral homeland from which they were unjustly ejected by the Romans nineteen centuries ago. Jews have an a priori right to return there and create a Jewish state. This right takes precedence over any other people who have lived there, either before the Jewish presence in antiquity or since.); and (3) that the return of the Jews to their homeland, and their founding of a state there, is a messianic event. Although it may not yet be fully messianic, it can be called the beginning of redemption. Return, resettlement, and the establishment of Jewish sovereignty in Palestine is itself an unequivocal good that must be evaluated as redemptive. This redemptive good stands over against, not only the Holocaust as the extremity of evil, but also against any Jewish life lived outside the land.

THE JEWS: RELIGIOUS COMMUNITY OR NATION?

Periods of Jewish sovereignty over parts of Palestine were brief in antiquity. Jews more typically lived under a series of empires (Persian, Hellenistic, Roman) whose policy was to depose local political leadership but use religious leadership as the national representatives of subject communities. Already in the Persian period Jewish religious leadership saw itself as superceding the ancient kingship. In this period the religious leadership also began to develop, through the Law and the synagogue, the means of maintaining religious, communal existence outside the national territory.

Contrary to the Zionist myth that all Jews were forcibly ejected from their homes and have lived ever since longing to return, it is evident already in the Persian period that many Jews emigrated to the Diaspora by preference and were not interested in return. Rabbinic developments after C.E. 133–36 further legitimated the Diaspora as the normal religious state of Jews prior to the messianic age. Proselytism also made Jews a universal community drawn from many nations, distinguished by a religious-communal way of life. The ghetto of Jews among the nations was created as much by internal religious regulations that demanded separatism as by external anti-Semitism. Indeed the two reinforced each other.

The emancipation in the eighteenth and nineteenth centuries reflected both an external dissolution of the barriers against Jews in civil society and an internal revolt against these religious restrictions. Jews moving out into the larger quasi-secularized Christian world met a secularized anti-Semitism based on racial nationalism and were also pulled back by their own fears of disappearance through assimilation. Zionism was constructed in response to both these forces. Secular Zionists borrowed from romantic, racialist nationalism to declare that Jews were not a religious community but a nation and a race.

Zionism took over this view and proclaimed that Jews would be safe from anti-Semitism only when they returned to their ancestral soil and reconstructed themselves as a nation-state. Religious Zionists also sought to reconstitute the walls of religious separation that kept Jews apart from the "unholy" gentile world. The State of Israel reveals both these kinds of reghettoization: the racial, nationalist wall erected by the Jewish state against the Palestinians and the religious wall that has arisen to separate Orthodox observant Jews from secular Israelis, as well as from Gentiles.

Prior to World War II, Zionism was a minority movement among world Jewry. Reform and secular Jews rejected it because they were committed to citizenship in secular, democratic states. Orthodox

Jews rejected Zionism as a heresy that sought to do by unholy hands a task that could only be accomplished by the Messiah. But the Second World War and the shock of the Holocaust made it possible for Zionists to capture control of Jewish organizations in the Diaspora and cement the official loyalty of world Jewry to the Jewish state.[11]

But this official loyalty conceals a massive silent defection. Only 20 percent of the world's Jews have moved to Israel and made it their nation, and many of these did not come in a fully voluntary manner. Of these, one-seventh (.5 million out of 3.5 million) live permanently abroad with dual citizenship. The way Israeli society has developed has made it increasingly less representative of world Jewry. Most Diaspora Jews are Reform, Conservative, or secular, while only Orthodox Judaism is recognized in Israel. Most Diaspora Jews are democratic humanists. But increasingly these values are seen as incompatible with a Jewish state and are being rejected by many Israelis. Most Diaspora Jews are Ashkenazi, while the majority of Israelis (60 percent) are from the Arab world.[12]

The notion that Jews are a nation, in the sense of being a "race," was drawn from European racist, anti-Semitic concepts of nationalism. But in Israel the assemblage of Jews from many lands has made it evident that Jews are both a multiracial and a multicultural group, who have through the centuries assimilated the many cultures and physical characteristics of the peoples among whom they have lived. What tied them together as Jews was a religiously based communal life, which was carried on independently of political sovereignty. Within Israel, cultural differences divide not only Jews from Palestinians but the many cultures of Jews from each other, especially Ashkenazi from Oriental Jews.

By several means, Jews in the Diaspora are made to feel that Israel is their state, even though they do not chose to move there. First, as Judaism as the basis of religious community erodes for many Jews, activity for Zionism is used to replace Judaism as the basis of Jewish identity.[13] Second, fears of anti-Semitism and a "second Holocaust" are kept alive by constant evocation of these as imminent dangers. Diaspora Jews are made to feel that each of them can be safe from such a danger by getting on the next plane and escaping to Israel. Israel is the haven that assures each Diaspora Jew of ultimate security against the danger of anti-Semitism.

The idea that the State of Israel could actually provide a haven for all of world Jewry is a cruel chimera. In reality there is no place today where a Jew is more likely to be killed because he or she is a Jew than in Israel. Thousands of Jews have died in Israel in the last forty years, most of them soldiers who died in wars.[14] The conflicts created by territorial expansion in 1967 and 1982 have become so severe that pullback from both of these expansionist attempts will be necessary if Israel is to become an economically viable state. Thus Israel cannot, in reality, accommodate a massive influx of new Jewish population. Despite the promises implied by the "Law of Return," new immigration will most probably be limited to replacement of the present population lost through emigration.

Israel has failed to be the center of moral and religious renewal that socialist and spiritual Zionists promised. It has not constructed an appealing expression of religious life, but it is locked into a style of orthodoxy rejected by most Diaspora Jews. It has become less a "light to the nations" of exemplary social justice and equality than an expression of militarism and intercommunal discrimination and hatred. It is not even an economically viable state, but its military expansionism has been purchased by more than $4 billion of American foreign aid a year, as well as a constant flow of contributions from world Jewry. Israel is a sign of redemption for many Jews, but it has also become a moral and financial liability to world Jewry.

There are signs of new restiveness toward Israel among Diaspora Jewry. This is expressed in a variety of new movements of social and religious renewal. The New Jewish Agenda attempts to recapture the Jewish commitments to justice both within the American national community and internationally. While not turning away from concern for Israel, its militarism and injustice is criticized as one such issue among many in a global pattern, although one for which Jews have special responsibility as Jews. The *Havurah* movement seeks to create a spiritually and morally uplifting renewal of Judaism in communities of study and celebration. Something like parallel Christian movements of liberation theology and base communities, the *Havurot* seek to reconnect spirituality and social justice. Jewish feminism, concern for world peace, and concern for ecology are some of the issues that are being expressed through the *havurot* communities.[15]

These expressions of renewal of Jewish life in the Diaspora break down the Zionist myth that the Diaspora is *galuth*, or exile, and is a doomed option. They point to the possibility of a revival of that alternative view of the Diaspora as mission. Jews are dispersed among the nations to be witnesses to ethical monotheism. Or perhaps Jews have no need to have a special reason to live everywhere, other than the fact that they do live everywhere. In fact, the Diaspora has been "normal" for most of Jewish history, not atypical, and even in antiquity it was mostly voluntary rather than forced.

If life is not perfectly just and whole for Jews, it is hardly better for most other human groups. Indeed many other communities at present live under harsher conditions of repression or homelessness than the Jewish community. Alienation and lack of fullness of life is a human condition, not a specifically Jewish condition. Any new genocide will more likely be directed at other groups of people or at the planet as a whole rather than specifically at the Jewish community. Thus, it becomes scarcely credible to separate Jewish survival from human survival, as Zionism has sought to do.

While affirming their own specific communal particularity and perspective, a redevelopment of those links of Jewish life with universal human life would seem more fruitful than tying itself to an Israeli nationalism that implicitly denies Diaspora Jewry the legitimacy of their national identification with the many nations in which they hold citizenship. Israel would remain a special concern of world Jewry but not their goal or destiny, except for a particular group of Jews who are Israelis. This shift in relationship between the State of Israel and world Jewry is suggested in the recent identity statement released by the Conservative movement.[16]

The State of Israel has failed to vindicate the thesis that Jewishness is a nationality separable from religion. When faced with the question of "who is a Jew" for purposes of providing legal guidelines for the "Law of Return," secular atheist Zionists had to turn to the Orthodox rabbinate for the guidelines. There exists no secular definition of who is a Jew but only the one based on religious law.[17] As world Jewry declines to increase the numbers of those who opt for Israeli citizenship, and as Israel remains a nation where most Jews are secular, and one that includes a significant minority of Christians and Muslims, the definitions of being an Israeli citizen and of being a member of the Jewish people drift apart. An Israeli is a citizen of the State of Israel, who may be a Jew, a Christian, or a Muslim. A Jew is a member of a religiously defined global community, a part of which is Israeli by nationality.

JEWISH ELECTION AND THE PROMISED LAND

The notion that Palestine has been promised to the Jews by God, and that this divine promise supercedes the rights of any other group of people who has ever lived there, is foundational to Zionist ideology. It is the basis of the claim that this area is the national homeland of the Jewish people. Secular Zionists, while not believing in the God upon whom this religious promise was based, used the religious belief to draw the loyalty of less secularized Jews. The belief that the Jews have an a priori right to Palestine, which was granted them by God, has also been central in attracting Christian support for the State of Israel.

However, the use of this religious myth entangles Zionism in several contradictions. The religious vision of a Promised Land in the Bible has undefined borders. It points Israel toward an expansionism not only toward the West Bank, which was the heart of the ancient Hebrew settlements, but also into the territories of the twelve tribes in the Book of Joshua. This would include the east bank of the Jordan and southern Lebanon. Since Menachem Begin came to power in 1977, militarist expansionists and religious messianists have joined together in a fanatical dream of reconquering the "whole" of this territory. Rabbis of the militarist, messianist perspective have proclaimed it a sin to return "one inch" of the Promised Land and have defined the very existence of aliens (Palestinians) on this land as a pollution.

But this effort to use *halachic* (religious-legal) tradition for military expansion flounders on the fact that the secular nonobservant life of the Israeli majority, as well as the violence and injustice of the military messianists, constitutes greater pollution of the land, according to biblical norms, than the mere existence there of Christian and Muslims who are also monotheists rooted in biblical ethics. The messianists cannot claim biblical promises and *halachic* norms and totally ignore the ethical traditions of Judaism.

The biblical and rabbinic traditions do not claim that the Promised Land is a real estate deed given to the Jews by God. Rather they suggest that it is a usufruct, dependent on living according to the commandments. To occupy the land and violate the commandments is, in fact, to bring down the wrath of God, expressed ultimately in expulsion from the land. Thus, the appeal to religious tradition by those who do not intend to observe the fullness of the commandments leads to its own denouement. It puts one under the threat of divine expulsion.[18]

Secular Israelis who do not believe in God, or are perhaps theists but without belief that they should observe the whole of the Torah, can hardly appeal to such divine promises as the basis of their right to the land. At most, they can appeal to cultural memory as a part of Jewish historical identity. But this gives them no more rights than any other group who has lived there and feels deep attachment to the area. Do not Palestinians also feel deep attachment to the land and constitute their communal identity through memories of living or having lived there?

Palestinian residence there has been continuous. They can speak of their fathers and mothers, grandparents, and great-grandparents having lived in Palestinian villages and towns. Jews arriving from Poland or the United States appeal to ancient long-broken roots, not recent life in the region. No non-Israeli court of law gives people the right to uproot those presently living in houses and land on the basis of two-thousand-year-old memories. Since most of the world's people have immigrated to their present homes and lands from other parts of the world, it is scarcely imaginable what would happen if such ancient memories would be constructed as a priori rights for any other group of people. The appeal to rights to the land as secular national memory and culture is inconclusive. It throws the Zionism back on the religious basis of the claims, with the contradictions that we have noted.

The constantly reiterated insistence in Zionist rhetoric that other people, Palestinians and Arabs, but also the rest of the world, recognize "Israel's right to exist," is really a covert appeal to this religious myth that Jews have an a priori right to exist as a nation in a particular territory. However, we suggest that nations and national lands are not God-given absolutes but relative historical realities that arise through the processes by which groups of people settle in particular lands, put down roots, and build up a culture and identity in that place.

Almost everywhere today nation-states are a mix of people living within national boundaries. The task of every nation today is to construct just political communities that take into account the actual plurality of cultural groups living within their borders. The ethnically exclusive nation-state is a nineteenth-century European ideology that has failed in the face of contrary reality. Most states are made up of people who have migrated there from some other area, either recently or in more ancient times. There are few people who, for as long as one can remember, have always lived in the region where they now live. Palestinian peasants probably have as good a claim to this status of indigeneity as any.

Migrating people have often subjugated the earlier people who they found living in the region. The conflict between earlier people and those who seek to migrate and settle in an area can be resolved in one of three ways. The settler people can exterminate or expel the earlier people and thereby silence their protest. This has been the pattern of white European settlers toward the American Indians and other aborigines in the Americas and Australia. Another way is for the colonized people to rise up in a protest that refuses to be crushed. Eventually most of the settlers return to their former homes or immigrate to another area more accepting of them. The area is left to the indigenous nationalist community. This has been the pattern of European colonialism and de-colonization in most of Africa and Asia.

A third pattern is for both groups to continue to maintain deep ties of identification with the area and neither succeed in subjugating or expelling the other. This demands a reconciliation and the forging of a pluralist political identity that can accommodate both peoples. Although Israel has sought to solve its conflicts with the Palestinians in the first way, and the Palestinians to solve the conflict in the second way, the third pattern seems to be the only real option. This means that, until such accommodation is developed, a settler community will remain partially illegitimate in the eyes of the earlier people. This is particularly true if the indigenous community is part of a larger cultural community in the surrounding region, as is the case with the Palestinians.

Until such an accommodation is developed that the Palestinian people can accept, there is no way to remove the onus of illegitimacy from the State of Israel in the eyes of the Palestinian and Arab people. No efforts to batter on the walls of the world conscience with claims of Israel's "right to exist" will have an effect on Arab feelings. Only genuine political accommodation to Palestinian national rights can change this picture from rejection to mutual accommodation.

This claim of an a priori right of the State of Israel to exist prior to such accommodation rests, as we have suggested, on the religious myth of the Promised Land. This myth depends for its credibility on the acceptance of a tribalist and exclusive concept of God. Already within the Bible this tribalist concept of God was being questioned in favor of a more universalist concept of God as Creator of all nations. Rabbinic Judaism constituted itself outside the land by drawing on a more universalist concept of God. Christianity and Islam also have expressed more universalist views of the monotheistic God by transcending ethnocentric concepts of peoplehood and territorial views of God's presence. But none of the monotheistic faiths has adequately freed itself from ethnocentric views of itself in relation to God and other people.

Zionism, in its definition of Jews as a nation and Palestine as its Promised Land, reverts back to an ethnocentric view of God as one who elects only one people and is concerned with only one territory, to the exclusion of Palestinians and their rights to live in this land. But Palestine has actually been a crossroads of all people of the Middle East. It is the font of all three monotheistic religions. If God is indeed universal and ethical, not tribal and partial, then Palestine can only be seen as the land that this God calls all its historic peoples to share with one another.

THE STATE OF ISRAEL AND THE BEGINNING OF REDEMPTION

Zionism drew not only on ancient Jewish religious beliefs in the Promised Land but also on prophetic and rabbinic beliefs that a return of the Jews from exile and the founding of a new Jewish kingdom would be an integral part of a future redemption. According to classical rabbinic tradition, this could only be accomplished by the Messiah. Orthodox Jews rejected the capacity of secular, unbelieving Jews to being this redemptive project.

But a few Orthodox rabbis, steeped in Kabbalistic doctrines and also open to nationalism, began the integration of religious messianism and Zionism. Rabbi Abraham Isaac Kook was the most important architect of religious Zionism. Kook argued that secular Zionists unknowingly were the instruments of divine providence. They were beginning the redemptive project simply by regaining the land and settling it. Once the land was regained and settled by Jews, this would lead to the next stage, the building of a Torah-observant national community.

In classical Judaism there are three pillars of Jewish life: people-hood, Torah, and land. Traditionally, Torah and peoplehood are first: the people of Israel are constituted through the giving of the Law and called to be faithful to it. Only when obedience to Torah is achieved will the Messiah come to restore the kingdom in the land. Restoration of the land thus stands as an eschatological fulfill-ment of the historical task of obedience to Torah. Kook reversed this relationship. The settlement of the land becomes first. This will reconstitute the people of Israel. Faithfulness to Torah becomes the culmination of this process. Kook saw this as a cosmic process that would heal all nations through the reunification of Israel with its land.

Kook's son, Rabbi Zvi Kook, abandoned the universalist side of his father's thought. He became the teacher of the militant fun-damentalist *Gush Emunim*. For Zvi Kook the primary redemptive act is the settlement of Jews on the land, displacing the Palestinians. The very presence of Jews on the land redeems the land from unholiness, caused by the dwelling there of unholy people. For Abraham Kook, the holiness of the people of Israel and its land suffuses the unholiness of other nations and lands and communi-cates redemption to them. For Zvi Kook, this concept of the superior holiness of Jews loses any positive relation to other peo-ples. It becomes solely an argument for separation from and exclu-sion of other, profane people from contact with Jews and their land.[19] However, both versions of this concept of the superior holi-ness of the Jews and their land materializes holiness and translates into religious racism the call of the Jews to holiness.

Kabbalistic religious Zionism is not the only line of messianism in Zionism. One can say that each of the various schools of Zionism had a messianic aspect. Each, in one way or another, claimed that its type of Zionism was redemptive. For example, labor Zionism appealed to socialist visions of a redeemed society of shared eco-nomic power where class hierarchy would be overcome. Israel was to be a model of socialist justice. Romantic utopian Zionists appealed to the mystique of an intuitive, cosmic relationship between peoplehood and national soil. They saw the Diaspora as having created a weak, alienated Jew, lacking in wholistic humanity. The "conquest of the land" by which Jews would work their ancestral land with their own hands, was seen as having innate, redemptive effects. Jews would regain integration of mind and body. The transformation of urban Jews into agriculturalists would simultaneously redeem the land and redeem the alienated psycho-physical being of Jews.

Military Zionism cast this promise of the psycho-physical redemption of the Jew into a messianic mystique of the sword. Jews of the Diaspora had become weak and effeminate by being disarmed and subjugated people. Reclaiming the land would make them, above all, warriors. The sword and the plowshare are not in conflict, as in Isaiah, but they are complementary. The new Jewish man, redeemed from the pale effeminacy of cities and schools, would defend his land with his sword. This vision of the heroic new Jew was the collective myth of a generation of *sabra* militarists.[20]

The Holocaust has provided another powerful dimension to the idea that the founding of the State of Israel would redeem Jews from exile and save them from anti-Semitism. The chapter on Jewish and Christian Holocaust theology discussed the emergence of a collective redemption myth in which Israel stands as the sign of resurrection and new life, in contrast to the manifestation of the demonic in Nazism and the Holocaust. Particularly since 1967, with the occupation of "greater Israel," this link of Israel as redemption from the Holocaust has gained broad acceptance in Diaspora Reform and Conservative Judaism, uniting religious feeling with Zionism as the focus of a secularized Jewish identity. This link also depends on constantly feeding the fears of Diaspora Jewry that they themselves face "another Holocaust" and that the State of Israel, itself ever on the brink of annihilation from the Arab world, is all that separates world Jewry from disaster.

All of these forms of progressive, socialist, romantic, militaristic, religious, and catastrophic messianism contain deep contradictions. Each of them has been largely disproven by the historial reality of Israel. Only fervid mythmaking that conceals this contrary reality prevents the myth from collapsing. Let us briefly examine each of these kinds of messianism.

The religious messianic tradition allowed a secular reclaiming of the land and building of a state only if there was movement toward a theocratic development of the state. The state can be seen as redemptive only if it increasingly accepts Torah as its sole law and incorporates all Jews into observance of Torah. Ben-Gurion made major concessions to this religious perspective in the founding of the state by ceding to the Orthodox rabbinate key areas of control of social life. For this reason, Israel remains without a secular constitution. But the majority of Israeli Jews remain secular. Further encroachment of the Orthodox rabbinate on daily life has created a deepening *kulturkampf* within Israel between religious and secular Jews.

Increasingly, religious Jews withdraw into their own separate enclaves, refusing to have any contact with their fellow Jewish citizens on the grounds that they are unobservant and hence unclean. The Orthodox make violent raids on Israeli secular life, burning bus stands with advertisements of bikini-clad females, stoning vehicles traveling on the Sabbath, and assaulting archaeologists digging in what might be areas of ancient Jewish cemeteries.[21]

The ultra-Orthodox have become the source of extremely dangerous kinds of political violence in their fanatical efforts to create settlements in the midst of sites holy to Muslims, such as Hebron, or to occupy the Temple Mount in preparation for the rebuilding of the Jewish Temple. Thus religious messianism, far from being healing and unifying, has become one of the major sources of inter-Jewish violence, as well as violence with Palestinians.

The various other forms of Zionist messianism have also found their denouement in hard realities. The *sabra*, redeemed from Diaspora weakness, with a gun in one hand and a plow in the other, has become a military-political-industrial ruling elite. Many Jews no longer work the land with their own hands or do any kind of manual labor. For many, such labor is now seen as "Arab work," unbefitting a Jew. Some Israelis have become an urban managerial elite, ruling over lower classes and races who do the manual labor. The dream of redemption through labor has evaporated in the reality of a colonialist, capitalist organization of the economy. The class and race hierarchy of labor, relegation of Palestinians to third-class citizens or stateless subjects of military rule, also destroys the messianic myth of Israel as model social democracy, a "light to the nations," in terms of democratic and socialist ideals.

The denouement of these various forms of Zionist messianisms points to a common conclusion: Zionism is a bearer of false messianism. This does not mean that many of these hopes are not valid ethical and religious hopes. Creating a land of democratic freedom and socialist justice; a land where head and heart, head and hand are integrated; a refuge for the persecuted; a land of faithfulness to God—each of these are valid expressions of human longing for redemption. But these hopes have been falsely construed in relation to reality and translated into fallacious ideologies.

False messianism rests on a false construction of the relationship between unredeemed human reality and human hopes. False messianism evokes a dream of redeemed life, whether that be expressed in romantic, liberal, socialist, or religious norms. It uses this dream to cover up contrary realities. Symbol is separated from ethical substance and then used to conceal the contradiction between symbol and ethical substance. False messianism demands deception. Those who glorify their activities as redemptive must lie about contradictory realities. The deception, in turn, must be covered up, and those who would expose it vilified. The large amount of deception, coverup of deception, and vilification of those who seek the truth has been typical of Israeli state propaganda. This pattern of deception is not unlike that found in other modern forms of failed messianism, such as state communism, fascism, and even the American self-perception of its foreign policy as "making the world safe for democracy."

Authentic relationship to Ultimate Reality generates, not a need for deception, but the confidence to tell the truth. It is expressed in compassion, not hardness of heart. This might be called prophetic hope, in contrast to false messianism. Prophetic hope situates itself in a self-critical and transformative relationship to the divine call and future hope. This call and hope judges historical reality in its true distance from the ideals; it does not cover up this distance with deceptive self-glorification. Prophetic hope grounds the critic in a confident trust in Ultimate Reality that empowers truthful self-knowledge. It calls the critic to a struggle to reform reality, beginning with oneself, to bring self and society closer to the divine ideal. It is by keeping human hopes and ideals as critical measuring rods to judge historical reality, rather than using them as ideological self-sacralization, that one keeps redemptive hopes from being turned in false messianism.

This does not mean that every moment in history is equally unredeemed. There are sabbatical moments when one experiences the "signs" of redemptive presence. Those are the graced times when one person's good is not another's evil; one peoples' redemption is not another peoples' damnation. Graced moments are moments of repentance that create reconciliation and overcome enmity. False messianism, by contrast, is built on a presumed right to vengeance. It assumes that our success is measured by our triumph over our enemies; our redemption is the annihilation of others, who become the representatives of Satan. False messianism is built on adversarial dualism. Two human groups become identified with the ultimate dualisms of good and evil, God and Satan. Divine beneficence toward one group means divine wrath and punishment against the other. Jewish, Christian, and Muslim fundamentalisms all partake in this kind of religious paranoia.

Zionist ideology, both religious and secular, has had a strong element of this vengeance·seeking relation to the Western and Arab worlds. Gaining the lands for the Jews has been seen as a righteous ousting of Palestinians as inferior and evil. Redemption of the Jews from exile also was perceived as receiving justified compensation from the Christian world for Jewish suffering. Redemption built on the psychology of vengeance generates a cycle of violence. The vanquished and displaced seek their own vengeance. Then the victors must reassert, with yet more devastating blows, their superiority, to vindicate their divinely favored status.

The face of the enemy takes on more and more untrue proportions. The other become, first, animals, then pestilent vermin, and, finally, Satan. The Israeli rhetoric toward Palestinians as "two-legged animals," "cockroaches," and "Nazis" represents this demonization process.[22] A similar process toward Zionism has also gone on in the Arab world, which has eagerly adopted as its own some of the worst of the literature of Western anti·Semitism, such as the *Protocols of the Elders of Zion*.[23] The demonic myth on one side feeds the demonic myth on the other.

False messianism also becomes caught in its own contradictions. For those persons free enough to discern the contradiction between ideology and reality, these contradictions become more and more intolerable. Finally they begin to criticize these failures, in hopes of bringing change, and find themselves the target of official vilification as "traitors."[24] Assaulted by their own community, the prophetic critics are faced with several alternatives. They can simply leave the community in disgust. This was the route of the Argentinian human rights activist, Jacobo Timerman, who immigrated to Israel in the late 1970s and left again shortly after the 1982 war, disillusioned by what he perceived as the reality of Israel.[25]

Another response is to cover up the contradiction with cynical *Realpolitik*. This has been the response of many morally sensitive Israelis, such as Moshe Sharett, who gradually adjusted themselves to the deceptions of power.[26] A third alternative is to reaffirm one's relation to the community as a prophetic voice for truth. Israel Shahak, president of the Israeli League for Human and Civil Rights, who has carried on his personal crusade for truth and justice towards the Palestinians for many years, is an example of this response.[27]

Perseverence in prophetic commitment of this type requires a shift in one's relationship to oneself and one's community. One puts one's trust in an Ultimate Reality, whether that is understood as God or as Truth or as the good of humanity as a whole, rather than in the immediate successes of one's projects. Love for one's people can then be sustained, in spite of its failures to live up to its ideals. Particularity and universality are linked in a positive way. Concern for truth and justice for one's own people demands a like concern for the other people that it faces. One side cannot be redeemed as long as the other side is violated. In the words of classical Jewish ethical wisdom: "If I am not for myself, who will be for me? If I am only for myself, what kind of a human being am I? And if not now, when?"[28]

CONCLUSIONS

The struggle for justice and peace between Israelis and Palestinians has also become a battle within Israel between those who put territorial expansion over ethical values and those who want to give up the Occupied Territories in order to retain what they see as key ethical values and principles. This conflict is referred to as the conflict between the land of Israel and the "soul" of Israel.[29] Those who believe that the 1967 Occupied Territories must be given up, in order to retain the "soul" of Israel, see the occupation as exacerbating to the breaking point all the contradictions that divide Israeli society.

Expansion of land means feeding the militarists who believe that Israel's security lies entirely in military power. Expansion also feeds the religious ultraright who base themselves on a literalistic and maximalist doctrine of the Promised Land and the messianic timetable. Holding onto the Territories means an endless cycle of violence against the Palestinians. Because the Palestinians can neither be expelled *en masse* (because of world opinion) or enfranchised (without changing the concept of the Jewish state), they can only be repressed. Repression corrodes whatever democratic and humane values remain in Israeli culture and shapes the new generation of young people to be ever more hardened to their task of beating, gassing, and shooting Palestinians.

Holding on to the 1967 Territories also means increasing inflation, indebtedness, and dependency of the Israeli economy upon foreign, especially American, aid. This makes Israel, not just the puppet state of American interests, but a conspiratorial ally; the tail that wags the dog of American imperialism. Continued military occupation of conquered territories, land confiscation, and settlements thwart, indefinitely, peace negotiations with the Arab world. It also earns the opprobium of Third World nations.

Many Jews are wont to claim that the Arabs are moved by an irrational hatred and desire to destroy Israel, and so there can be no peace with them. But this absolutizing of Arab enmity refuses to see that this enmity is rooted in concrete political conflicts that are capable of amelioration. Surrounding Arab states certainly harbor little good will toward Israel at this point. Security issues are real and will continue to be for some time. Arab enmity is rooted in objections to Israel as a Jewish state and as a colonial settler state created by Western imperialism. But it has also been exacerbated by forty years of warfare in which the surrounding Arab nations have suffered enormous losses of life and property at the hands of the Israeli military.

Anger fueled by this loss of life, land, and property will not disappear in the foreseeable future. But it can be significantly ameliorated by political negotiations that recognize Palestinian national rights. The readiness of the Palestinian and Arab world for this solution to the Palestinian component of the Middle East conflict has been available for fifteen years, since 1973. It is Israel and the United States who are the primary impediments to these negotiations.

When pressed to move on this issue of Palestinian rights, Zionists tend to see themselves as embattled by a universal hatred. The claim that "the whole world is against us" has become a part of the Israeli national mythology.[30] But as far as the Western Christian world is concerned, in fact, Israel continues to enjoy uniquely favored status. There is great willingness among Christians to believe that Israel has a divinely given "right to exist" and that it is a land of superior social morals. When this latter belief is unmasked by negative realities, this is not welcome news for most Christians. Many translate this bad news into a worried concern that indicates their continued good will. In short, Christian criticism of Israel has been based primarily on the discovery of historical facts, not an a priori malice.

One has to ask whether part of the intransigence toward territorial compromise among Israeli leaders does not lie in the need to maintain a perceived threat of the outside Arab world in order to paper over internal conflicts within Israeli society. Maintaining the crisis psychology of war for survival silences the divisions between religious and secular Jews, Ashkenazi and Oriental Jews. Fomenting new dangers, planning new wars of "survival" against the Arabs, prevents Israel from flying apart from internal conflicts.[31]

If this is true, then trading the Territories for peace also would mean facing these internal contradictions. If peace were made with the Arab world, the size of the present military and secret police establishments would lose its justification. Many of their practices would become questionable. It would become necessary to reshape the Israel Defense Forces into a normal army of national defense, not a warrior cult engaged in covert expansion and violent repression of noncitizens. This would also mean facing the militarization of the whole of Israeli society, the virtual autonomy of the military from the civil government, and the domination of the economy by military production. One would also have to curb the expanding secret intelligence services, the *Mossad* and *Shin Bet*, which threaten to make Israel a police state for Jews, as well as Palestinians.

Such reshaping of Israeli society offers many promises. Israel could reconstitute its relationship with the Arab world as a partner in Middle East development. It could cease to be so dependent on American aid and cease to be called in as arms trader and trainer of mercenary armies to bring down popular Third World revolutions.

It could pursue a more positive foreign policy with Third World nations. Also, on the domestic side, it could cease to starve its welfare budget to feed its warfare budget. This would allow it to address the growing economic gaps between wealthy, mainly Ashkenazi, and poor, mainly Oriental, Jews, which threatens to turn into intercultural class warfare. Finally its democratic institutions and humanist values could be reclaimed and redeveloped.

But the decision to make peace by ceding the Territories will not succeed if it is undertaken as a misleading charade, or a new scheme to keep the land while ceding the Palestinian residents to the political control of Jordan. The "peace" proposals of both the so-called moderates (Peres) and hardliners (Shamir) have fallen into different versions of this scheme. This 'Jordanian Solution' may no longer be available, since the July 31, 1988 announcement by King Hussein that Jordan no longer claimed legal or financial responsibility for the West Bank. There must be genuine recognition of Palestinian political autonomy and self-government within at least a mini-region.

The claim that this would create an intolerable "security danger" is questionable. Demilitarization of the Palestinian region can be part of the autonomy negotiations. This might begin by the replacement of Israeli troops with UN troops to assure that there are no armed incursions across the borders. This, or course, means not simply that Palestinians could not send armed men across the border but that Israel could not send its armies into Palestinian territory. The Israeli military would have to accept a limitation of its aggression into Palestinian or other Arab lands, which Israel has never accepted since 1948.

The phobia against Palestinian autonomy in a region next to Israel is fed by a self-terrorization of Israeli people, convinced that its Arab neighbors desire its annihilation. This has become increasingly unreal, as both the Arab and the Palestinians have repeatedly indicated their willingness to settle with Israel on the basis of a territory restricted to and defined by 1949 borders. The power of the Israeli military, including its possession of nuclear weaponry, means that no Arab state seriously wants to go to war with it, despite posturing rhetoric aimed at placating militant elements in Arab societies.

Moreover, with the Palestinian issue settled, much of the impetus for this rhetoric would also decline. Israel might even become, as some of its early binationalist thinkers had hoped, a part of the Arab League, redefined as a Middle Eastern or "Semitic" league. It could then trade with the Arab nations as a partner, rather than being a pariah nation in the Middle East. The increasing proportion of Oriental Jews in Israeli society, who will eventually assume the leadership of its government, would also make it seem more acceptably a part of the Arab world, rather than a "colonial settler state" of Europeans. Without giving up the advantages of Western education and skills, these Oriental Jews could relearn Arabic and reintegrate their Arab cultural roots into their Israeli identity as an advantage, rather than a disadvantage, in dealing with their Semitic cousins.

Limiting Israel's territorial claims and allowing it to redevelop its culture and institutions in this direction means giving up three cherished Zionist myths: (1) that Jews have an a priori right to the whole of Palestine, (2) that the other people resident there historically, the Arab Palestinians, do not have a parallel claim on the land as a national community, and (3) that Israel must be an outpost of European people and culture, not a part of the "Levant." It is these three Zionist myths that have walled Israel into a segregated, hostile, and violent relationship to the rest of the communities of people that live around it.

Giving up these three myths would demand a fundamental shift in the understanding of Jewish identity or, rather, a decision in favor of a pluralist, rather than an ethnocentric, understanding of Jewish identity. We have suggested throughout this study that there are two different ways of construing the relationship of the particular and the universal. Both of these ways have existed in the Jewish tradition. One of these ways is to construe one's particular identity, in this case as a national, ethnic, and religious community, as unique and incomparable with the particularity of any other community. One's particularity separates this people from all other people and calls them to special obedience to God. This separation from other nations is construed as conferring a special holiness on the Jewish people. The gift of the land is seen as giving Jews a priori rights to the land that supercedes that of any other people.

These ethnocentric views of election misconstrue the religious idea of election by transferring it to superior innate qualities of Jews themselves. The religious idea of election does not claim any innate superiority for Jews but only a calling to be faithful to God by observing the commandments. If they do not do this, they are no more holy than any other people and their land is as unholy as any other land.[32]

The universalist tradition affirms Jewish particularity in solidarity with the particularity of other people. Concern for Jewish distinctiveness grounds an equal concern for the rights of other people to exist in distinct ways. Human beings must limit the claims of their own distinctiveness in order to accommodate themselves to the rights of others to live, side by side, with themselves. This is the fundamental biblical ethic of "loving the neighbor as oneself."

This ethic of mutual solidarity does not mean an anonymous universalism. Anonymous universalism generally conceals a hidden agenda of one group to set itself up as the "normative universal." This was the false universalism of Hellenism and of Christianity, which demanded that Jews stop being distinct in order to merge into a Greek or a Christian-defined "universal humanity." This type of false universalism has rightly been resisted by Jews through the ages. Rather, mutual solidarity means pursuing that mode of being for oneself that obliges one, at the same time, to be for others. This is the authentic ethic of mutuality that both Jewish and Christian ethics have sought, the one tending to err in the direction of ethnocentrism and the other in the direction of an imperialist false universalism.

To love one's neighbor as oneself means also that one cannot love everyone "equally." Human beings and cultural communities are finite. The ability to imagine and relate to infinite varieties of people is limited. Real uniqueness in persons and peoples is not affirmed by a generic diffuseness, which has no real content. Rather one must locate it in the concrete relations between different people who are actually called, either by choice or by historical circumstances, to live side by side with each other. The quest of Israeli Jews and Palestinian Arabs for a just and peaceful coexistence is an instance of the difficulty and challenge of that ethical commandment.

The struggle of Israeli Jews and Palestinian Arabs to find a way, personally and politically, to live together in one land reflects a worldwide dilemma and challenge. Is not, in fact, every land, every nation today a microcosm of many nations, many peoples? The nationalist myth of one land, one state for each ethnic, racial group has evaporated in the reality of global migrations and settlements of human groups. The task of creating justice and peace between Israelis and Palestinians, as two people claiming one land, mirrors the task of creating justice and peace between all peoples on one earth.

If we are to claim that God is the God of all nations, this can no longer mean a demand that all nations convert to one religion but a recognition that there is one ultimate unity behind the many names for divinity. We must see ourselves as children of the one God from whom all peoples spring. People have shaped themselves into distinctive historical communities. We are summoned to become sibling people to one another and caretakers of the one earth we all share.

Notes

CHAPTER 1. PEOPLEHOOD, COVENANT, AND LAND IN JUDAISM, CHRISTIANITY, AND ISLAM

1. See Albrecht Alt, "The Settlement of the Israelites in Palestine," in *Essays in Old Testament History and Religion* (Oxford: Blackwell, 1966), 173–222.
2. W. D. Davies, *The Gospel and the Land: Early Christianity and Jewish Territorial Doctrine* (Berkeley, CA: University of California Press, 1974), 17–18.
3. Norman K. Gottwald has proposed a theory of the origins of the Israelites as a federation of tribes already *in situ* in the hill regions on both sides of the Jordan, in rebellion against Egyptian and Philistine overlordship, in *Tribes of Yahweh: A Sociology of the Religion of Liberated Israel, 1250–1050 B.C.* (Maryknoll, NY: Orbis, 1979).
4. 2 Sam. 23:8–39; also 1 Chron. 11:10–47.
5. 2 Chron. 2:17 tells of a census of aliens in the land taken by Solomon in order to make this group do forced labor. But *1* Kings *5:13* reveals that, in fact, it was Israel that had to send contingents of forced labor to neighboring kings in Lebanon.
6. W. D. Davies, *The Territorial Dimension of Judaism* (Berkeley, CA: University of California Press, *1982*), *55–56*.
7. Delbert R. Hillers, *Covenant: The History of a Biblical Idea* (Baltimore, MD: John Hopkins University Press, *1969*), *46–71*.
8. Davies, *Gospel and Land*, *118*.
9. Ellis Rivkin, *A Hidden Revolution* (Nashville, TN: Abingdon Press, *1978*), 242, 289, 294.
10. Ibid., *34*.
11. Jacob Neusner, *From Politics to Piety: The Emergence of Pharisaic Judaism* (New York: Ktav, *1979*), *45–66*.
12. Ibid., *50*.
13. Davies, *Gospel and Land*, *52–54*.
14. Jacob Neusner, *A Life of Rabban Yohanan ben Zakkai* (Leiden: Brill, *1962*).
15. Rivkin, *Hidden Revolution*, *211–252*.
16. J. S. Brown, *Temple and Sacrifice in Rabbinic Judaism* (Evanston, IL: Seabury-Western Theological Seminary, *1963*), *26ff*.
17. Ellas Rivkin, *The Shaping of Jewish History* (New York: Charles Scribner's Sons, *1971*), *50*.
18. Jacob Neusner, "Man Without Territory: Mishnah's System of Sacrifice and Sanctuary," *History of Religions* 19 (November *1979*): *103–27*.
19. Davies, *Gospel and Land*, *67–8*.
20. Davies, *Territorial Dimension*, *34–35*.
21. Some Orthodox groups of Jews, most notably Neturei Karta, hold this view today even within the State of Israel; see Yerachimiel Domb, "Neturei Karta," in *Zionism Reconsidered: The Rejection of Jewish Normalcy*, ed. Michael Selzer (New York: Macmillan, *1970*), *23–48*.

22. Neusner, *ben Zakkai, 130-46.*
23. Raphael Patai, *Hebrew Goddess, 159-62, 258-69.*
24. *Pesikta Rabbati* 160a; see W. D. Davies, *Territorial Dimension, 103.*
25. Rabbi Eleaser of Modiim (C.E. 120-40) said, "God scattered Israel among the nations for the sole end that proselytes should wax numerous among them." T. B. Pes. 87b), see W. D. Davies, *Gospel and Land, 119-20.*
26. Bernard J. Bamberger, *Proselytism in the Talmudic Period* (New York: Ktav, *1968*).
27. Ibid.
28. Philo, "On the Migration of Abraham," II, in *The Essential Philo,* ed. Nahum N. Glatzer (New York: Schocken, *1971*).
29. Philo, "On Dreams, that they are God-sent," I, *215*, in vol. 5 of *Philo,* trans. F. H. Colsen and G. H. Whitaker, Loeb Classical Library, (Cambridge, MA: Harvard University Press, *1934*), 413.
30. Philo, *On Monarchy,* I, V.
31. R. B. Charles, *The Apocrypha and Pseudepigrapha of the Old Testament* (Oxford: Clarendon Press, *1913*), 2:463.
32. Ibid., *259*.
33. Davies, *Gospel and Land, 125.*
34. Ibid., *123-24*.
35. Philo, in "The Migration of Abraham," enjoins the observance of the laws and feasts with these words: "Nor does it follow, because the feast is the symbol of the joy of the soul and of its gratitude toward God, that we are to repudiate the assemblies ordained at the periodical seasons of the year; nor because the rite of circumcision is an emblem of the excision of pleasures and of all the passions, and of the destruction of that impious opinion, according to which the mind has imagined itself to be by itself competent to produce offspring, does it follow that we are to annul the law which has been enacted about circumcision . . . this class of things resembles the body and the other class the soul: therefore, just as we take care of the body because it is the abode of the soul, so also must we take care of the laws that are enacted in plain terms, for while they are regarded, those things also will be more clearly understood, of which these laws are the symbol. . . ." Glatzer, *Essential Philo,* 17:159-60.
36. Rosemary Ruether, *Faith and Fratricide: The Theological Roots of Anti-Semitism* (New York: Seabury Press, 1974), 149-65.
37. Rom. 7:7-12.
38. Rom. 2:14-24.
39. Lloyd Gaston, "Paul and the Torah," in *Anti-Semitism and the Formation of Christianity* (New York: Paulist Press, 1979), 48-71, argues that Paul's strictures against the Law apply only to gentile converts to Christianity.
40. Ruether, *Faith and Fratricide,* 131-37.
41. Ibid., 133-34, 147-48.
42. *Letter to Diogenes,* vol. 2 of *The Apostolic Fathers,* trans. Kirsopp Lake (Cambridge, MA: Harvard University Press, 1913), 350-79.
43. Eusebius of Caesaria, *Oration in Praise of Constantine,* vol. 1 of *Select Library of the Nicene and Post-Nicene Fathers,* 2d ser. (New York: Christian Literature, 1890), 581ff.
44. W. H. C. Frend, "The Roman Empire in the Eyes of Western Schismatics During the Fourth Century," in *Miscellanea Historiae Ecclesiasticae* (Louvain, 1961), 9-22.
45. Aurelius Prudentius Clemens's *Apotheosis* celebrates the exile of the Jews and the triumph of Christianity within the Roman Empire in these words:
Judaea, do you not deplore your crime? . . .
What judgment you deserve Titus has taught,
And Pompey, too; by their cohorts dispersed.

Your race is borne through every land and sea.
The Jew in exile wanders far and wide
Since he was banished from his fatherland,
And stained with blood of Christ, whom he denied,
Has paid the penalty his crime deserved.
See how the ancient virtue has declined!
The noble heir of the faithful patriarchs
Has been enslaved and is an outcast now.
The thrall adopts the faith of recent times,
So great its power, Confessing Christ, a race
Once infidel prevails, but subject now
To faithful lords, is that which doubted Christ.

lls. 503, 538–52.

Poems, vol. 52 of *Fathers of the Church*, trans. Sr. M. Clement Eagan (Washington, DC: Catholic University Press, 1962), 22–23.

46. Ruether, *Faith and Fratricide*, 183–95.
47. Gregory the Great, founder of the medieval papacy, faithfully reflected this policy of repression and protection of the Jews; see Ruether, *Faith and Fratricide*, 199–200.
48. Norman Stillman, *The Jews of Arab Lands: A History and Source Book* (Philadelphia: Jewish Publication Society of America, 1979), 22–24.
49. Tor Andrae, *Mohammed: The Man and His Faith* (New York: Harper & Row, 1960), 97–8.
50. Louis Ginsberg, *The Legends of the Jews* (Philadelphia: Jewish Publication Society of America, 1925), 223, n. 82, and 234, n. 136.
51. See "Ibrahim" and "Isma'il," in *Shorter Encyclopaedia of Islam*, ed. H. A. R. Gibb and J. H. Kramers (Leiden: Brill, 1953), 154–55, 178–79.
52. Mohammed Marmaduke Pickthall, trans., *The Meaning of the Glorious Koran* (New York: New American Library, 1953), 45.
53. Introductory commentary by Abdullah Yusuf Ali, *The Holy Qur'an* (Cambridge, MA: Khalil al-Rawal, 1946), 1–12.
54. W. Montgomery Watt, "Muhammed," in *The Central Islamic Lands*, vol. 1 of *The Cambridge History of Islam*, ed. P. M. Holt, Ann K. S. Lambton, and Bernard Lewis (Cambridge: Cambridge University Press, 1970), 43–44.
55. Sūra IV:46.
56. Sūras IV:171 and V:73.
57. "Djizya," in vol. 2 of *The Encyclopaedia of Islam*, H. A. R. Gibb et al. (Leiden: Brill, 1965), 559–67.
58. "Dhimma," in vol. 2 of *Encyclopaedia of Islam*, 227–31.
59. Translation by Abdullah Yusuf Ali, *Holy Qur'an*, 447.
60. C. E. Bosworth, "The Concept of Dhimma in Early Islam," in *Christians and Jews in the Ottoman Empire: The Functioning of a Plural Society* (New York: Holmes and Meier, 1982), 37–51.
61. Ibid., 8–9; also Stillman, *Jews of Arab Lands*, 63.
62. S. D. Goitein, *Jews and Arabs: Their Contacts Through the Ages* (New York: Schocken, 1974), 89–124.
63. Bosworth, "Concept of Dhimma," 48–49.
64. Travelers to Jerusalem in the nineteenth century remarked on the poverty-stricken appearance of the Jewish houses and clothes, but those who were invited into these Jewish homes were surprised to find these same Jews wearing fine clothes and having elegant home interiors: see Martin Gilbert, *Jerusalem, Rebirth of a City* (New York: Viking Penguin, 1985), 37–38.

65. Bernard Lewis, *The Jews of Islam* (Princeton, NJ: Princeton University Press, 1984), 54.

66. Goitein, *Jews and Arabs*, 87–88.

67. Lewis, *Jews of Islam*, 8–10.

68. See "Dar al-Islam," "Dar al-Harb," and "Dar al-Sulk" in vol. 2 of the *Encyclopaedia of Islam*, 126, 127–28, and 131.

69. Sūra V:23–29.

70. W. Montgomery Watt, "Muhammed," 44.

71. See "The Religious Status of Jerusalem and Palestine in Medieval Islam," in Y. Porath, *The Emergence of the Palestinian-Arab National Movement, 1918–1929* (London: Frank Cass, 1974), 1–4; also S. D. Goitein, "The Sanctity of Jerusalem and Palestine in Early Islam" in *Studies in Islamic History and Institutions* (Leiden: Brill, 1966), 135–48.

72. See "al-Kuds" in vol. 5 of the *Encyclopaedia of Islam*, 322–44.

73. Ibid., 330–31.

74. Y. Porath, *Emergence of the Palestinian-Arab National Movement*, 7.

75. Isa. 2:2–3 speaks of all nations going up to the mountain of the Lord, "to the house of the God of Jacob, that he may teach us his ways and that we may walk in his paths, for out of Zion shall go forth the Law and the word of the Lord from Jerusalem." The Christian tradition declares that after the Gentiles have been converted to Christ, the Jews also will lose their "hardness of heart" and be converted: Rom. 11:25–26. Islam claims that it is the true, original, monotheistic religion that both Judaism and Christianity corrupted. Jews and Christians are saved by sharing in that one true faith of Islam, and if they do not they will be punished: see Qur'an, V:18.

76. For Jewish views of tolerance, see Jacob Katz, *Exclusivism and Tolerance: Jewish-Gentile Relations in Medieval and Modern Times* (New York: Schocken, 1967). For Christian theologians who seek an egalitarian universalism with other world religions, see John Hick and Paul Knitter, *The Myth of Christian Uniqueness: Toward a Pluralistic Theology of Religions* (Maryknoll, NY: Orbis, 1987). For a Muslim account of tolerance, see Fazlur Rahman, *Islam and Modernity: Transformation of an Intellectual Tradition* (Chicago: Chicago University Press, 1982).

77. See particularly chapter 6 on Christian and Jewish fundamentalisms. For Islamic fundamentalism, see R. Hrair Dekmejian, *Islam in Revolution: Fundamentalism in the Arab World* (Syracuse, NY: Syracuse University Press, 1985).

CHAPTER 2. RELIGIOUS AND SECULAR ROOTS OF ZIONISM

1. David Biale, *Power and Powerlessness in Jewish History* (New York: Schocken Books, 1986), 47–57.

2. Julius H. Greenstone, *The Messianic Idea in Jewish History* (Philadelphia: Jewish Publication Society of America, 1906), 142–51.

3. Ibid., 182.

4. Leon Poliakov, *The History of Anti-Semitism: From Voltaire to Wagner* (New York: Vanguard Press, 1968), 217, 518, n. 10.

5. Bernard D. Weinryb, "Eastern European Jewry Since the Partition of Poland" in vol. 1 of *The Jews: Their History, Culture and Religion*, ed. Louis Finkelstein, (New York: Harper & Row, 1960), 321–71.

6. Shlomo Avineri, *The Making of Modern Zionism: The Intellectual Origins of the Jewish State* (New York: Basic Books, 1981), 36–46.
7. Excerpts from Yehudah Alkalai, *The Third Redemption* (1843), and Zvi Hirsch Kalischer, *Seeking Zion* (1862), are translated in Arthur Hertzberg, *The Zionist Idea: A Historical Analysis and Reader* (New York: Meridian, 1960), 102–14. See also Avineri, *Making of Modern Zionism*, 47–55.
8. Leo Pinsker, *Auto-Emancipation*, trans. D. S. Blondheim, 2d ed. (New York: Federation of American Zionists, 1916). See also Avineri, *Making of Modern Zionism*, 73–82.
9. Aaron David Gordon, "Our Tasks Ahead" (1920), in Hertzberg, *Zionist Idea*, 379–81.
10. Ahad Ha'am, *Nationalism and the Jewish Ethic*, ed. Hans Kohn (New York: Herzl Press, 1962), 203–4.
11. See Pamela Ann Smith, *Palestine and the Palestinians*, 1876–1983 (New York: St. Martin's Press, 1984), 44–53.
12. Itzhak Ben-Zvi, "Eretz Israel under Ottoman Rule," in *The Jews*, ed. Finkelstein, 602–89.
13. For Herzl's analysis of how Zionism should benefit anti-Semites, see his *The Jewish State* (New York: American Zionist Emergency Council, 1946), 80–81.
14. For Herzl's negotiations with heads of state, see especially *The Diaries of Theodor Herzl*, ed. Marvin Lowenthan (New York: Dial Press, 1956), for the period between June 2, 1895, and May 16, 1904.
15. In Herzl's utopian novel, he describes the sophisticated European culture that would characterize his ideal Jewish state: *Old-New Land*, trans. Lotta Levensohn (New York: Bloch, 1941).
16. Herzl, *The Jewish State*, 98–152.
17. See Klaus Herrmann, "Politics and Divine Promise," in *Judaism or Zionism: What Difference for the Middle East*, ed. EAFORD and AJAZ (London: Zed Books, 1986), 29–30. The traditional Orthodox rejection of Zionism continues to be maintained by some small Orthodox groups, most notably the Neturei Karta; see *Zionism Reconsidered: The Rejection of Jewish Normalcy*, ed. Michael Selzer (London: Macmillan, 1970), 23–48.
18. *Reform Judaism: A Historical Perspective*, ed. Joseph Blau (New York: Ktav, 1973).
19. Louis L. Snyder, *Varieties of Nationalism: A Comparative Study* (Hinsdale, IL: Dryden Press, 1976), 122–24.
20. Bernard Avishai, *The Tragedy of Zionism: Revolution and Democracy in the Land of Israel* (New York: Farrar, Straus & Giroux, 1985), 94.
21. Abraham Isaac Kook, "Lights for Rebirth," in Hertzberg, *Zionist Idea*, 430. For a new translation of Kook's writings and introduction to his thought, see Abraham Isaac Kook, *The Lights of Penitence, the Moral Principles Lights of Holiness, Essays, Letters and Poems*, trans. Ben Zion Bokser (New York: Paulist Press, 1978).
22. Kook, "The Land of Israel" in Hertzberg, *Zionist Idea*, 419–421; also Avineri, *Making of Modern Zionism*, 190.
23. Hertzberg, *Zionist Idea*, 419–21.
24. Avineri, *Making of Modern Zionism*, 194–95; also Ben Zion Bokser, ed., *Lights of Penitence*, 6–10.
25. Zeev Jabotinsky, *Ktavim* (Works), vol. 1 (Jerusalem and Tel Aviv, 1947), 28–29, cited in Avineri, *Making of Modern Zionism*, 163.
26. Avineri, *Making of Modern Zionism*, 172; see also Jabotinsky's novel, *Samson the Nazirite*, trans. Cyrus Brooks (London: M. Secker, 1930), where the Philistines are presented as a fascist society that the Jews are to emulate, over against the decadent Canaanites.

27. Avineri, *Making of Modern Zionism*, 162.
28. Joseph Scheerman, *Rebel and Statesman: The Vladimir Jabotinsky Story* (New York: Thomas Yoseloff, 1956), 250–51, 399–415. Also Lenni Brenner, *The Iron Wall: Zionist Revisionism from Jabotinsky to Shamir* (London: Zed Books, 1984), 66–71.
29. See Edwin Black, *The Transfer Agreement: The Untold Story of the Secret Agreement Between the Third Reich and Jewish Palestine* (New York: Macmillan, 1984), esp. 380.
30. Ibid., 380–400.
31. Brenner, *Iron Wall*, 194–99, translates the document of the *Irgun* to the Axis powers for the solution to the Jewish question and the alliance of the *Irgun* with the Axis against the Allies.
32. See the evaluation of Weizmann's and Ben-Gurion's views of the Palestinians, and their similarity with those of Jabotinsky, in Simha Flapan, *Zionism and the Palestinians* (New York: Barnes and Noble, 1979), 17–120, 131–48.
33. Avineri, *Making of Modern Zionism*, 180.
34. Flapan, *Zionism and the Palestinians*, 142–45.
35. "We shall try to spirit the penniless population across the border by procuring employment for them in the transit countries while denying any employment in our country," *Diaries of Theodor Herzl*, 188.
36. See Michael Palumbo, *The Palestinian Catastrophe: The 1948 Expulsion of a People from Their Homeland* (London: Faber and Faber, 1987), 2–4.
37. Avineri, *Making of Modern Zionism*, 198–216.
38. Flapan, *Zionism and the Palestinians*, 163–64.
39. Hertzberg, *Zionist Idea*, 444–49.
40. "Toward a Jewish State: The Biltmore Program," *The Israel-Arab Reader*, ed. Walter Laqueur (New York: Bantam Books, 1969), 77–78.
41. Judah Magnes and Martin Buber, *Arab-Jewish Unity: Testimony before the Anglo-American Commission for the Ihud (Union) Association* (London: Victor Gollancz, 1947), 42.
42. See Simha Flapan, *The Birth of Israel: Myths and Realities* (New York: Pantheon, 1987), 3–12.

CHAPTER 3.   CHRISTIANITY AND ZIONISM

1. Cecil Roth, *A History of the Marranos* (Philadelphia: Jewish Publication Society of America, 1947).
2. Yosef Hayim Yerushalmi, *From Spanish Court to Italian Ghetto: Isaac Cordoso: A Study in Seventeenth Century Marranos and Jewish Apocalyptic* (New York: Columbia University Press, 1971), 14–16.
3. John Lilburne, leader of the Leveller party during the English Civil War, in a 1647 letter to William Prinne, declared that "Jesus alone is King of his saints and lawgiver to his Church and people," in William Haller, *Liberty and Reformation in the Puritan Revolution* (New York: Columbia University Press, 1955), 260.
4. Ibid., 353–54.
5. See Gershom Scholem, "The Kabbalist R. Abraham b. Eliezer ha-Levi (Hebrew)," *Kiryath Sepher* 2 (1925): 101–4, 269–73, and 7 (1931): 149–65, 440–56.
6. Most seventeenth-century restorationists believed that the Jews should be converted and then return to Palestine, but some, such as Isaac de la Peyrere (who may have been a Marrano), envisioned them returning in the unconverted state; see Lawrence Epstein, *Zion's Call: Christian Contributions to the Development of Israel* (New York: University Press of America, 1984), 14.

7. Regina Sharif, *Non-Jewish Zionism: Its Roots in Western History* (London: Zed Press, 1983), 17.

8. Ibid., 18.

9. Ibid.

10. This material on the restoration of the Jews occurs in the apocalyptic tract by Mary Cary (Rande), *The Little Horns Doom and Downfall, a New and More Exact Mappe of New Jerusalem's Glory,* April 17, 1651 (Thomason Tracts).

11. Ibid., 161.

12. Sharif, *Non-Jewish Zionism,* 25.

13. See Lucien Wolf, *Manasseh ben Israel's Mission to Oliver Cromwell* (London: Jewish Historical Society, 1901), which contains the text of his *Hope of Israel.*

14. Sharif, *Non-Jewish Zionism,* 27.

15. Ibid., 28.

16. Barbara Tuchman, *Bible and Sword: England and Palestine from the Bronze Age to Balfour* (New York: New York University Press), 105.

17. Ibid., 213–14, 216.

18. Ibid., 216.

19. Ibid., 113–17, 126–28.

20. Alexander was consecrated by the Archbishop of Canterbury, November 12, 1841, and dispatched to Palestine November 29 of that year; Tuchman, *Bible and Sword,* 118, 133.

21. Col. Claude R. Condor, *Tent Work in Palestine: A Record of Discovery and Adventure,* 2 vols. (New York: Palestine Exploration Fund, 1878). Condor wrote numerous other works on biblical history and archaeology; see Tuchman, *Bible and Sword,* 153–54, 157–60.

22. Lucien Wolf, *Sir Moses Montefiore* (London: J. Murray, 1884).

23. Tuchman, *Bible and Sword,* 165–66.

24. Ibid., 119–20.

25. Ibid., 203–17.

26. Ibid., 20.

27. Blanche Dugdale, *Arthur James Balfour* (New York: G. P. Putnam, 1937), 2:58.

28. David S. Wyman, *The Abandonment of the Jews: America and the Holocaust, 1941–1945* (New York: Pantheon, 1948), 311f; Bernard Wasserstein, *Britain and the Jews of Europe, 1939–1945* (Oxford: Clarendon Press, 1979).

29. For example, in Cotton Mather, *Soldiers Counselled* (1689); see Richard Slotkin, *Regeneration through Violence: The Mythology of the American Frontier, 1600–1860* (Middletown, CT: Wesleyan University Press, 1973).

30. Conrad Cherry, *God's New Israel: Religious Interpretations of America's Destiny* (Englewood Cliffs, NJ: Prentice-Hall, 1971).

31. Peter Grose, *Israel in the Mind of America* (New York: Knopf, 1983), 55.

32. United States aid (military and economic) to Israel has moved from $2.5 billion in the early 1980s to more than $5 billion a year in 1987 and 1988. Total figures are difficult to ascertain because significant amounts are given under categories not conventionally used for foreign military aid—economic assistance, grants, and credits. See Report by the Comptroller General of the United States, *U.S. Assistance to the State of Israel* (Washington, D.C.: General Accounting Office, June 24, 1983), also published under the title *American Aid to Israel: Nature and Impact,* eds. Mohamed Khawas and Samir Aded-Rabbo (Brattleboro, VT: Amana Books, 1984). For recent figures see *U.S. Statistical Abstract* (Washington, D.C.: GPO, 1987 and 1988).

33. Samuel H. Levine, "Palestine in the Literature of the United States to 1867," in Isidore S. Meyer, *Early History of Zionism in America* (New York: American Jewish Historical Society, 1958).

34. David A. Rausch, *Zionism within Early American Fundamentalism, 1878–1918* (New York: Edwin Mellen Press, 1979), 79–125.

35. Ibid., 65–71, 79–125.

36. Ronald R. Stockton, "Christian Zionism—Prophecy and Public Opinion," *Middle East Journal* 49 (Spring 1987): 234–54.

37. Grose, *Israel in the Mind of America*, 35–37; for the Blackstone Memorial, see W. E. Blackstone, *Palestine for the Jews* (1891), reprinted in *Christian Protagonists for Jewish Restoration* (New York: Arno Press, 1977).

38. Rausch, *Zionism*, 88.

39. Ibid., 95.

40. Joseph P. Sternstein, "Reform Judaism and Zionism, 1895–1984," in *Herzl Year Book* (New York: Theodor Herzl Foundation, 1963), 5:11–31.

41. In 1914 less than 1 percent of American Jews belonged to Zionist organizations; by 1918 the number had increased to 8 percent; see Grose, *Israel in the Mind of America*, 45, 51.

42. Herzel Fishman, *American Protestantism and a Jewish State* (Detroit: Wayne State University Press, 1973), 72–77.

43. Grose, *Israel in the Mind of America*, 134–58, 244–51.

44. Ibid., 184–205, 276–98.

45. Ibid., 256, 293.

CHAPTER 4. THE EMERGENCE AND SURVIVAL OF PALESTINIAN NATIONALISM

1. Simha Flapan, *Zionism and the Palestinians* (London: Croom Helm, 1979), 70–83, 131–48.

2. R. Hrair Dekmejian, *Islam in Revolution: Fundamentalism in the Arab World* (Syracuse, NY: Syracuse University Press, 1985), esp. 3–75.

3. Ibid., 99–101. In the trial of the *Jihad* leaders for the assassination of President Sadat, the work of Muhammed abd al-Salam Faraj, *Al-Jihad: The Forgotten Pillar* was shown to be a foundational text. This work argues that the assassination of apostate Arab Muslim leaders is the sixth pillar or duty of the observant Muslim.

4. Barry Rubin, *The Arab States and the Palestinian Conflict* (Syracuse, NY: Syracuse University Press, 1981).

5. For the diplomatic history of the Arab states vis-à-vis the League of Nations and the United Nations on the Palestine question, see particularly Fred J. Khouri, *The Arab-Israeli Dilemma*, 3d ed. (Syracuse, NY: Syracuse University Press, 1985).

6. George Antonius, *The Arab Awakening: The Story of the Arab National Movement* (London: Hamish Hamilton, 1983), 292–94. Original edition, 1938.

7. Ibid., 111–12, 119–20. See also Bassim Tibi, *Arab Nationalism: A Critical Enquiry* (New York: Macmillan, 1981; German 1971), 69–96.

8. Antonius, *Arab Awakening*, 135–42.

9. Ibid., 163–85 and appendix A: The McMahon correspondence was not officially released by the British government until 1939, after Antonius's book was published. For British hearings on the correspondence, see Walid Khalidi, *From Haven to Conquest: Readings in Zionism and the Palestinian Problem until 1948* (Washington, D.C.: Institute for Palestine Studies, 1987), 219–21.

10. Antonius, *Arab Awakening*, 252–53.

11. Ibid., appendix D.

12. Ibid., appendix E.

13. Ibid., 292–94.

14. Ibid., 305.

15. Ibid., 325–49.

16. Ibid., 368–86.

17. This attitude is summed up in the oft-quoted statement of Golda Meir: "There is no such thing as Palestinians. . . . It was not as though there was a Palestinian people in Palestine considering itself as a Palestinian people and we came and threw them out and took their country away from them. They did not exist." Interview with Frank Giles in the *Sunday Times*, June 15, 1969.

18. Y. Porath, *The Emergence of the Palestinian-Arab National Movement, 1918–1929* (London: Frank Cass, 1974), 4–7.

19. Ibid., 7–8.

20. Ibid., 121–83.

21. Ibid., 32–34, 90–93.

22. Ibid., 39–63.

23. Ibid., 144, 147–58, 172–73.

24. Ibid., 184–207.

25. For the mufti's activities in Iraq and Axis Europe, see J. C. Hurewitz, *The Struggle for Palestine* (New York: Schocken, 1976), 146–55. For an account of the mufti's leadership prior to his flight, from a Palestinian perspective, see Taysir Jbara, *Palestinian Leader, Hajj Amin al-Husayni, Mufti of Jerusalem* (Princeton, NJ: Kingston Press, 1985).

26. Hurewitz, *Struggle for Palestine*, 60–63; also Y. Porath, *The Palestinian-Arab National Movement. From Riots to Rebellion*, vol. 2, *1929–1939* (London: Frank Cass, 1977), 49–79, 165–66.

27. For the wavering of Arab nationalist leaders between alignment with the Axis or the Allied powers in the early stages of the war, see Rubin, *Arab States*, 117–32.

28. For the usefulness of the boycott in cementing the exclusiveness of the Jewish *Yishuv*, see Flapan, *Zionism and the Palestinians*, 217–23.

29. See Barbara Kalkas, "The Revolt of 1936: A Chronicle of Events," in *The Transformation of Palestine: Essays on the Origin and Development of the Arab-Israeli Conflict*, ed. Ibrahim Abu-Lughod (Evanston, IL: Northwestern University Press, 1971), 237–74. Also Porath, *Palestinian-Arab National Movement*, 2:233–73 and Hurewitz, *Struggle for Palestine*, 67–92.

30. For the Peel Commission Report, see Walter Laqueur, ed. *The Israel-Arab Reader*, (New York: Bantam Books, 1969), 56–57.

31. Hurewitz, *Struggle for Palestine*, 77–78, on the struggles over the Peel Commission Report in the Jewish Agency.

32. Ibid., 78–80, for the Zionist and Arab rejections of the Peel Commission Report.

33. See Laqueur, *Israel-Arab Reader*, 64–75.

34. Hurewitz, *Struggle for Palestine*, 94–111.

35. Laqueur, *Israel-Arab Reader*, 76–77.

36. Hurewitz, *Struggle for Palestine*, 146–52.

37. Ibid., 152–55.

38. Ibid., 112–23.

39. Ibid., 249–53.

40. For Abdullah's and Egyptian views of the mufti, see Rubin, *Arab States, 185–204.*

41. For Ben-Gurion's satisfaction at the mufti's sabotage of moderate leadership, see Simha Flapan, *The Birth of Israel: Myths and Realities* (New York: Pantheon, 1987), 67.

42. Ibid., 55–80.

43. Rubin, *Arab States*, 205–15.

44. Ibid., 206.

45. Khouri, *Arab-Israeli Dilemma*, 61–63. For the struggle between Truman and the State Department in the early months of 1948, see Peter Grose, *Israel in the Mind of America* (New York: Random House, 1983), 255–75.

46. See Rubin, *Arab States*, 196–97; also Dekmejian, *Islam in Revolution*, 82.

47. For the military strength of the Palestinian Arabs and the Arab Liberation Army between January and May 15, 1948, see Khalidi, *From Haven to Conquest*, 858–60.

48. For a dramatic description of this period of the war before May 1948 and the buildup of Israeli armaments, see Larry Collins and Dominique Lapierre, *O Jerusalem* (New York: Simon & Schuster, 1972), esp. chaps. 4 and 5.

49. For the seizure of arms and ammunition by the British authorities from Arabs compared to those seized from Jews, see Khalidi, *From Haven to Conquest*, 845. For the development of the *Haganah* in the pre-state period, see M. P. Waters, *Haganah: The Story of Jewish Self-Defense in Palestine* (London: Newman Wolsey, 1947).

50. Walid Kahlidi estimated that the total Arab strength on May 15, 1948, was 19,269, with 13,876 in the combined five Arab armies; 1,563 in the Palestinian local militias; and 3,869 in the Arab Liberation Army: *From Haven to Conquest*, 858–60, 867–71. He estimated that Jewish strength at that time was 27,400 with more than 90,000 who could be mobilized: 32,000 in the reserves; 15,410 in the settlement police; 9,000 in youth militia; 32,000 in the homeguard; and about 4,000 in dissident groups.

Ben-Gurion noted in his *Diary* on May 15, 1948, that he had 24,000 in the brigades; 4,161 in service units; and 1,719 in training; or a total of 29,880. (See Flapan, *Zionism and the Palestinians*, 349, n. 14; Flapan, however, totals the number as 30,574.)

Khouri estimates *Haganah* strength in May as 60,000–70,000, perhaps counting both the first-line troops and the reserves. He estimates Israeli strength in October as 75,000–120,000, which includes tens of thousands of new immigrants and foreign volunteers; *Arab-Israeli Dilemma*, 85. The difficulty in counting Israeli troops' strength comes from the various categories of troops, the first-line troops, Palmach and KHISH, and the various second-line troops created for home defense: garrison troops, settlement police, and home guard, plus the unofficial *Irgun*, which was incorporated into the *Haganah* by the end of the war.

51. Khouri, *Arab-Israeli Dilemma*, 73–81.

52. Ibid., 84–98.

53. Michael Palumbo, *The Palestinian Catastrophe: The 1948 Expulsion of a People from Their Homeland* (London: Faber and Faber, 1987), 166–67.

54. Rubin, *Arab States*, 205.

55. Khouri, *Arab-Israeli Dilemma*, 123–81.

56. UN Resolution #194 of December 11, 1948, resolved that "the refugees wishing to return to their homes and live at peace with their neighbors should be permitted to do so at the earliest practicable date, and that compensation should be paid for the property of those choosing not to return and for loss of or damage to property which, under principles of international law or in equity, should be

made good by the Governments or authorities responsible." This resolution was regularly reaffirmed by the United Nations, and all these reaffirmations were reaffirmed in the December 19, 1967, UN General Assembly Resolution #234A, in response to the report of the commissioner-general of UNRWA for Palestine refugees in the Near East: see Khouri, *Arab-Israeli Dilemma*, 412, 421. In 1949 the Syrians offered to resettle 300,000 refugees, but this was ignored by Ben-Gurion. See Palumbo, *Palestinian Catastrophe*, 182.

57. Khouri, *Arab-Israeli Dilemma*, 168–71.

58. On the importance of the familial network, see Rosemary Sayigh, *Palestinians: From Peasants to Revolutionaries* (London: Zed Press, 1979), 23–24.

59. Helena Cobban, *The Palestinian Liberation Organization: People, Power and Politics* (Cambridge: Cambridge University Press, 1984), 21–23. Also Abdullah Frangi, *The PLO and Palestine* (London: Zed Press, 1982), 94–99.

60. Cobban, *Palestinian Liberation Organization*, 15–16, 24.

61. Ibid., 10, 28–30.

62. Ibid., 140–52.

63. Ibid., 157–61.

64. Ibid., 165–67.

65. Ibid., 11–14; also Frangi, *PLO and Palestine*, 145–57; Cheryl Rubenberg, *The Palestinian Liberation Organization: Its Institutional Infrastructure* (Belmont, MA: Institute of Arab Studies, 1983).

66. Cobban, *Palestinian Liberation Organization*, 41–42.

67. Ibid., 49–53.

68. On the development of policies of reprisals and preemptive strikes, see David Hirst, *The Gun and the Olive Branch: The Roots of Violence in The Middle East*, 2d ed., (London: Faber and Faber, 1984), 177–84.

69. Cobban, *Palestinian Liberation Organization: People, Power, and Politics*, 55, 232. See also Yossi Melman, *The Master Terrorist: The True Story of Abu-Nidal* (New York: Adama Books, 1986), esp. 135.

70. UN Resolution #3236. Text available in Jorgen S. Nielsen, ed., *International Documents on Palestine* (Beirut: The Institute of Palestine Studies, 1974), 186–87.

71. Cobban, *Palestinian Liberation Organization: People, Power and Politics*, 215–41.

72. On September 1, 1975, as part of the second Egyptian-Israeli Sinai agreement, the United States, in a secret memorandum, promised Israel that it would not recognize or negotiate with the PLO as long as the PLO does not "recognize Israel's right to exist and does not accept Security Resolutions 242 and 338." For the text of the memorandum, which was leaked to the *New York Times* in mid-September, 1975, see Cobban, *Palestinian Liberation Organization: People, Power and Politics*, 67.

73. The basic framework for a peace conference in Geneva to settle the Israeli-Palestinian conflict has been in place since 1976 and generally accepted by the Arab states, the PLO, Second and Third World nations and Western Europe. The United Staes and Israel have created the major stumbling blocks to holding this conference through the unwillingness to allow the PLO to be seated as a recognized partner in the negotiations and to accept the return of the Occupied Territories: see Khouri, *Arab-Israeli Dilemma*, 402–3.

74. Cobban, *Palestinian Liberation Organization: People, Power and Politics*, 62.

75. Ibid., 84–86.

76. Rashid Khalidi, *Under Siege: P.L.O. Decisionmaking During the 1982 War* (New York: Columbia University Press, 1986), 20–41.

77. Cobban, *Palestinian Liberation Organization: People, Power and Politics*, 73; see also Jonathan C. Randal, *Going All the Way: Christian Warlords, Israeli Adventurers and the War in Lebanon* (New York: Viking Press, 1983), 84.

78. Already in 1948, Ben-Gurion and other leaders had developed a "master plan" of Israel's expansion that included annexation of the West Bank and Gaza Strip, control of southern Lebanon to the Litani River and the installation of a Christian regime dependent on Israel. See Michael Palumbo, *The Palestinian Catastrophe* (London: Faber and Faber, 1987), 183.

79. Cobban, *Palestinian Liberation Organization: People, Power and Politics*, 94–95.

80. Khalidi, *Under Siege*, 37–39.

81. For the "Sharon plan" for the Lebanon war, see Hirst, *The Gun and the Olive Branch*, 402–3. Also Khalidi, *Under Siege*, 46–47.

82. According to the official Lebanese police report, the wartime casualties were 19,085 killed and 30,302 wounded. Of the casualties in Beirut, 84 percent were civilians. Khalidi, *Under Siege*, 200, n. 5.

83. Khalidi, *Under Siege*, 132.

84. Ibid., 132–35.

85. Ibid., 99–165. The Israeli siege continued more than two weeks after the PLO had accepted the Habib plan to evacuate, because the Israelis still hoped to destroy the PLO leaders and eliminate the PLO altogether as a military and political force. See George W. Ball, *Error and Betrayal in Lebanon* (Washington, DC: Foundation for Middle East Peace, 1984).

86. Since Beirut was filled with journalists, the massacres of Sabra and Shatila were extensively covered by the press. For an account that gathers together testimonies of survivors, see Abdallah Frangi, *The PLO and Palestine* (London: Zed Press, 1983), 222–40. Also Jean Genet, "Four Hours in Shatila," *Journal of Palestine Studies* 12: (Spring 1983): 3–22.

87. Israeli Commission of Inquiry into the Events at the Refugee Camps in Beirut, *The Beirut Massacre: The Complete Kahan Commission Report* (Tel Aviv: Kohl-Carz, 1983). See also Ammon Kapeliouk, *Sabra and Shatila: Inquiry into a Massacre* (Belmont, MA: Association of Arab-American University Graduates, 1984).

88. See Emile F. Sahliyeh, *The PLO After the Lebanon War* (Boulder, CO: Westview Press, 1986), 87–101. Also G. H. Jansen, "Arafat's Chance to Rebuild the PLO: The 17th PNC in Amman," *Middle East International*, no. 238 (Nov. 23, 1984): 4–5; and G. H. Jansen, "The Mandate for Moderation," *Middle East International*, no. 239 (December 7, 1984): 3–4.

89. Lamis Andoni, "The 18th PNC: No to the US; Yes to the USSR," *Middle East International*, no. 299 (May 1, 1987): 3–4.

90. The poll was published as a pamphlet by Al-Fajr (E. Jerusalem, 1986).

91. Data from the Palestine Human Rights Information Center, June 25, 1988 (P. O. Box 20479, Jerusalem). For harassment of hospital workers and arrests of the wounded in hospitals, see Etan Vlessing, "Intimidating Palestine's Health Workers," *Middle East Internatinal*, no. 321 (March 19, 1988): 17–18.

92. See Mubarak Awad, "Non-Violent Resistance: A Strategy for the Occupied Territories," *Journal of Palestine Studies*, 13: (Summer 1984), 22–36.

93. See "A Palestinian Finds Support among Sympathetic Jews," *Washington Post*, Nov. 22, 1987, section A. Oz veShalom-Netivot Shalom, a religious Zionist group, has published an information packet on Mubarak Awad and the struggle to prevent his deportation, December, 1987 (P. O. Box 4433, Jerusalem 91043). Also Israel Shahak, "Violence against Non-Violence," *Middle East International*, no. 302 (June 12, 1987) 16–17. On the deportation of Mubarak Awad, see Uli Schmetzer, "Despite Plea from Schultz, Israel Rules Activist will be Deported," *Boston Globe*, June 8, 1988, pp. 1,6. Also Marvine Howe, "Ousted Palestinian-American says 'Shamir Made me a Hero' ", *New York Times*, June 15, 1988, p. 6.

94. "Arafat Links Recognition of Israel to Peace Talks," *Chicago Tribune*, January 15, 1988 (from Baghdad, Iraq).

95. In August 1986 the joint Labor-Likud government amended the 1948 Prevention of Terrorism ordinance to make "the establishment of contact by an Israeli citizen or resident, knowingly and without lawful authorization, within or beyond the boundaries of the State of Israel, with any persons holding any position with any organization that the Israeli government has declared a terrorist organization" a criminal offense, carrying a penalty of three years in prison. On November 7, 1986, four of the delegates returning from a symposium on peace held in Rumania with PLO officials present were arrested on return to Israel. *MERIP Report* 17 (March-April 1987): 42.

96. "Trampling on the Law: Legal Ramifications of Closing the Two PLO Offices in the United States," *Palestine Human Rights News Letter* (October-November 1987): 11.

97. Cobban, *Palestinian Liberation Organization: People, Power and Politics*, 267–68.

98. UN General Assembly Resolution #3379 (November 10, 1975).

99. Alain Gresh, *The PLO: The Struggle Within: Toward an Independent Palestinian State* (London: Zed Press, 1985).

CHAPTER 5. CONTRADICTIONS OF THE JEWISH STATE

1. See above, chapter 2.

2. The statement that Israel is the only democracy in the Middle East is a Zionist commonplace. It is repeated endlessly with no effort to recognize the lack of democratic rights for Palestinians and also the erosion of democracy for Israelis. For concerns among Israelis over growing racist and fascist trends in Israel, see *Israeli Settler Violence, 1980–1984* (Chicago: Palestine Human Rights Campaign, 1985), 68–71.

3. Shabtai Teveth, *Ben-Gurion and the Palestinian Arabs: From Peace to War* (New York: Oxford University Press, 1985), 179–84.

4. Royal Commission on Palestine, *Palestine Royal Commission Report* (London: His Majesty's Stationery Office, 1937).

5. *The Jewish Case: Before the Anglo-American Committee of Inquiry on Palestine as Presented by the Jewish Agency for Palestine* (Jerusalem: Jewish Agency for Palestine, 1947), 71.

6. Teveth, *Ben-Gurion*, 188. Teveth cites several statements made by Ben-Gurion in 1937 and 1938 showing that he regarded the partition of Palestine as acceptable as the basis of a Jewish state only as a beginning for a continually expanding state.

7. The literature on the 1948 flight-expulsion of the Palestinians, and the creation of the refugees, is extensive. The Israeli government has denied expelling the Palestinians and has claimed that the Arab governments called them to come out. Careful studies of the radio broadcasts of the Arab states to the Palestinians have shown that no such broadcasts were made and indeed the Arab states were urging the Palestinians not to flee. For a detailed study of the whole history of the flight and expulsion of the Palestinians in 1948–49, see Michael Palumbo, *The Palestinian Catastrophe* (London: Faber and Faber, 1987). A detailed study of the expulsion of Palestinians from Galilee, drawn from firsthand testimony of refugees, is Nafz Nazzal, *The Palestinian Exodus from Galilee: 1948* (Washington, DC: Institute for Palestine Studies, 1978).

8. United Nations General Resolution #194, of December 11, 1948.

9. Uri Davis, *Israel: An Apartheid State* (London: Zed Books, 1987), 44–49. See also Uri Davis and Walter Lehn, "And the Fund Still Lives," *Journal of Palestine Studies* 7: (Summer 1987): 3–33.

10. Davis, *Israel*, 40.

11. Ibid., 20.

12. Janet Abu-Lughod, "The Demographic War for Palestine," *The Link* 19 (December 1986): 4.

13. Ibid., 5.

14. Ibid., 8.

15. The 1988 *World Almanac* gives the official figures of Israel's population as 4,208,000; 83 percent as Jewish. This would give a figure of 715,250 for "non-Jews," most of whom would be Palestinians.

16. Popular Zionist theory, exemplified in Joan Peters, *From Time Immemorial* (New York: Harper & Row, 1984), has argued that Palestine was almost uninhabited in 1900 and most of the Palestinians emigrated there in the 1920s in response to improving conditions created by Zionists. Janet Abu-Lughod, comparing Turkish with British census figures for the period, shows that the Palestinians were in place in the Ottoman period, that the increase from 630,000 to 677,000 between 1914 and 1922 shows that there was probably some out-migration, the increase being lower than would be expected from natural increase: "Demographic War," 7.

17. The phrase *non-Jews* used for Palestinians in the Balfour Declaration is a striking indication of British discriminatory bias, when it is remembered that Palestinians at this time made up 88 percent of the population.

18. "The White Paper of 1939," in *The Israel-Arab Reader*, ed. Walter Laqueur (New York: Bantam Books, 1969), 64ff.

19. Henry Feingold, *The Politics of Rescue* (New Brunswick, NJ: Rutgers University Press, 1970), 70; also Peter Grose, *Israel in the Mind of America* (New York: Knopf, 1983), 108, 110–12. The Zionist group, the *Irgun*, led a passionate campaign against this mainstream American Jewish inaction on rescue, but with little effect.

20. *Ray Tzair Bizaron* (Oct. 1943): 1–13, in Leon W. Wells, *Who Speaks for the Vanquished: American Judaism and the Holocaust* (New York: Peter Lang Press, 1987), 184. Wells, a death camp survivor, argues that the main reason for American Jewish inaction on rescue was the unwillingness to integrate large numbers of indigent refugees into the American Jewish community. Insisting that the refugees should go to Palestine was the way to avoid this. Peter Grose, *Israel in the Mind of America*, suggests the same underlying motivation.

21. *Fakten und Meinungen* (September 1943): 11, in Leon W. Wells, *Who Speaks for the Vanquished*, 186.

22. Grose, *Israel in the Mind of America*, 196–201, 208–11, 232–98.

23. Ibid., 210.

24. Jacob Lestschinsky, "Jewish Migrations, 1840–1956," in *The Jews: Their History, Culture and Religion*, ed. Louis Finkelstein, 3d ed. (New York: Harper & Row, 1960), 1581–84; also Janet Abu-Lughod, "Demographic War," 4.

25. Bernard Lewis, *The Jews of Islam* (Princeton, NJ: Princeton University Press, 1984), 154–91.

26. Milton Himmelfarb, "Jews Outside of Israel, the United States and the Soviet Empire," in Finkelstein, *The Jews*, 1680, 1688.

27. David Hirst, *The Gun and the Olive Branch: The Roots of Violence in The Middle East*, 2d. ed., (London: Faber and Faber, 1984), 155–64. For the deterioration of the situation of the Iraqi Jews in the nineteeth to twentieth centuries, see Nissim Rejwan, *The Jews of Iraq: 3000 Years of History and Culture* (Boulder, CO: Westview Press, 1985), 210–48.

28. These figures are from Howard Morley Sachar, *Diaspora: An Inquiry into the Contemporary Jewish World* (New York: Harper & Row, 1985), 284–5. However, the 1988 *World Almanac* gives 8,050,100 for the Jewish population of North America and 3,177,380 for the Jewish population of the USSR. (p. 51).

29. See Ari L. Goldman, "Israel Asking U.S. to Bar Soviet Jews," *New York Times*, March 1, 1987.

30. Ian Lustick, *Arabs in the Jewish State: Israel's Control of a National Minority* (Austin, TX: University of Texas Press, 1980), 65–81.

31. Elia T. Zureik, *The Palestinians in Israel: A Study in Internal Colonialism* (London: Routledge and Kegan Paul, 1979), 142–65.

32. Lustick, *Arabs in the Jewish State*, 82–149.

33. Ibid., 150–97.

34. Ibid., 198–231.

35. The Koenig memorandum was leaked to the Israeli press and published in *Al-Hamishmar*, the official organ of the Mapam party. Translated in SWASIA (Washington, DC) 3, no. 41 (October 15, 1976): 1–8; see Lustick, *Arabs in the Jewish State*, 68–69.

36. Lustick, *Arabs in the Jewish State*, 107–8.

37. Ibid., 167.

38. Davis, *Israel*, 49–55; also Lustick, *Arabs in the Jewish State*, 96–7.

39. Zureik, *Palestinians in Israel*, 149–59; also Lustick, *Arabs in the Jewish State*, 168–69.

40. For a general study of the crisis of religious politics in Israel, see Norman Zucker, *The Coming Crisis in Israel: Private Faith and Public Policy* (Cambridge, MA: M.I.T. Press, 1973).

41. Because of the lack of civil marriage in Israel, not only is marriage between Jew and non-Jew forbidden, but also between any combination of Christians, Moslems, and Druze. See Lustick, *Arabs in the Jewish State*, 133–34.

42. Ibid., 189–90.

43. Ibid., 137–43, 241, 247.

44. Michael Jansen, *Dissonance in Zion* (London: Zed Press, 1987), 19–23.

45. See the *Report of the Anglo-American Committee of Inquiry* (Cmd. 6808) 1946, issued by His Majesty's Stationery Office. Also Jansen, *Dissonance*, 23.

46. On August 8, 1982, in a speech at the National Defense College, Prime Minister Begin defended the 1982 war in Lebanon as a war by choice, rather than one forced upon Israel by outside invasion, by stating that the 1956 and 1967 wars were also such wars by choice. This statement indicated the disparity between Begin's own understanding of these past wars and the official government and IDF ideology, which always claimed that these past wars were forced upon Israel and there was no alternative. See *Jerusalem Post International Edition*, August 22–28, 1982; also Jansen, *Dissonance*, 67.

47. Jansen, *Dissonance*, 93–94.

48. Ibid., 143–45.

49. An important witness to the cultural and economic discrimination against Sephardic Jews, including those of ancient family and culture, is found in the autobiography of Elie Eliachar, a Sephardic Jew whose ancestors had lived in Palestine since their immigration from Spain in the sixteenth century: *Living with Jews* (London: Weidenfeld and Nicolson, 1983). Eliachar also is pointed in his remarks about mishandling of Palestinians and makes clear from his personal and family memories that Palestinians were not newcomers to Palestine but were already, in Ottoman times, a people with a distinct national identity in the Arab world.

50. See "The Second Israel," in Georges Friedman, *The End of the Jewish People* (Garden City, NY: Doubleday, 1967), 146–71.

51. Abu-Lughod, "Demographic War," 9.

52. According to the Geneva Convention on Protection of Civilian Persons in Times of War, August 12, 1949, it is illegal to apply collective punishment for crimes not committed by the individuals so punished. It is also illegal to annex territory, change laws, or deport persons individually or en masse.

53. Lecture by Salem Tamari of Bir Zeit University, in Jerusalem, January 30, 1987.

54. Raja Shehadeh, *Occupier's Law: Israel and the West Bank* (Washington, DC: Institute for Palestine Studies, 1985), 15–37.

55. Ibid., 39–40.

56. Jan D. Abu-Shakrah et al., *Israel's Settler Violence in the Occupied Territories, 1980–1984* (Chicago: Palestinian Human Rights Campaign, 1985).

57. Shehadeh, *Occupier's Law*, 54.

58. Ibid., 153–54.

59. Lecture, Salem Tamari (see note 53); also interview with Mustafa Natsche, former mayor of Hebron, February, 1987.

60. There has been a conflict between Israel and the European Economic Community (EEC) about independent marketing of Palestinian agricultural goods to the EEC, which was resolved in spring of 1987 in favor of the Palestinian agriculturalists.

61. Shehadeh, *Occupier's Law*, 76–100.

62. Ibid., 133–47, 154–55.

63. Jonathan Kuttab, from "Law in the Service of Man," Ramallah, West Bank, lecture on the legal structure of the military occupation, Tantur, Israel, January 1987.

64. An English translation of the results of the poll was published by *Al-Fajr*, Jerusalem (Summer 1986). See also R. Friedman, "Israel's Censorship of the Palestinian Press," *Journal of Palestine Studies* (Fall 1983): 93–101.

65. Interview with Fathy Chapin, Jabalia Camp, Gaza Strip, February 19, 1987.

66. Interview with Karim Khalaf, Ramallah, August 18, 1981, and with Basaam Shaka'a, February, 1987, in his home in Nablus; see also the interview of Jan Abu-Shakrah with Basaan Shaka'a on May 10, 1985, in *Settler Violence*, 99–101.

67. Shehadeh, *Occupier's Law*, 174–82.

68. "An Najah University President Deported: Public Relations Director Forced to Resign," *Palestinian Human Rights News Letter* 6 (September 1986): 1–5; see also the quarterly bulletin *Education Under Occupation: The Palestinian University*, published by North American Academics in Solidarity with Palestinian Universities, first issue (Spring 1986).

69. Shehadeh, *Occupier's Law*, 161–73.

70. Ibid., 124–28, 147–52; also from an interview with Raji Surani, Gazan human rights lawyer, who described his arrest and torture without trial or charges in the summer of 1985, after he had written in May 1985 to Israeli legal and military authorities to complain of human rights violations of his clients. Surani described his torture as continuing for forty-two days and consisting of such tortures as manacling, covering his head with a wet sack into which tear gas was continuously injected, and constant deprivation of sleep. Surani was threatened with deportation and allowed to remain in Gaza only on the condition that he is forbidden to represent political prisoners.

71. According to the Palestine Human Rights Information Center, there were 13 killings and 20 serious injuries to Palestinians from the occupation army or settlers in 1985; 21 killings and 52 serious injuries in 1986; 60 killings and 530 serious

injuries in the first eleven months of 1987; and 149 killings and about 30,000 injuries between December 1987 and March 20, 1988. By September 27, 1988 the killings had grown to 374 and the injuries were uncountable. As of April 6, 1988, one Israeli soldier had been killed in the Occupied Territories. A fourteen-year-old girl was also killed, probably by a bullet fired by the gun of a settler guard.

72. The DataBase Project on Palestinian Human Rights, established in Jerusalem and Chicago in May 1986, is a major example of such documentation; contact 1 Quincy Court, Suite 1308, Chicago, IL 60604.

73. The Arab Studies Society in East Jerusalem has made a historical map of the destroyed Palestinian villages and, in 1987, was in the process of updating the map. The Arab Studies Society was closed and sealed by the Israelis on July 30, 1988.

74. See Rosemary Ruether, "Women of Palestine: Steadfastness and Self-Help," *Christianity and Crisis* 14 (December 14, 1987): 434–38.

CHAPTER 6. CONTEMPORARY CHRISTIAN RESPONSES TO JUDAISM AND TO ZIONISM

1. It is common among Christian Zionists to claim that the pope's failure to recognize the State of Israel is derived from this Christian tradition of Jewish exile (see chap. 7 of this book). For Herzl's meeting with Pius X, see his *Diaries*, ed. Marvin Lowenthal (New York: Dial Press, 1956), 427–30.

2. *Declaration on the Relationship of the Church to Non-Christian Religions* (October 28, 1965), in *Documents of Vatican II*, ed. Willilam M. Abbott (New York: America Press, 1966), 661–62.

3. Hans Küng, *Christianity and World Religions: Paths of Dialogue with Islam, Hinduism and Buddhism.* (Garden City, NY: Doubleday, 1986).

4. Abbott, *Documents of Vatican II*, 666.

5. George E. Irani, *The Papacy and the Middle East: The Role of the Holy See in the Arab-Israeli Conflict, 1962–1984* (Notre Dame, IN: Notre Dame University Press, 1986), 17.

6. Ibid., 37–40.

7. Ibid., 88–89.

8. Ibid., 91–93.

9. Ibid., 81–82.

10. Ibid., 30–34.

11. Ibid., 28–30.

12. Ibid., 41–42.

13. Helga Croner, ed., *Stepping Stones to Further Jewish-Christian Relations: An Unabridged Collection of Christian Documents* (London: Stimulus Books, 1977), 91–107.

14. Ibid., 69–73.

15. Ibid., 73–85.

16. Larry Ekin, *Enduring Witness: The Churches and the Palestinians* (Geneva: World Council of Churches, 1985), 17–25.

17. Ibid., 44.

18. "Documents and Statements of the World Council of Churches on the Palestinian Question from Amsterdam, 1948, to Geneva, 1980," in Michael C. King, *The Palestinians and the Churches, 1940–1956* (Geneva: WCC, 1981), 130–31.

19. Ibid., 133, 134.

20. Ibid., 135. The *Middle East Policy Statement*, adopted by the governing board of the National Council of Churches of Christ in the U.S.A., November 6, 1980,

declares that "Israel must officially declare its recognition of the right of the Palestinians to self-determination, including the option of a sovereign state apart from the Hashemite Kingdom of Jordan and of its acceptance of the Palestine Liberation Organization as a participant in the peace negotiations."

21. Ibid., 135–37.
22. Ibid., 130, pt. 7.
23. First published by Zondervan, 1970.
24. Lawrence J. Epstein, *Zion's Call: Christian Contributions to the Origins and Development of Israel* (New York: University Press of America, 1984), 149–51.
25. Merrill Simon, *Jerry Falwell and the Jews* (Middle Village, NY: Jonathan David Publishers, 1984).
26. Ibid., 11–38.
27. Ibid., 41–48.
28. Ibid., 63–64, 71–72.
29. Ibid., 62–64, 79–85.
30. Ibid., 9.
31. Ibid., 48.
32. Ibid., 24–26.
33. Ibid., 65–66, 70–71.
34. Ibid., 84.
35. Ibid., 75–78, 82–89.
36. Ibid., 73.
37. See chapter 2 in this book.
38. Simon, *Jerry Falwell*, 15–16, 64.
39. Mike Evans, *Israel — America's Key to Survival* (Plainfield, NJ: Logos International, 1981); Evans also organized the TV special, *Jerusalem, DC.* (David's Capital), with major American evangelical leaders; Hal Lindsey, *The Late Great Planet Earth* (Grand Rapids, MI: Zondervan, 1970) and *The 1980s, Countdown to Armageddon* (New York: Bantam, 1981); David Allen Lewis, *Magog 1982 Cancelled* (Harrison, AK: New Leaf Press, 1982); Lewis has served as president of the National Christian Leadership Conference for Israel.
40. Reprinted from *Torat Hamelukhah*, 102–3, in Uriel Tal, "The Land and the State of Israel in Israeli Religious Life," *Proceedings of the Rabbinical Assembly of the 76th Annual Convention* (Grossinger, NY: Rabbinical Assembly, 1977), 9.
41. Ibid., 10.
42. See Rosemary Ruether, "Religion of Survival in the Holy Land," *National Catholic Reporter*, April 10, 1987.
43. Edward W. Said, "Attacks on Al-Aqsa," *The Link* 17 (August-September 1984): 10–13.
44. Grace Halsell, "Shrine under Siege," *The Link* 17 (August-September 1984): 2.
45. Ibid., 3; also Grace Halsell, *Prophecy and Politics: Militant Evangelists on the Road to Nuclear War* (Westport, CT: Lawrence Hill, 1986), 96–100.
46. Ibid., 96–97.
47. Halsell, "Shrine under Siege," *The Link*, 4; also Halsell, *Prophecy and Politics*, 98, 119.
48. Halsell, "Shrine under Siege," *The Link*, 4. In April 1988 the Christian Embassy hosted the Second Christian Zionist Congress in Jerusalem. This was strongly criticized by Middle Eastern Christian leaders. See "Declaration by the General Secretary of the Middle East Council of Churches" and the "Statement by the Heads of Jerusalem Churches," both dated April 15, 1988, P. O. Box 4259, Limassol, Cyprus; also Don Wagner, "The Program of the Christian Zionists," *Middle East International*, (14 May 1988), 19.
49. Halsell, "Shrine Under Siege", 6.

50. Robert Branton Betts, *Christians in the Arab East* (Philadelphia: John Knox Press, 1978).
51. Larry Ekin, *Enduring Witness: The Churches and the Palestinians* (Geneva: WCC, 1985), appendix, 130–35.
52. Ibid., 131.
53. Ibid., 133.
54. Ibid., 134.
55. Ibid., 135.
56. Na'em Ateek, *Toward a Strategy for the Episcopal Church in Israel, with Special Focus on the Political Situation: Analysis and Prospect* (San Anselmo, CA: 1982), chapter 3.

CHAPTER 7. JEWISH AND CHRISTIAN RESPONSES TO THE HOLOCAUST

1. Arthur C. Cochrane, *The Church's Confession Under Hitler* (Philadelphia: Westminster Press, 1962), 206–8.
2. Emil L. Fackenheim, "The People Israel Lives," *Christian Century*, May 6, 1970, p. 563.
3. Reader's response: Richard Rubenstein, *Christian Century* (July 29, 1970): 919–21.
4. Richard Rubenstein, *After Auschwitz: Radical Theology and Contemporary Judaism* (New York: Bobbs-Merrill, 1966), 9–11, 56–58, 85 and *passim*.
5. Richard Rubenstein, *The Cunning of History: Mass Death and the American Future* (New York: Harper & Row, 1975), 21.
6. Ibid., 95–97.
7. Rubenstein, *After Auschwitz*, 131–42, 154. "The Canaanites" were a group of intellectuals in the Jewish *Yishuv* in the 1940s who claimed to be Hebrew-speaking Canaanites, not Jews; see Akiva Orr, *The UnJewish State: The Politics of Jewish Identity in Israel* (London: Ithaca Press, 1983), 95.
8. Rubenstein, *After Auschwitz*, 196, 222.
9. Note 2, above.
10. In Rubenstein's reply to Fackenheim (note 3, above), he somewhat nastily points out that raising Jewish children is indeed an ethical decision for Fackenheim, since his wife is a Christian and, therefore, according to Jewish law, his children are not Jews. To become Jews they must be converted to Judaism.
11. Emil L. Fackenheim, "The Holocaust and the State of Israel: Their Relation," in *Auschwitz: Beginning of a New Era? Reflections on the Holocaust*, ed. Eva Fleischner (New York: Ktav, 1977), 205–14.
12. The phrase is found in a prayer for the State of Israel by the Israeli chief rabbinate, quoted by Fackenheim, "Holocaust and the State of Israel," 205.
13. Ibid., 208.
14. Ibid., 212–14.
15. Ibid., 214.
16. See chapter 1 of this book on Islamic views of the Jews as a people of the Book.
17. Irving Greenberg, "Cloud of Smoke, Pillar of Fire: Judaism, Christianity and Modernity After the Holocaust," in Fleischner, ed., *Auschwitz: Beginning of a New Era*, 7–55.
18. See Michael Berenbaum, *The Vision of the Void: Theological Reflections on the Work of Elie Weisel* (Middletown, CT: Wesleyan University Press, 1979), 160–71, for an analysis of the differences between the religious language of Weisel and that of Rubenstein.

19. Greenberg, "Cloud of Smoke," 44.
20. Irving Greenberg, "On the Third Era of Jewish History: Power and Politics," in *Perspectives (New York: National Jewish Resource Center,* 1980), 11, and "The Third Great Cycle in Jewish History," in *Perspectives* (1981), 27–35.
21. Marc Ellis, *Toward a Jewish Theology of Liberation* (Maryknoll, NY: Orbis, 1987), 32–36.
22. "Declaration on the Relationship of the Church to Non-Christian Religions," in *Documents of Vatican II,* ed. Walter Abbott (New York: America Press, 1966), 663–66.
23. Rat der Evangelischen Kirche in Deutschland, *Christen und Juden: Eine Studie des Rates der Evangelischen Kirche in Deutschland* (Gütersloh: Gütersloher Verlagshaus Gerd Möhn, 1975).
24. For Christian documents on Jewish-Christian relations published between 1965 and 1976, see *Stepping Stones to Further Jewish-Christian Relations: An Unabridged Collection of Christian Documents,* ed. Helga Croner (London: Stimulus Press, 1977).
25. Eliezer Berkovits, *Faith After the Holocaust* (New York: Ktav, 1973).
26. Rosemary Ruether, *Faith and Fratricide: The Theological Roots of Anti-Semitism* (New York: Seabury Press, 1974), esp. 246.
27. Ibid., 184–94.
28. Ibid., 226–61.
29. Ibid., 227–28.
30. *Long Night's Journey into Day: Life and Faith After the Holocaust* (Detroit: Wayne State University Press, 1982) and *Jews and Christians: The Contemporary Meeting* (Bloomington, IN: Indiana University Press, 1986).
31. For Eckardts' critique of Christology, see *Long Night's Journey,* 125–33.
32. See Eckardts' *Jews and Christians,* 79–81.
33. Ibid., 78.
34. Eckardt, *Long Night's Journey,* 134.
35. Eckardt, *Jews and Christians,* 80–81.
36. Liberia was founded in 1822 by U.S. black freed slaves who believed that it would be impossible to ever win integration and equal rights for blacks in U.S. society. They were assisted by white anti-slavery groups who believed that slavery should be abolished but also that blacks should be sent back to Africa. The Americo-Liberians looked down on the native Africans and established a system of class domination over them that has only recently begun to be challenged.
37. Ibid. The Eckardts completely accept the discredited work by Joan Peters (see ch. 5, n. 16).
38. Franklin Littrell, *The Anabaptist Concept of the Church* (Hartford, CT: American Society of Church History, 1952).
39. Franklin Littell, *The German Phoenix* (New York: Doubleday, 1960).
40. Franklin Littell, *The Crucifixion of the Jews* (New York: Harper & Row, 1975), 68.
41. Ibid., 88.
42. Ibid., 95–96.
43. Ibid., 83–84.
44. Paul Van Buren, *A Christian Theology of the People Israel* (New York: Seabury Press, 1983).
45. For Karl Barth's christocentric anthropology, see his *Christ and Adam: Man and Humanity in Romans 5* (New York: Macmillan, 1956).
46. Van Buren, *Christian Theology of the People Israel,* 70–76 and 116–28.
47. On Kabbalistic light-darkness language, see above, chapter 2.
48. Van Buren, *Christian Theology of the People Israel,* 350.

49. Ibid., 268–94 and *passim.*
50. Ibid., 33–37.
51. Ibid., 272–74.
52. Ibid., 277–82.
53. Ibid., 240–64.
54. Ibid., 316–19.
55. Ibid., 161–62 and 195–97.
56. Ibid., 334–37.
57. Ibid., 337.
58. Ibid., 127–28 and 312–3.
59. Ibid., 338–41.
60. See Arnold Forster and Benjamin R. Epstein, *The New Anti-Semitism* (New York: McGraw-Hill, 1974), 125–54 and *passim.*
61. Arthur Waskow is presently completing a new book, *The Rainbow Sign*, that will develop this connection of the Holocaust and universal solidarity in the face of the threat of the final holocaust of nuclear war.
62. Ellis, *Toward a Jewish Theology of Liberation*, 110–22.

CHAPTER 8.   ZIONISM AND INTER-NATIONAL JUSTICE

1. So far no group has attempted to compile a comprehensive account of the num- ber of Palestinians killed or severely injured in the conflicts within Israel and in the Occupied Territories or in the surrounding Arab states. The Database Project on Palestinian Human Rights has figures for the Occupied Territories only from 1982 to the present. From 1982 through 1987 (exclusive of December 1987) there were 123 killings and 477 severe injuries. Between December 9, 1987, and 1988, there have been deaths and an estimated 38,000 severe injuries (as of February 1988).

   Any effort to compile comprehensive statistics would have to take account of (1) deaths and injuries in the 1947–49 period (at least several thousand deaths); (2) major massacres, such as the Black September massacre of Palestinians by the Jordanian army in 1971 (more than 3,000); Tel al-Zatar, 1976 (1,500 killed); Sabra and Shatila (about 3,000, 37 percent Palestinians); and a number of other smaller massacres, such as Burj al-Barajneh, summer 1986 (200 killed, about 1,000 severe injuries); (3) the continual raids on Palestinian camps and villages from 1949 on, in which scores and even hundreds have been killed, such as the invasion of southern Lebanon in 1978 by the Israeli army in which 700 died (Lebanese and Palestinian); (4) the number of Palestinians who were among the more than 19,000 who died in the Lebanese war, other than in Sabra and Shatila, and (5) the number of those killed and injured in the Occupied Territo- ries since 1967.

   From these figures alone it is clear that Palestinians have suffered at least 15,000 to 20,000 deaths and probably more than 100,000 severe injuries in the forty-year period, probably more than half at the hands of Arab armies.

2. The phrase *purity of arms* is a standard expression of IDF ideology. When these authors were in Israel in January-February 1987, the term was used on a number of occasions to describe the high moral conduct of the Israel armed forces, not only by government spokespersons, but also by Israeli peace groups. Only in one interview, with long-term Israel pacifist Amos Guvritz, was the term criti- cized as a "contradiction in terms."

3. Simha Flapan, *The Birth of Israel: Myths and Realities* (New York: Pantheon, 1987).

4. See, for example, Arnold Forster and Benjamin R. Epstein, *The New Anti-Semitism* (New York: McGraw-Hill, 1974), 85–88, which labels the American Friend's Service Committee study, *Search for Peace in the Middle East* (1970), as anti-Semitic.

5. On the bias in favor of Israel in American State Department reports on human rights violations, see Louise Cainkar and Jan Abu-Shakrah, "A Critique of the U.S. State Department's 1986 Country Report on Human Rights Practices in the 1967 Israeli Occupied Territories," *Journal of Palestine Studies* 18 (Autumn 1987): 91–96.

6. See Fred Axelgard and Peretz Kidron, "Pollard: The Flak Flies in the U.S. and in Israel," *Middle East International* (March 20, 1987): 2–6.

7. See, for example, the coverage of the 1987–88 uprisings in articles by Jonathan Broder in the *Chicago Tribune*, January 1–30, 1988.

8. Two such recent statements are "Time to Disassociate from Israel," a statement by American Jews of national prominence that appeared in the *Nation* (February 13, 1988): 191, and "Arab-Israeli Conflict: Jews Against Occupation call for a Negotiated Mid-East Peace," in *Seattle Post-Intelligencer*, January 22, 1988.

9. Mordechai Venunu, an Israeli nuclear technician, revealed the existence of the Israeli nuclear capacity to the London *Sunday Times* in September 1986. He was subsequently captured by the *Mossad*, imprisoned, and put on trial in Israel. See J. M. Wall, "Nuclear Arms and the Missing Man," *Christian Century* 103 (November 19, 1986): 1019–20. For the report of his conviction, see the *Chicago Tribune*, March 25, 1988.

10. The assertion that it is Palestinians who must assure Israelis of their peacefulness and assuage Jewish fear is one we heard frequently in Israel. The sentiment was expressed in a television conversation between David Hartman and Sari Nusseibeh, who replied that this was like telling a person who was in jail surrounded by armed guards that they were supposed to assuage the fear of their armed guards. CBS documentary, "The West Bank: 20 Years Later" (1987).

11. See Elmer Berger, *Memoirs of an Anti-Zionist Jew* (Washington, DC: Institute of Palestine Studies, 1978).

12. Michael Jansen, *Dissonance in Zion* (London: Zed Press, 1987): 98–99.

13. Irving Greenberg has suggested that Jewish institutions designed to support the State of Israel are actually the new expression of Judaism: "On the Third Era of Jewish History: Power and Politics," in *Perspectives* (New York: National Jewish Resource Center, 1981).

14. Over 13,000 Israeli soldiers have died in wars and military conflicts between 1947 and 1983. See *Israeli Society and Its Defense Establishment: The Social and Political Impact of a Protracted Violent Conflict*, ed. Moshe Lissak (London: Frank Cass, 1984), 17. (The figure of 500 for the 1982 war is given; by 1983 this had increased to over 600.)

15. See Arthur Waskow, *These Holy Sparks: The Rebirth of the Jewish People* (San Francisco: Harper & Row, 1983); also Marc Ellis, *Toward a Jewish Theology of Liberation* (Maryknoll, NY: Orbis, 1987), 47–65.

16. *Report of the American Conservative Movement*, March 12, 1988.

17. Akiva Orr, *The UnJewish State: The Politics of Jewish Identity in Israel* (London: Ithaca Press, 1983), 216–20, 226–29.

18. Yeshayahu Leibowitz, scientist at Hebrew University, editor of several volumes of the *Encyclopaedia Hebraica* and writer on Jewish philosophy, has developed the arguments against the use of *halachic* arguments for settlement, which are key to the movement of religious Zionists for Peace (Oz VeShalom) in their critique of the *Gush Emunim*: Jansen, *Dissonance in Zion*, 79.

19. See chapter 2 and chapter 6, above.

20. Ammon Rubenstein, *The Zionist Dream Revisited: From Herzl to Gush Emunim and Back* (New York: Schocken, 1984), 127–55.

21. Jansen, *Dissonance in Zion*, 15–17, 114.

22. The release of the Kahan report in 1983 precipitated a new level of verbal violence between Israeli Jews as well as against Palestinians. Prime Minister Begin habitually referred to Palestinians as "two-legged animals," while Army Chief of Staff Raphael Eitan declared that the Palestinians under occupation should become "like drugged cockroaches in a bottle." Accusations of becoming Nazis were traded back and forth by each side. See Jansen, *Dissonance in Zion*, 16; also Amos Oz, *In the Land of Israel* (New York: Vintage, 1983).

23. See Yehoshafat Harkabi, "Contemporary Arab Anti-Semitism: Its Causes and Roots," in *The Persisting Question: Sociological Perspectives and Contexts of Modern Anti-Semitism*, ed. Helen Fein (Berlin/New York: Walter de Gruyter, 1987), 419–20.

24. Jansen, *Dissonance in Zion*, 105.

25. Jacob Timerman, *The Longest War: Israel in Lebanon* (New York: Knopf, 1982), was written while Timerman was in Israel and shows his disenchantment with the state.

26. See particularly Simha Flapan's analysis of the character of Moshe Sharett, in *Zionism and the Palestinians* (New York: Barnes and Noble, 1979), 148–59. Sharett confided his discomfort with the ruthlessness and mendacity of Israeli policies to his private diary, which was published in Hebrew in 1970.

27. Israel Shahak has issued his human rights reports periodically under the title *The Shahak Report*. See also his *Israel's Global Role: Weapons for Repression*, special report, series no. 4, American Arab University Graduates, 1982.

28. From the *Pirke Aboth* I, 14: *The Mishnah*, ed. H. Danby (Oxford: Clarendon Press, 1933), 447.

29. Jansen, *Dissonance in Zion*, 98.

30. The phrase *Ha'alam kulo negdeinu* (the whole world is against us) is frequently evoked in Israeli national life and has become a defiant national slogan, like "We shall overcome." It was even made into a popular national song in 1967. See Orr, *The UnJewish State*, 232.

31. Jansen, *Dissonance in Zion*, 115–30.

32. See Orr, *The UnJewish State*, 4, for a critique of the religio-nationalist materialization of holiness as a "blasphemy."

Index